Will Pearson is a journalist, broadcaster and writer. When the first Gulf War broke out, realising there was a great story waiting to be told, he approached RAF pilot Flt Lt John Peters and navigator Flt Lt John Nichol – who had been shot down and captured by the Iraqis – to write the best-selling *Tornado Down*. Since then, he has written five more books, including *The Shooting Gallery*, a searing account of life in the SAS. He lives in London with his wife and two children.

DEATH WARRANT

Kenneth Noye,
the Brink's-Mat Robbery
and the Gold

WILL PEARSON

An Orion paperback

First published in Great Britain in 2006
by Orion
This paperback edition published in 2007
by Orion Books Ltd,
Orion House, 5 Upper St Martin's Lane,
London WC2H 9EA

1 3 5 7 9 10 8 6 4 2

A CIP catalogue record for this book is available
from the British Library.

ISBN-13 978-0-7528-7809-6

Printed and bound in Great Britain by Clays Ltd, St Ives plc

The Orion Publishing Group's policy is to use papers that
are natural, renewable and recyclable products and
made from wood grown in sustainable forests. The logging
and manufacturing processes are expected to conform to
the environmental regulations of the country of origin.

www.orionbooks.co.uk

Acknowledgements

This book owes much to many: former Metropolitan Police officers Commander Roy Ramm and Detective Sergeant Tony Curtis; former Brink's Mat guard Robin Riseley; and others who do not wish to be named. They all gave freely of their knowledge and time.

The mass of documentary evidence Bob McCunn provided was invaluable when it came to unravelling the post-heist financial and legal web. Thanks, Bob.

Special thanks go to Mark Hayhurst of Blast Films for allowing unrestricted use of his excellent drama-documentary about the robbery.

Bullion, the 1988 account of the heist by *Sunday Times* journalists Andrew Hogg, Jim McDougall and Robin Morgan, was a great touchstone.

Malcolm Edwards of Orion saw that there was gold to be mined from a murky seam of criminal history. Alan Samson, Lucinda McNeile and designer Sue Michniewicz helped get stuck in with the pick-axes, and copy-editor Steve Cox did a great job of spotting the mistakes.

Mark Lucas and his team are the kind of agents you want on your side.

Last but not least, love to Gaynor Aaltonen, best and sternest critic, and to my children, Juliet and Lewis, without whom, to paraphrase Frederick Forsyth, this book would have been finished much sooner but in less happy circumstances.

Preface

This book is based on: interviews with serving and retired Metropolitan Police officers; former Brink's-Mat employees; accounts in press, television and book form; court transcripts; other legal documents, and the testimony of some who wish to remain nameless.

1

There was nothing unusual about the battered blue Ford Transit van parked opposite Unit 7 that morning.

It was 0620 on Saturday, 26 November 1983, and apart from the occasional roar of an inbound plane, the roads surrounding the Brink's-Mat high-security warehouse were quiet. A bleak collection of storage sheds and offices built to service the adjacent airport whose perimeter fence lay less than a mile distant, the Heathrow International Trading Estate was never going to win any prizes for its architecture. But then, looks hardly mattered. The 'estate' was a collection of big functional sheds: why would anyone worry about their design?

From the outside, one large, ugly, prefabricated steel and brick box looks much like another – and in fact there was so little external difference between Unit 7 and its neighbours that it had a large figure '7' marked on its sides to help people find it. But this particular shed was, in fact, quite exceptional: one of the most secure and technologically advanced storage facilities in the country, it was a commercial fortress, its contents protected by a rolling daytime shift of at least six security guards; omnipresent CCTV cameras; state-of-the-art electronic alarm systems and some of the world's most advanced deadlocks.

At the heart of the building lay a reinforced concrete vault. About 4 metres high by 11 in length, its steel-hardened walls were more than 15cm thick. In essence a gigantic safe, this box within a box was Unit 7's treasure chest, a redoubt that was meant to be proof against all comers.

As he climbed out of his family runabout and walked towards his place of work, Michael Scouse shivered in his dark-blue parka. The smoky November air had a bitter edge and the prospect of a long shift in a barren warehouse while his family and friends were out shopping, relaxing at home or watching the football did nothing to lessen the wintry chill. As 'Key Man' for the shift that day, he had to be first in. The side-door through which he and the other guards entered the warehouse was protected by an automatic alarm system, set to release at 0630 and not a moment before. The only member of the security crew with a key to this external door, Scouse had to be on time. But then, he was always on time.

The next member of the shift to arrive was crew leader Robin Riseley. A quiet, well-built, easygoing man of medium height who liked to keep in good physical shape, Riseley was an ex-British Army soldier who had seen the rough end of active service with the 3rd Battalion, The Queen's Regiment in Northern Ireland. He had joined up at fifteen, and been shot at more than once trying to control riots in Belfast. Riseley was also the man who had the other half of the vault access and safe codes stored in his memory. Three more members of the shift followed in short order: Peter Bentley, Ron Clarke and Richard Holliday. They waited with Scouse in the gradually lightening darkness until the night alarm released.

Anthony Black, the sixth guard scheduled for duty that day, was late.

Scouse held most of the building's keys; he knew half the access codes to the vault and the three safes inside it by heart, and he also had front-line responsibility for the vault's contents. These varied from gold and other precious metals to large amounts of cash held in transit between banks, bullion merchants and corporations worldwide.

Glancing at his wristwatch, Scouse saw that it was 0631: the tamper-proof alarm system, preset by the outgoing shift the night before, should by now have switched itself off. As he stooped to unlock the door the rugged, dependable face creased in a momentary frown that cleared as he stood and withdrew the key. At least he had the company of the other five guards to help relieve the boredom: they were a good bunch, liked a laugh, and, given the miserable basic pay rate that pertained even in this high-profile sector of the security business, the overtime for a weekend duty was worth having.

Pushing through the main door, which he relocked behind him, the Key Man stepped inside to the familiar high-pitched whine. Unlocking a second, inner door to the hall he went to the control box, inserted the appropriate key and gave it a quick anti-clockwise twist. Silence rewarded him. After the ear-splitting screech, the quiet was a blessed relief. The building's perimeter alarms were now deactivated.

Scouse now went back out to the main door and let in the rest of the guards. Once the four men who had arrived on time were safely inside, he reactivated the perimeter alarms, relocked the main door and followed them upstairs. He had been in the security business longer than he might have liked, but the familiarity of his surroundings and the routine of the procedures did not stop him from being careful. Scouse was always careful – it was one reason why the Brink's-Mat company had promoted him.

On his way up to the crew-room, Holliday switched on the CCTV cameras and the radio aerials.

Few people pass up the chance to make their lives more comfortable if they can, and over the years the crew-room had been turned into a cosy, heated refuge nestling egg-like within the cold, draughty shell of the main building. Situated on the first floor and accessed by a set of stairs leading up from the side-door, the room held a fridge, a radio tuned just then to a local London pop music station, a TV monitor hooked up to the inner loading bay surveillance camera, a sink with a kettle and a jumble of coffee and tea things, and an array of notices pinned up on a wall-mounted noticeboard. Desks formed three sides of a square in the middle of the room, and there were several office-style swivel chairs scattered about. A window let into the back wall in one corner of the room gave an uninterrupted view of the internal loading bay. This big, concrete floored space was protected by electronically controlled steel doors. Operated from a control box situated next to the observation window, these doors were kept permanently locked except when a shipment was scheduled in or out.

Nothing cheers the British on a cold morning like a hot cup of tea, and Peter Bentley, a big, experienced guard and the third man to arrive, put the kettle on with his customary, 'We'll have a bit of a brew then, shall we, lads?' He began rattling around with the mugs and the milk and the tea things. There was a pleasant sense of routine, of the day's work beginning in a familiar and reassuring ritual: despite, or perhaps because of the fact that its occupants were male and for the most part ex-military, the atmosphere inside the crew-room was one of snug domestic well-being.

Discussion turned briefly to their duties. In keeping with standard operating procedures, none of the guards knew the exact details of the shipment they were meant to be guarding that day. Often it was cash – in the region of between one and two million pounds. Today, according to the advance whispers, it included gold. But until Scouse read the entry in the logbook left on the desk by the outgoing shift, no one knew how much.

The Key Man let out a suppressed whistle when he saw the value of the shipment written out in figures on the page. It was astronomical – the largest he had ever seen. In fact, he'd be surprised if it wasn't the largest amount of gold bullion ever shipped through a British airport. He repeated the figure softly to himself to make sure that he hadn't misread it.

He had not. He glanced around at the others, warming their hands on the fresh mugs of tea, and felt glad of their good-natured bantering – it meant they were awake.

In theory, their task on that Saturday morning was simple: to load the bullion into one of the armoured company security vans parked downstairs in the loading bay, and then escort it to Gatwick airport for on-shipment to the banks and businesses in Hong Kong that had ordered and, in part, already paid for it. He showed Robin Riseley the consignment's all-up weight. 'Best take the Mercedes, then,' said the crew leader, phlegmatic as always. 'Bentley can drive; I'll ride shotgun with him up front. If Rich [Richard Holliday] goes in the back, then Ron Clarke can follow us in the Escort and Black can work the radio as usual.' He gave a wry smile. 'If he turns up for work, that is.'

The Key Man's gaze flicked up to the digital wall clock. It showed 0636 – six minutes past the scheduled start of the shift, and Black had still not yet reported for work. Scouse looked through some of the paperwork, ensuring that it was all in order and that the Gatwick airport security passes were up to date. When he was satisfied, he looked up and caught Riseley's eye. It was now 0640. 'Any idea where Tony is, Rob?' Riseley shrugged his shoulders. 'Expect he's overslept again.' The other men laughed. Black had a habit of indifferent timekeeping – nothing very serious, just the odd few minutes nipped from the start of a shift. But Black was 'radio man' that day: Scouse needed him to man the communications link between the armoured truck, Unit 7 and Gatwick airport.

As if on cue, the doorbell rang. Scouse put down his tea, stood up and reached for the keys. 'Speak of the devil,' he grunted. He went downstairs, unfastened the catch on the inner door and peered out through the armoured glass panel set in the outer one. Black was standing on the threshold waiting to be let in. Scouse unlocked the door and pulled it open. Slim and slightly built, with long, black hair and a drooping, Zapata-style moustache, Black – who bore a passing resemblance to the young Peter Sellers – looked a little peaky in the grey autumnal light: the thin, pale face was pinched a little tighter than usual, while the dark-brown, deep-set eyes held a curious glint. Black shifted from one foot to the other. 'Sorry I'm late.' He stood back so that Scouse could relock the outer door. Before doing so, the Key Man gave the outside area a quick once-over.

He saw nothing amiss. There was an old blue Ford Transit van parked some little way up the side road opposite and at a slight angle to Unit 7. The Transit was the van of choice for moving small loads around Heathrow airport – dozens of them criss-crossed the area night and day. Transit vans were part of the landscape, one more or less in Scouse's field of vision did not signify. He relocked the outer door, refastened the inner door for what he hoped was the last time before the armoured truck arrived, and then followed the latecomer upstairs.

As he reached the crew-room door, Black suddenly stopped. Bentley called out, 'You look a bit rough.' Everyone laughed except Black. Scouse lifted an eyebrow and tilted his head. Black muttered, 'Overslept,' turned on his heel and headed back down the stairs. Scouse stared at the guard's retreating back. After hanging up his coat, Black's usual routine was to grab a mug of tea, find a chair and join in the early morning chit-chat. Bentley had also picked up on Black's unusual behaviour. 'Typical Tony – hasn't even started work yet and he's off back home already.' They all laughed again. 0643.

Black did not go to the toilet. Ear cocked like a gun dog, he listened intently at the foot of the stairs for a few seconds. Satisfied all was well, he released the catch on Unit 7's inner front door: the same one he had just watched Michael Scouse refasten. Moving through into the lobby he stepped up to the armoured glass panel in the outer door, raised his right hand and gave a quick wave. Then, leaving the inner door standing ajar, he nipped back upstairs and rejoined the others, still chatting happily over their tea.

Forty seconds later, the lock in the outer door clicked open.

2

Scouse was standing behind his desk at the back of the room when he heard an odd scuffling sound from the stairwell. He glanced up. A ghoul figure charged in through the doorway. A figure from nightmare; dark-yellow mask, trilby hat, a pistol in the outstretched hand. The hole cut in the balaclava worked up and down as the mouth behind it opened and shut: 'GET DOWN ON THE FLOOR, NOW! GET DOWN ON THE FUCKING FLOOR! . . . STAY DOWN! STAY DOWN ON THE FLOOR!' More masked men came pile-driving in behind him, boots thumping and squeaking on the linoleum floor. *Armed robbers*.

Scouse stared as the blood drained from his face and hands. This could not be happening. It was not possible. He had locked the outside door himself – it was impregnable – only a rocket-propelled grenade . . . Reality caught up with him, like a door slamming in his face. An avalanche was on the room, a rolling explosion of armed and masked men. They scythed through the guards, pistols chopping round and down in flat, vicious arcs.

Trilby was the leader: the ochre stocking mask on his face cut with three jagged holes: Freddy Kruger one year before he screened. With its herringbone pattern, the hat lent him an extra, jaunty horror. Four or five men in the gang, it was hard to count – the figures moved too fast, blurring with the guards as they smashed through them. To make things even more confused, some of them seemed to be wearing bits of Brink's-Mat uniform. Scouse could not work it out: fear stopped his mind, the noise in the crew-room was deafening. They were all screaming the same order: 'GET DOWN! ON THE FLOOR! STAY DOWN! STAY DOWN ON THE FLOOR!' They meant to put the fear of Christ into the guards, and they succeeded. In ten seconds, twenty, the room was a shambles. Guards, tables, chairs, everything blown to the four winds. Turning his head slightly, flat on the floor, Scouse tried to take in the destruction. His men had been smashed flat, cut down like corn in a gale. Except for one who was still standing: Bentley. It would be Peter: at more than six feet and strongly built, of all the guards Bentley was most likely to carry the fight. Scouse opened his mouth to shout a warning, but it was too late. Quick as thought, Yellow Mask raised the pistol high above his head and smacked the butt down hard into Bentley's scalp, splitting the flesh like a ripe plum. 'I SAID, GET FUCKING DOWN!'

Bentley folded up like a concertina. Blood streamed from the gash, dripping red on his white shirt. He let out a soft groan as he sank to the floor.

Scouse watched the pistols and boots come his way. He curled into a ball, arms round his head, waiting his turn. Speed, aggression and surprise, the stock Special Forces recipe: gives the victims no chance to fight back. There were hidden panic buttons dotted around the room, but it was already too late for those. There was no chance to cry out, or even think. They'd been sipping their tea, snug as beetles in oak, and now . . . This could not be. There were locks and alarms that could not have been forced. The lock on the front door . . . Denial was useless. This was happening, it was real, he had to deal with it.

'GET DOWN! ON THE FLOOR! GET YOUR HANDS UP BEHIND YOUR BACK! DON'T MOVE OR YOU'RE FUCKING DEAD!' Scouse saw in fragments. In snatches, he made out the radio's banal twittering. In the maelstrom of violence the sound was surreal.

They were on him, then. Gloved hands yanked his arms up behind his back. Steel handcuffs snapped tight on his wrists; masking tape around his lower legs. A canvas hood rammed down over his head. The rough sacking clung to his face, blocking nostrils and mouth: a new terror speared through Scouse, the cold fear of suffocation. They had become prisoners of their own fortress: all of Unit 7's extraordinary, ultra-high security now worked against them. No chance of rescue, no means of calling for help. At the mercy of men who did not know the word. They were not scheduled to make any radio calls for the best part of an hour. Unless they were lucky, no one would even know they were under attack.

They were not lucky.

Trilby was shouting, voice like a road drill, 'Who's the Key Man? Which one of you fucking wankers is Scouse?' In his thirties, about five feet and ten inches, stocky and strongly built; the lead robber's dark eyes burned from the ragged slits in the ochre mask. Not a man you might notice, except for the stare. Not an especially big, broad or tall man – but ruthless, admired for his violence by those in the trade.

'I'm Scouse. it's me.' Yellow Mask pounced like a dog on a rat: screwed the muzzle of his pistol into the back of Scouse's head. 'Get up. GET UP!'

There was an empty office next to the crew-room: the manager's office. The radio room was on the other side, directly above the vault. The robbers seemed to know this, they knew everything, it was shocking how much information they had. Except for the one thing they needed to know most: the vault codes. They bundled Scouse into the manager's office and shoved him back down flat on his face. Scouse understood what they wanted; no need to be Brain of Britain to work that one out. He also knew they would do anything to get it.

Another man took over now, Black Mask: tall and heavily built, a little older than Trilby from the way he moved. He stooped close and gave Scouse the news in a flat tone. 'We know where you live, Scouse: in Ruislip, over the TV shop with your family. We've been watching you for a year now, so don't fuck about – right?'

Right.

A third robber lumbered up, even bigger than the man who had just spoken. He had the meaty upper body of a cruiserweight boxer, arms like a lesser man's thighs. A slab-sided bruiser, coarse stubble showing at the edge of the ski mask. A heavy, a 'slag' – the muscle you called on when force was the thing. Not the sharpest knife in the box, but good with one. A blade in his hand now. He stuck the curved point of the diver's knife in through Scouse's flies, twisted it so the razor edge caught in the fabric and sliced up. The uniform trousers fell open, exposing the Key Man's lower half.

A red plastic petrol container, the kind used for roadside emergencies. A fourth masked man shook it. Scouse shrank back from the sound, he had nowhere to go. They had him pinned like an insect, the soft parts exposed.

The robbers were ice slick. They had done it a hundred times, practised till they had the routine down pat. Masked and armed, in their coveralls and boots and gloves they were more like a Special Forces hit team than a South London firm. The petrol man unscrewed the cap. Stuck the spout in under the edge of Scouse's hood. 'Breathe in.' The Key Man gagged, rearing back from the acrid stink. 'Breathe in, or you'll get cut.' Scouse took a deep breath. They held him, forcing him to inhale the fumes.

'You know what this is?' He gave the can another shake. Scouse wished he didn't know. 'Petrol.'

'Clever boy.'

Trilby shook the box in his hand. Its contents made a dry rattle. 'And these?'

'Matches.'

'Hold him.'

Petrol splashed onto Scouse's groin, soaking his genitals and thighs. Trilby put his mouth up to Scouse's ear, the drill voice the substance of menace itself. 'Listen carefully, you cunt: we're taking you down to the vault. And when we get down there, you'll tell us the combination. Or I'll barbecue YOUR FUCKING COCK!' He paused to let the threat sink in. 'If the alarms go off, if the police turn up, if we don't get what we want, I'll put a match to you and put a bullet through your head.' The words punched into Scouse, he believed every one of them. The robbers dropped him, left him lying there while they dealt with the rest.

They dragged Clarke and Holliday into a separate office and handcuffed them to the heating pipes. Bentley had stopped bleeding but he was still groggy. They locked him into an electrical cupboard. It was Scouse and Riseley they wanted. They were the ones who knew the combination to the Brink's-Mat high-security vault. They were all that now stood between the gang and a fortune.

0648. Trilby wanted the job done and out of there by 0730.

Riseley was still in the crew-room. 'Are you Riseley? The Combination Man?'

'Yes.'

They dragged him through into the same room as Scouse. The knife man walked up to Riseley, stooped and sliced his trousers wide with a quick slashing curve of the knife. The petrol man stepped up and launched a jet that soaked Riseley's groin and legs. Yellow Mask rattled the matches again. A neat routine they had going: gang theatre.

One guard was left in the crew-room with Riseley – Anthony Black. Trilby padded over to him. 'You Black?' Black nodded, blind in the canvas hood. 'Get up.' When Black was on his feet the gang leader stuck the pistol in the small of his back and prodded him over to the corner where the internal window looked down on the loading bay. He ripped the hood from Black's head, uncuffed him and pointed to the wall-mounted control box. 'You know how to use this?' Black nodded again.

'Then do it.'

Black held down two buttons and the huge steel doors began to swing open. The instant they were wide enough, the blue Transit that had been parked opposite the warehouse raced into the outer loading bay and shuddered to a halt in a squeal of tyres. Yellow Mask moved closer to Black. 'Stay right where you are now and don't move a muscle. Got it?'

'Got it.' Black faced into the corner like little Jack Horner, hands newly cuffed behind his back. A good boy, not moving, eyes on the back wall.

Two men hauled Riseley to his feet, took him by the arms and half-carried, half-dragged him out into the corridor. Scouse was already there, held in the same way. 'Downstairs. The vault. MOVE!' Trousers round their ankles, neither Riseley nor Scouse could walk. Swearing and shouting, the robbers manhandled them down the stairs and into the vault area.

There was the outer shell of the warehouse with the outer loading bay at the rear; a second, enclosed, drive-in section of the loading bay known as the 'safe area'; and finally the vault proper, a reinforced concrete blockhouse fitted with twin 20cm steel doors that opened outwards. First you had to get past the state-of-the-art deadlock and alarm combination set in the massive grey-painted steel doors protecting the safe area. Unless both the lock and the alarm on this first set of armoured doors were correctly released in tandem, it was no go. Once past the outer doors, you entered the safe area, an inner loading space adjoining the vault – which vehicles could still access. You then faced the thick, green-painted steel doors to the vault proper. These were protected by a separate and similar alarm/deadlock combination, which would release only when the outer doors had been opened in the correct way and then relocked.

The access and alarm systems were complex and elaborate, but ensured that the Brink's-Mat treasure was protected at all times by at least one set of dual-locked, reinforced steel doors.

The robbers stood for a moment, awed by the sheer size and strength of the outer steel doors. Large enough to admit an armoured truck, they looked impregnable. Ripping the hood back up enough that Scouse could see, Trilby broke the silence. 'You – Scouse – how do we unlock these doors?'

'There's no point me telling you what to do. There's a sequence. Let me do it, or you'll set the alarms off.' The dark eyes in the yellow mask glared at him suspiciously. 'Do it, then.' Scouse hesitated a fraction too long. The gang leader put the pistol to his head. 'Put your numbers in, or that's it.'

Scouse shouted, '45-75-55-85.' One of the robbers put in the sequence. The first lock sprang open with a loud *click*. Trilby grabbed Scouse by the hair, pulled his head back and put the ragged eyeholes up into his face. 'The keys.' The gang leader rammed the Browning's muzzle up under his chin. 'WHERE ARE THE FUCKING KEYS?'

'Upstairs. The crew-room. The box on the far wall. Brown pouch.' The pouch contained the keys to all the ground-floor doors, including the vault door. One of the gang ran to fetch it.

They still had to get through a second set of doors, protected by the same tandem combination and deadlock system. This barrier was linked directly to the headquarters of the Group 4 security firm. Scouse opened the alarm box to the left of the doors and turned the two dials inside to the correct numbers: 11-11. With the alarm now deactivated, he pulled the deadbolts and the doors swung open. He moved through into the space beyond, selected a new key from the pouch and switched off yet another alarm.

Now the robbers only had to defeat the door to the vault proper.

Scouse felt Riseley to his left, bundled up to join him. Each man put in his own half of the vault code.

It worked.

They were in.

There was one last-ditch barrier: the wire-mesh grille protecting the fortune beyond. But after all that they had already overcome, this one was easy: Scouse reached into the bag, selected the correct key and turned the lock.

They had done it. They were inside Aladdin's cave.

Three large steel safes caught the robbers' attention. In all of the excitement, they had momentarily forgotten about the gold.

Yellow Mask grabbed Scouse by the scruff of the neck and frogmarched him up to the combination wheel on the first safe. 'Put your numbers in – HURRY UP!'

Scouse looked at the hand-wheel. He was freezing cold except for where the petrol burned his skin and there was a madman in a yellow mask and a trilby hat pointing a gun at him. Why couldn't he think? If he could just think. There was a hard knot in his stomach and below that a kind of watery void. He'd been shot at and threatened before, but this was different. He'd blanked, and the knowledge that he'd blanked made the vacuum where his memory was supposed to be feel emptier still.

The codes were changed regularly and without warning, usually once every three or four weeks. Like all of the company's Key Men, Scouse was required to memorize his half of each combination by heart – no cribs, nothing on paper for anyone unauthorized to find. On any other day he would have input the numbers without a second's thought. But the 9mm handgun boring into the top of his spine seemed to have done something fatal to his memory. He stood there sweating, staring at the combination wheel set dead centre of the doors, with the shreds of his clothing splayed around his feet. His body reeked of petrol – he could feel it burning into the soft skin of his thighs and groin. He wanted to scratch at it madly. His mind went blank.

The shout blasted through the lofty space: 'COME ON, YOU CUNT – HURRY UP AND OPEN IT!' Scouse tried to think, but nothing happened. He hadn't just forgotten the vault code: he could hardly remember his own name. Slowly, eyes on the Key Man, the gang leader raised his gun arm. Put the pistol's muzzle into Scouse's face. Everything went quiet. The threat of violence was like a separate presence in the room.

Riseley shuffled up to the door. Watching Scouse, he had learned the Key Man's numbers by heart. He twisted them in quickly, and then stood back.

The first safe held more than £1 million in cash – Mick had told him that. But without the crew leader's half of the combination they weren't going to get it. Riseley's teeth chattered. He might have learned Scouse's numbers, but now it was his turn to blank. All the safe combinations had been changed recently. Against regulations, and as a way of helping him remember them, he had the numbers written in a little book, which he now distinctly remembered he had left at home. He could visualize the notebook sitting on this bedside table. What were the new numbers? He cast around wildly, looking for help. There was none coming. The eyes in the Yellow Mask glistened with rage. The yell rained a fine spray of spit in his ear. 'What the FUCK are you waiting for? Open it, NOW!'

Riseley knew he was done for unless he remembered. But the numbers would not come: the space inside him was filled up and hollow at the same time. The harder he tried, the less he could remember. Yellow Mask sprang at him, lashing and clubbing. Riseley reeled backwards, hands raised to shield his face. Battered and hobbled, he stumbled and fell backwards, sprawling awkwardly on the floor.

'ARE YOU CUNTS HAVING A LAUGH, OR WHAT? OPEN THE FUCKING SAFE!'

'I can't,' Riseley mumbled. 'I've forgotten the numbers.'

The masked face was right in his own. The gravel voice whispered: 'What did you say?'

Riseley looked to Scouse, but the Key Man shook his head. He had not memorized Riseley's numbers. He could not return the favour. Riseley said faintly, 'The numbers have gone.'

The gang leader grabbed Riseley, lifted him bodily and slammed him into the wall. 'DON'T. FUCK. ABOUT. You hear me? DON'T

FUCK ABOUT!' He took out a match, struck it and held it down near the petrol-soaked clothing at Riseley's waist. Riseley tried to speak, but the muscles in his face had gone slack. The gang leader caught him by the throat and shook him. 'You're going to remember – I'm going to *make* you remember.'

Upstairs in the crew-room, the telephone rang. The caller was Alan Bullock, the manager of Norman Reeves Trucks in nearby Hayes: one of the Brink's-Mat vans sent in recently for service had been repaired and was ready for collection. When no one answered, Bullock put the phone back on the hook, waited a couple of minutes and then tried again. There was still no reply. Bullock thought this was unusual. He hesitated for a few seconds, hand over the phone. It was hardly his place to report it. In any case, what would he tell the police? The guards were too busy to answer the telephone?

Yellow Mask glanced at his wristwatch. It was 0705: time was running out. He shook his head. They had broken into Aladdin's cave, yet here they were half-an-hour later still empty-handed. It was unbelievable. No fucking way. He slid a razor-sharp diver's knife the same as the heavy's from its leather sheath. Held the blade up in front of Riseley's face. 'See this?'

Riseley nodded.

'Put in the combination.'

Riseley just looked at him. As a Section Leader at the head of an army foot patrol, he had faced death more than once in Northern Ireland. He did not want to die – but for the life of him he could not remember the safe code.

The gang leader stepped back, dropped the knife and brought it up in a short arc. Riseley put his hands up in front of his face. The point of the blade curved a line through the soft flesh of his outstretched palm. He gasped, clutching at the wound. Blood welled out from between his fingers and ran back down his forearm. Yellow Mask yanked him upright, put the knife in between Riseley's legs and moved it. 'Do you want to sing soprano? *Do you?* Because that's what's going to happen if you don't open the safe. Now, DO THE FUCKING NUMBERS!'

Scared as he was, Scouse could not stand by and watch Riseley get castrated. A fragment of training flashed into his mind. *Try and get friendly with the robbers: get them talking if you can, develop a rapport.* There was no way you could befriend a mad dog. But he had to do something, anything to stop what was about to happen. He nodded his head at the gasping Riseley. 'You think he's bad now? You should see what he's like in the week.' The joke might be weak, but it was his best shot.

It was also an act of insane courage.

With a snarl of rage the gang leader launched himself at Scouse, clubbing at him. Scouse hit a box with the back of his legs, fell and lay sprawled in his turn. The gang leader screwed the pistol into his ear. 'Get up. *Stand up!* What's that there?'

Scouse followed the direction of the gloved finger. The robber was pointing at what looked like a half-size metal beer keg. 'It's scrap,' he said, 'scrap metal.' It was scrap, true enough – scrap silver, worth thousands of pounds in its own right. A second keg stood next to it. 'And that one?'

Scouse told the truth. 'That's palladium sponge.'

'You what?' Palladium is a rare and valuable element sometimes used in the manufacture of delicate electronics. In the jewellery trade it is alloyed with yellow gold to make white. 'Open them!' McAvoy barked. Scouse knelt and removed the lids. The scrap inside looked worthless, dull little lumps of metal waste. Trilby and Man in Black exchanged glances: it was now well past 7 o'clock, and still they had nothing to show for their work.

The dark eyes in the ochre mask flicked wildly round the vault; came to rest on two wooden pallets. The pallets were stacked to about chest height with grey cardboard boxes. The boxes looked nondescript, like shoe boxes. The gold? Why had they forgotten that? The trilby hat jerked in their direction. 'What's in those boxes? WHAT'S IN THEM?'

Scouse shook his head. 'No idea.' They were bullion boxes – he had handled hundreds in his time. Their eyes locked. Something unspoken passed between the two men. The gang leader walked up to the nearest stack. The boxes were secured with thin metal straps. Slowly, as if he were pushing it through water, he slid the knife blade in through the thick cardboard and sawed. It parted. He tore back the cut section.

He stood looking down for a long time. The box seemed to radiate an odd yellow glow, almost as if it were lit from the inside. Silence stretched out in the echoing vault. The robber in black broke it. 'What is it, Mickey? What's in there?'

The drill voice was quiet, now: 'It's gold.'

The others moved forward, as if drawn by wires. The leader reached in and lifted something out: a bright yellow bar of metal, gleaming and buttery. He turned the brilliant slab in his gloved hand, making it flash in the harsh light. The assay mark stamped on the back caught his gaze. 'It's four nines,' he murmured.

He was right: the bar he was holding was bullion: 99.99 per cent pure gold: so soft he could have moulded it between his fingers; so pure that if he had sliced off a matchbox-sized chunk and beaten it out to airy thinness, the foil would cover the surface of a tennis court. All he thought about was the fact that it would make him incredibly rich. He hefted the little ingot, relishing its mass and weight before laying it gently back to rest in the box. 'Must be a ton of it.' It was hard to keep the headlong, rushing excitement out of his voice.

He was wrong. There were seventy-six boxes stacked on the pallets, ninety ingots to a box: 6,840 bars of fine gold, 2,670kg, or getting on for 3 tons. The size and shape of a small confectionery bar, each of the ingots weighed just under 400g, and each was worth around £3,000. Depending on the latest gold fix, the heist's total value was in the region of £26,500,000.

A fortune beyond dreams. A conquistador haul, that people would suffer, risk death to obtain. Theirs for the taking. He came back to himself. 'You know what, Brian – we're going to need another set of wheels.' The man in the black balaclava nodded. 'You're right, Mickey.' He turned his head. 'Tony, sort it. The rest of us – there's a trolley over there – let's get this lot shifted.'

There was more in the vault: several bars of pure platinum; a leather pouch with £100,000 in uncut diamonds – worth far more in their finished state – and a box containing hundreds of blank traveller's cheques. The gang fetched and carried, sweating in their coveralls: it was hard work, but worth every drop.

0745: fifteen minutes past the original deadline. But the gold was on the motors. Nothing else mattered.

Yellow Mask and Man in Black jumped into the battered Transit. It was ancient, knackered, severely overladen, and they were neither of them small men. For a moment, it threatened to collapse under the enormous weight. It buckled visibly, axles bowing and engine protesting as it laboured to pick up speed. The gang leader had his foot hard down on the accelerator, but even so they were moving at little better than running pace. He thumped the steering column with the heels of his hands. 'Come on!' he roared at the lumbering jalopy. 'Get fucking going!' He caught his companion's eye. 'How much do you weigh?'

'Fourteen stone twelve. You?'

'Thirteen stone eight. One of us has to get out.'

That started them. Trilby had tears running down his face; it was all he could do to drive. Aftershock had hit them, 'robber's high' – a heady mix of adrenalin, euphoria and pure relief. They had gone into Unit 7 expecting to get away with a few hundred thousand pounds, a million, tops. Instead, they had committed the biggest daylight robbery in British history. Enough to make each and every one of them a multi-millionaire.

All they had to do now was hang on to it.

3

The Brink's-Mat robbery burst like a thunderclap on a Britain already reeling from inner-city riots, strikes, economic uncertainty and a general sense of social and cultural unease. High on the list of social ills was the epidemic of violent crime. The increase in armed robbery was exponential, and looked out of control even to the casual observer. In the ten years before the Brink's-Mat raid, the number of armed robberies had risen from 380 to 1,772 per annum – an increase of some 340 per cent. The mother and father of all heists, the Brink's-Mat raid definitely wasn't helping, either with UK crime statistics that were already among the worst, per capita, in Western Europe or with the image of the Metropolitan Police. In 1982, the 1,772 armed robberies in the London Metropolitan Police area netted thieves more than £12 million from banks, building societies, security vans, supermarkets, post offices and any other institution obliged to store or move cash in the capital.

News of the heist galvanized the top floor of New Scotland Yard, sending senior police officers scurrying in all directions. The biggest and most audacious robbery ever committed anywhere in the world: the press and public reaction – both national and international – was seismic. The story made the front page of all the British national newspapers and many foreign ones, dominating UK news bulletins for days. The question on everyone's lips was: how had the thieves managed to penetrate some of the world's tightest security in broad daylight, load several tons of gold onto one or more vehicles, and escape without anyone noticing?

And where was the missing gold? Despite the immediate posting of a record £2 million reward for information leading to its recovery, no one was talking.

As the Yard's phones rang a frantic chorus, senior Metropolitan Police officers convened in crisis meeting. They included Commander Frank Cater, appointed in January that same year as the new head of a much-expanded and – he hoped – corruption-free Flying Squad, the specialist unit originally set up to deal with a crime wave in the wake of the First World War; Assistant Commissioner (AC) Gilbert Kelland, and others. Ex-Royal Marine turned career policeman, Cater had made his name in the toughest of schools, by taking on – and breaking – the brutal and notorious criminal networks of both the Richardson family and the Kray twins. Cater and the others decided on two things: first, they had to get the gold back in order to stop it fuelling yet more serious crime on the UK mainland and beyond; second, they would do whatever it took to achieve this, in terms of allocating staff and resources.

In fact, the investigation was already in full swing. At 0820 Alan Bullock of Norman Reeves Trucks tried to call Unit 7 again. Using his teeth and a lot of initiative, guard Peter Bentley had managed to escape. He freed Scouse, who had been handcuffed to the heating pipes, and let Riseley and Black out of the cupboard where they had been shoved while the gang loaded the gold. Scouse tried to telephone the police, but the outside line had not been switched through. Bentley now went and did this, but Scouse, who had been through his own private version of hell, was unable to make the emergency operator understand what had happened. At this moment, Bullock rang. Scouse said, 'Call the police – we've been turned over.' Bullock wasted no time. As soon as the emergency 999 call came in, a Flying Squad team led by Detective Inspector (DI) Tony Brightwell raced to the scene, arriving at the Brink's-Mat depot minutes after the robbers had fled. Setting up a mobile control unit outside the warehouse, they found an empty, gaping vault and a group of terrified and shell-shocked security guards in various states of injury and undress. Apart from the masking tape that had been used to truss the guards, some handcuffs and a small amount of discarded clothing, they found no physical evidence. The robbers' boots, coveralls, masks and gloves had no doubt been burned, and there was no sign of the getaway vehicles, abandoned or otherwise, in the surrounding area.

Some months earlier, in a raid on a Security Express depot in the

East End of London, a gang disguised in monkey masks had escaped with £6 million in cash. Dubbed 'The Crime of the Decade' by the British press, this raid had dwarfed the title's previous holder, the 1963 Great Train Robbery in which thieves had netted a mere £2 million. Compared with the Brink's-Mat heist, both robberies – even combined – looked like also-rans.

One thing that interested Brightwell was the fact that a guard had also been doused in petrol and threatened in the course of the Security Express raid. Maybe this was the work of the same team, whose members had spent their formative years watching gangster movies. Maybe they had taken the petrol idea from Michael Winner's 1972 film *Scorpio*, in which, enraged at the murder of his wife, the character played by Burt Lancaster soaks a man in gasoline, lights a match and threatens him with immolation.

Brightwell's right-hand man was a no-nonsense Detective Sergeant (DS) named Tony Curtis. Curtis didn't know it yet, but he would spend the next thirteen years of his life – virtually the whole of his remaining police career – on the trail of the Brink's-Mat robbers and the missing gold. The pair had some useful help: not counting input from other elements like C11 (now SO11), Scotland Yard's intelligence branch, more than thirty experienced Metropolitan Police officers were instantly relieved of other duties and assigned exclusively to the case.

This was a big one – and as the minutes ticked away, it grew bigger: the fact that so much bullion had been snatched with such ease gave the gold markets the shakes. By the end of the day, the Brink's-Mat heist was worth around one million pounds more than when the robbers had stolen it twelve hours earlier – a bonus on their newly acquired capital.

A glance at the crime scene told Brightwell and Curtis that the robbery had been an inside job. The most glaring pointer was the fact that none of the locks – especially the formidable deadlock on Unit 7's pedestrian entrance – had been forced. None of the alarms had been triggered. And then there was the timing of the raid, which just happened to have taken place when the biggest bullion consignment ever handled by Brink's-Mat had been in transit.

Suspicion fell at once on the six guards. All of them·were badly shaken, Scouse, Riseley and Bentley most of all. Bentley's scalp and Riseley's sliced hand also needed medical attention. All the guards could have done with a long lie-down. But with the intense public and media gaze now focused on them, the police were under enormous pressure to come up with a quick result. Brightwell and his team set about interviewing the six men without delay.

To help him disentangle the sequence of events and get them clear in his mind, Brightwell staged the first-ever video reconstruction of a crime by the British police. The six guards – beginning with the Key Man, Michael Scouse – were asked to re-enact the raid from the moment when Scouse had arrived for work. For the very good reason that he *had* been the Key Man that day, the spotlight of immediate suspicion fell on Scouse. He was the one who had held the main door key, controlled the alarms, and knew most when it came to the overall security arrangements. True, he had been doused in petrol and threatened with a pistol, but he hadn't been physically harmed during the raid. The fact that he'd been both the first man in that morning and the one in charge of the front door might just, the police reasoned, have given him the opportunity to leave the entrance unlocked and tip the robbers the wink.

But when Curtis and Brightwell played back the video they had shot of the re-enactment, the body language of both Scouse and Riseley, the consistency and straightforwardness of their replies and their readiness to provide answers suggested that neither was involved. The exercise had not been a waste of time: it established where each guard had been during the raid, how the robbers had treated them, and it gave detectives a first impression of what, if anything, they were able to remember about the raiders.

When it came to explaining what he had seen in the course of the raid, the responses of one guard in particular raised a question mark.

Tasked with helping to interview Anthony Black, one of the Flying Squad team, Detective Constable (DC) Bill Miller, asked Black what had happened to him. A courteous Scot with a solid, wrestler's build, Miller was nobody's fool. When he asked you a question, you'd better be telling the truth. Lie, and there was every chance he would see through it. Black told Miller he'd come in slightly late for work that morning – the result, he claimed, of having overslept. This much, when Miller checked with Black's wife, was true. Black went on to say that he'd dumped his coat in the crew-room and then gone straight back downstairs to the toilet. An impressive officer with a penetrating stare, Brightwell jumped in. 'Did you say that was your intention to anyone, or did you just go?'

'No – I just went down to the toilet.' Black said that as soon as they burst into the crew-room the robbers had trussed and hooded him like the others. Then, some time later, they had asked for him by name, released him, removed his handcuffs and hood and forced him – at gunpoint – to open the internal loading bay doors. He explained that the controls to operate these doors were in the far left-hand corner of the crew-room, right next to the window overlooking the bay.

This was interesting. Brightwell decided they should re-enact it. The detectives and Black moved as a group to the corner, and stood for a moment looking down into the bay. Brightwell asked Black to show them exactly what he had done. Keeping his face averted towards the back wall, Black bent sideways to the controls and simultaneously pressed the two buttons that operated the doors. This looked odd to the watching police. Very odd.

'From where you were standing, could you see the doors opening?' Miller asked.

Black's thin shoulders hunched tighter. 'No,' he said, 'I was looking in the corner, like.'

'Did you see what vehicles were used to take the gold away?'

'No, no, I wasn't in a position to see out of the window.'

Brightwell and Miller stared at the guard. 'Are you standing in exactly the same position you were in at the time?' Black leaned further into the corner, pressing his face up against the wall in an effort to convince them how little he had been able to see. The detectives exchanged glances. There was something a little desperate about this pantomime. The guard was not just eager to have them believe him – he was falling over himself.

'I think I may have even been closer,' Black told them. 'I was doing it like that, rather than like that.' He made the same odd sideways-leaning movement with his upper body, fiddling with hands around the box to show how he had operated the door controls without looking at them. 'Must have ended up about here,' he added.

By now, he had his face squashed tight up into the corner angle of the room. To the watching officers, Black's re-enactment looked at once ridiculous and implausible. Miller walked across the room, asked Black to stand aside and took up the same position. Even with his face pressed tight up into the corner like Black, the window was so close – and so large – that he could still see almost the entire area of the loading bay without turning his head. He could certainly see the outside doors, and if there had been any vehicles in the bay he could not possibly have missed them.

'You didn't see any of the gang?' Brightwell's tone had a new edge.

Black hesitated. 'I can remember sort of seeing someone in the background. It wasn't, sort of clear, but there was someone in the background.' He sounded like William Brown trying to explain how the rare china figurine had unaccountably gone missing.

The police thanked Black for his cooperation and let him go. When he had gone, Brightwell turned to his team. 'All right,' he said, 'let's have a drains-up look at him.' In Metropolitan Police parlance, 'a drains-up look' means finding out everything there is to know about a suspect, right down to the colour of their Aunt Jemima's underwear.

Curtis and Miller got busy. Starting with Black's immediate family and friends, they began a trawl through his contacts, investigating his bank accounts, shining a bright forensic light into the secret corners of his life. A few days later, they came back to Brightwell. As soon as he clapped eyes on them, he knew they had found something.

'You two look like the cat that got the cream. Got a result?'

'Have we ever,' Curtis told him, pulling up a chair. 'Listen to this.'

When he'd heard them out, Brightwell sat back, put his hands behind his head and let out a long sigh. He'd spent several sleepless nights worrying about how to move the case forward. Everyone from the Assistant Commissioner for Crime to what seemed like the whole of Fleet Street and all the major TV news teams was on his back. Maybe now the case was beginning to break. 'Pick Black up at dawn tomorrow morning,' he ordered. 'And Tony?' Curtis stopped in the doorway and looked back. 'Do it by the book – I want him worried.'

Anthony Black was asleep when the police came for him. The

uniformed officers were stone-faced and silent, ignoring his anxious and repeated questions about why he was being taken for questioning. By the time they reached New Scotland Yard, his face had turned a grey colour much like the cold light struggling to break through the early morning overcast.

It was the morning of 4 December – eight days after the robbery.

When Black reached the interview room, he was surprised, and, to the watching Brightwell, obviously taken aback to find his personal work diary lying open on the desk in front of him. Brightwell asked Black to account for all the telephone numbers listed in it. In a voice that plainly betrayed his nervousness Black went through them one by one. Brightwell then asked him to explain some of the entries in the diary, especially the ones that were abbreviated, like 'W/A'.

'That's my wedding anniversary,' Black said blandly, recovering a little of his composure.

'All right. And who is "G. Harding"?'

'He used to work at Brink's-Mat. I do his car.'

Black didn't much seem to care for Brightwell's cat-and-mouse game. He liked it even less when Brightwell tightened the screw a couple of turns. 'This entry on the day of the robbery. Why did you write "6.30 a.m."?'

Black's voice was full of surprised innocence. 'That's what time I start.'

'You've never written it down before. Why did you write it down on this Saturday?'

'I dunno. No particular reason.' Black did not know that as soon as they had started the investigation, Brightwell and his team had photocopied every single page of the six guards' work diaries. Brightwell showed Black a photocopy of the original diary page taken on the day of the robbery, followed by a copy of the same page taken on the day after with the time inserted in Black's own handwriting. The evidence showed that the original diary page had been blank. There was no getting round it.

Brightwell kept his tone low and even, but there was no mistaking the underlying menace in his words. 'You changed your diary, Tony. I took a look at it, before we did the filming.' Black was silent. 'That's not the only change you made. Look here, where it says, "1.30" on the day of the robbery. That's been added, too. Why did you do that?'

Black had the look of a man who has suddenly been plunged into a vat of ice-cold water. He shook his head. 'I dunno.'

Brightwell's gaze was intent: his whole body seemed to point at Black, like a gun dog pointing at a downed game bird. 'Do you drink a lot, Tony?'

While it was a standard police interrogation ploy to throw in the odd disarming or non-essential question to keep the suspect talking, the change of tack seemed to disconcert Black further. 'Yeah, I like to have a light ale with the lads occasionally.'

Brightwell went for the throat. 'What does your brother-in-law, Brian Robinson, think about the robbery?'

Black recoiled as if he had been slapped hard across the face. 'I haven't spoken to him,' he stammered. 'I don't know what he thinks.' Brightwell nodded, but not in a way that would indicate belief. The 'drains-up look' had paid off: Curtis and Miller had found out that Anthony Black's sister Jennifer lived with a man named Brian Robinson. In fact, she was his common-law wife. Robinson was well known to the Flying Squad – as a diehard South London 'face'. Known as 'The Colonel' in the criminal backwaters south of the River Thames for his ability to plan and execute serious crime, Robinson was a career gangster. A big man in his early forties, he had a record that included fraud – and armed robbery.

Brightwell nodded to the police constable in the room with them. 'OK, take him down to the cells.' The officer led Black away. If Black had possessed a tail instead of a moustache, it would have dragged along the floor behind him.

Black had never been on the inside of a police cell before – and he did not like the experience one little bit. Brightwell left him to stew in the tiny, windowless room for a few hours. The cell was bare and stained, with a concrete floor and tiled walls that sweated grime. The only thing to sit on was a hard bench covered in filthy, ripped vinyl. With nothing to do but smoke, Black had plenty of time to reflect. And the more he reflected, the more the words, 'What does your brother-in-law, Brian Robinson, think about the robbery?' preyed on his mind. All he could think was that *the police knew*. In which case he had two equally unattractive options.

When he thought the suspect would be nicely done, Brightwell had Black brought back up again. He asked for a cup of tea, and an officer duly obliged. Black kept the steaming mug in front of his face, much as if he wanted to hide behind it. Brightwell, for his part, went on staring at the guard with an intense and discomfiting gaze. The seconds ticked by, and neither man spoke. Black looked everywhere but at his inquisitor. Brightwell looked only at him. At last, Black put the mug down, raised his eyes and met Brightwell's.

'Where do I start?'

Checking the momentary flare of triumph, Brightwell put his tea down carefully on the table between them. 'Let's start at the beginning, shall we, Tony?'

4

They began at the beginning, with Brian Robinson's Big Idea. This was hardly rocket science. Robinson had been living with Jennifer, Anthony Black's elder sister, since 1979. A professional criminal, he looked out for every opportunity to commit crime. When Black got the job at Brink's-Mat, Robinson was hardly going to hang back.

Black had served several years in the British Army, during which time he had been posted to Northern Ireland. Here he had met and married Vivien Sorrie, a local girl. They had a daughter, but the marriage did not go well – not least because when Black was posted to Germany he started a separate relationship with a woman named Suzanna Jahnke, and Vivien found out.

Despite this marital reverse, Black and Sorrie tried to patch things up. Black followed his wife and daughter back to Ulster, and when he left the army they decided to move to London and try again. Married and with a good record of army service, Black applied successfully to Brink's-Mat for a job as a driver/guard, starting work at the company's Arnold Street depot in the City of London late in 1976.

Six months later, and without any warning to his family, Black upped sticks and went back to Germany, and the open arms of Suzanna Jahnke. He drifted in and out of casual jobs, but in a matter of weeks this relationship, too, had crashed and burned. Black fled again, pitching up out of the blue at his parents' home in Bromley one evening. The very next day he went round to see his former supervisor at the Brink's-Mat office in Arnold Street, and begged for his old job back. It was and is very unusual to re-employ personnel in the security business, but after extracting a promise of some real commitment to the job this time round, the company took him on again. He restarted work on 29 January 1979.

At last, Black showed signs of settling down: he turned up regularly for work, made himself available for overtime and generally kept his nose clean. Finding a place to live anywhere near the City of London wasn't easy, but here his elder sister came to the rescue. Jennifer's new partner, Brian, had the keys to an empty flat in Ben Jonson Road, Stepney, above a row of shops – would Tony like to see it? Tony would: only a mile or so from the Brink's-Mat Arnold Street depot, the flat, while frayed around the edges and smack in the middle of an unprepossessing housing estate, was extremely convenient for work. In return for a down payment of 'key money', Black took the place on. Robinson and a friend of his – a huge, hard-looking man introduced simply as 'Tony' – helped the guard move in. Helping Black find accommodation gained his trust; it also put him in debt.

Robinson knew perfectly well what he was about: it wasn't every day you had a Brink's-Mat security guard in the family. There was no harm in looking after his brother-in-law – they were drinking partners, for one thing, and then you never knew when his insider knowledge might come in useful.

Black, meanwhile, divorced.

Some months passed uneventfully, until Black, delivering a cash shipment to the Twickenham branch of Lloyds Bank one bright summer's day, met a woman named Lynn Halliday employed there as a counter clerk. The two hit it off – so well that they married six months later, bought a maisonette a couple of miles from Heathrow airport and set up home.

One of Robinson's favourite ways of making money then was the 'stolen chequebook' scam. Since fraudsters often prey on those closest to them, he persuaded Black to hand over his personal chequebook. Unbeknownst to his new wife, Black falsely reported the chequebook stolen to the very same branch where she worked. Robinson went out and signed twenty-six fraudulent cheques in return for various goods and services – but instead of paying Black the £5 per cheque they had agreed, he gave him a black-and-white television set, some groceries, a few bottles of booze and a lawnmower.

It was a tawdry little crime, but the principle had been established – Black was prepared to help his brother-in-law 'cross the pavement', as the slang then had it for breaking the law. Robinson was well pleased: he had made a few bob, and if he could turn Black a little further from the paths of righteousness, then so much the better.

Black knew perfectly well that his brother-in-law had done several stretches in prison for a wide range of offences, including robbery. He also knew that in his position as a guard with one of the world's top security firms he should steer well clear of his sister's latest squeeze. Instead, like a groupie hanging round a rock star, he felt flattered by Robinson's attention and, far from thinking it wrong, looked on the other man's criminal lifestyle as somehow exciting, even glamorous. Being in with a top London villain made Black feel important, something more than a face in the crowd.

Black never took part in the stolen chequebook fraud again, but Robinson made sure to keep him on the criminal hook by slipping him the odd illegal goodie. Robinson knew Black was impulsive by nature: he had grandiose dreams, and he was fed up scraping by on the miserable wages of a security guard. Black made no bones about the fact that living in a maisonette set amidst the scruffy jumble of housing and light industrial units surrounding Heathrow airport, working 'earlies' and 'lates' for the Brink's-Mat company, was not how he wanted to spend the rest of his life. He also wanted to do better by Lynn.

Much better.

Robinson let things lie for some months. Then one day, out of the blue, he called in the favour he had done Black when it came to the flat. Handing Black a Polaroid camera, he asked him to photograph the interiors of the two main types of Brink's-Mat security vans then in use. Robinson said it was for a friend named 'Mickey'. Black might have hesitated – this was not so much crossing the pavement as taking a flying leap – but he agreed. A few days later, when they were alone in the council flat his brother-in-law shared with Jennifer in Rollins Street, New Cross, Black handed Robinson three rather blurred and shaky snaps. Quietly jubilant, Robinson led Black outside and round the corner into a sidestreet. There was a black BMW parked at the end of it. They walked up to the car and got in. A blocky, tow-headed terrier of a man with intense blue eyes and a disconcerting stare, the driver turned round in his seat and looked back at them. Robinson said, 'Tony, this is Mickey. Mickey, Tony.'

'Mickey' radiated violence. This was the genuine article, a top South London face – a flame for a gangster-moth like Black. Mickey did not waste time on the niceties, but he did do Black the courtesy of taking him seriously. Did he think a Land-Rover fitted with a makeshift battering ram would be able to punch through the rear doors of a Brink's-Mat security van? Black did not know. But he said he thought it would not work; the doors were too heavily armoured.

A few weeks later, in December 1980 when Black's memory of the meeting had faded, a gang of armed robbers smashed through the rear doors of a Brink's-Mat van with the jib of a mobile crane. The van was passing through Dulwich, South London, with £811,000 in cash on board.

They might have got away with it if the police had not been tipped off. Five shots were fired in the ensuing ambush and the whole gang arrested – except for the inside informant, who somehow managed to slip away.

Worried that his photographs might have been used in this robbery, Black asked Robinson if either he or 'Mickey' had been involved. Robinson said he knew a set-up when he smelled one, and they had neither of them been anywhere near it.

It wasn't until some two years later, in the autumn of 1982, that Robinson targeted Black again. Robinson knew Black liked fishing, and was more likely to be in a relaxed and receptive mood on the riverbank. He waited until his brother-in-law had disappeared through the door with his rod and keep-net, gave it an hour or so to let him get settled into that deep reverie so beloved of all fishermen, and then followed. Black had a favourite spot on an attractive reach of the Thames at Laleham. Robinson crossed the bridge and trudged along the footpath until he spotted his mark. Lowering his large bulk onto the grass next to Black, he shot him a friendly look. 'Tony, me old mate, how's it going?'

'All right, Brian – what brings you out here?'

Robinson nodded at the float bobbing in the water below them. 'Thought I'd come and see how you were doing. Had any luck?'

'Couple of tiddlers, like – threw them back in.'

Robinson got down to business. 'I was thinking, Tony – about your job.' This was always a sore point with Black, and immediately got his attention.

'What about it?'

'That lot – Brink's-Mat. How much are they paying you these days?'

Black kept his gaze focused on the float. 'Not enough.'

'Even with all of that shift work you do?'

It got him a look. 'Who's been talking? Jennifer?'

'No mate, it's nothing like that. It's just I was thinking. About the fact you guard all that money. Take all that risk. And Brink's-Mat pay you jack shit for doing it.'

Black's expression hardened. 'Too true, Brian. Too true.'

'Then why don't we do something about it?'

Black looked up at his brother-in-law, and then back down at the steel-grey water. You didn't need to be a genius to see where the conversation was headed: what with the chequebook scam and the security van photographs the pair of them had plenty of previous – and they had already had more than one conversation about the riches that daily passed under Black's nose.

'That warehouse you work in, up Heathrow – is there anything we can walk in on?' For the likes of Brian Robinson, Brink's-Mat Unit 7 and its contents were like the Holy Grail to the knights of Camelot: legendary among the ranks of London's criminal classes for the regularity and value of its shipments, it was always there, shimmering on the horizon. Waiting to be hit.

Black knew he was never going to get rich clocking on as a security guard. But he did stand every chance of staying poor. It really wasn't much of a choice. Unless, that is, you had a conscience. He said, 'There's a lot of stuff comes through there, as you know – especially at the weekends. But the place is like Fort Knox – it's got alarms and that everywhere.' He thought for a moment, and then added, 'An Aer Lingus currency shipment comes in every week. I go with the crew and collect the banknotes from their warehouse over by Egypt Air.' At the mention of the magical word 'banknotes', Robinson's dark, hungry gaze brightened. 'How much, for an average shipment?'

'A million.' Black said it in a flat tone. 'It's always at least a million quid.'

The mere fact that Black was still answering his questions made Brian Robinson a happy man: this wasn't petty stuff, like dodgy chequebooks – this could be the Big One. He handed Black a cigarette. They lit up and puffed away in companionable silence. Robinson said, 'You don't have to say anything right away, Tony. Have a think about it, we'll talk again tomorrow or whenever you want. It's just . . .'

'What?' The thin face turned upwards.

Robinson shrugged his meaty shoulders. 'You know – be nice to see my Jennifer and your Lynn get a bit of the gravy for a change. Buy themselves some new clothes, and that. We could maybe get them a couple of nice little houses somewhere.' The broad, lumpy face split in a wide grin. 'Or even, nice big ones.' He stopped there, right on the verge of conspiracy to rob. The last gambit, in which he had appealed to Black's love for his wife, and the guard's fear that unless he earned a lot more money she might soon leave him – it was like moulding putty. Robinson stubbed out his cigarette. He had sown the seeds: let Black mull it over, reach his own decision. He heaved himself upright, gave Black a last friendly wink, and made as if to saunter away down the footpath.

Black jumped to his feet. 'Wait! What would I have to do? Nothing dangerous or that?' Robinson turned, ambled back and laid a bear-like paw on Black's shoulder. 'Of course not, Tony – there'd be no risk for you, mate: no one's even going to know you were in on the job.' His eyes twinkled reassuringly. 'It's like I said, we just need a little information.'

Robinson saw fear buried deep in the brown eyes, and something else that pleased him more than anything Black could have said: the hard, metallic glint of greed – the same greed he nursed in his own heart.

'You're sure I wouldn't have to do anything except tell you what's what? Because I can't – you know – do any of that other stuff.'

By 'that other stuff' Black meant the nitty-gritty of armed robbery: like threatening his workmates with firearms; whacking them over the head; torturing and perhaps even shooting them if they tried to resist.

''Course you won't, Tony – we'll take care of all that. All you have to do is tell us a couple of details. Have a little think, like I said. And if you still want to come in on the job, we'll go and see Mickey again.'

'Mickey?' Black said quickly.

There was something of the mongoose sizing up the snake in Robinson's gaze. 'Yeah, Mick. You took some photographs for him – remember? Don't worry; he's sweet as a nut.' Robinson dropped his hand, turned and walked away, meaning it this time. 'Be seeing you, Tony. And remember – mum's the word.' Black went back to his fishing. But even if he'd hooked a world record-breaking pike, and fought an epic battle to land it, it's difficult to say whether the part of him that really mattered would have noticed.

5

When it came to it, Robinson's assurance that all they wanted from Black was a 'couple of details' turned out to be something of an understatement. What they wanted was everything Black already knew about Brink's-Mat Unit 7 high-security warehouse, plus everything else that he didn't but could find out. A raid on the Aer Lingus building was quickly rejected on the grounds that the police were routinely present in the area. It was Brink's-Mat or nothing.

And so the two men set to work, Robinson doing the fishing, while Black wriggled on the hook. They met a few days later in the New Cross flat while Jennifer Black was out at work. Robinson asked the questions, and Black, who had been at the Heathrow depot for more than a year, did his best to come up with the answers. The pair eventually concluded that the best time to strike the depot was on a Friday night, when, as Black explained, gold and currency shipments to the Far East – usually via the evening Cathay Pacific flight – were regularly held in transit. They discussed the ins and outs of it over the course of a few more meetings, and the simple fact of it was that, whichever way they looked at it, Friday was the night.

A few weeks later, in the middle of June 1983, Robinson invited Black to meet Mickey again, on the forecourt of Gibb's car showroom on the A30 at Bedfont, not far from Heathrow airport. When Black arrived he was surprised to find a third man in the other car – the same man who had helped him move into the flat over the shops in Stepney all those months ago. Robinson said, 'Tony, you already know Mickey.' 'Mickey' – real name Michael John McAvoy – said, 'Tony, this is Tony.' Pleased with his little joke, he treated them all to a mirthless grin.

Around forty and with the build of a heavyweight wrestler,

'Tony's' huge upper body made him look top-heavy. If Black had ever been in any doubt he was among thieves, meeting his 'friend' for the second time must have for ever banished it: this was no student of Socrates; here was a man majoring in Cosh Studies with Applied Extortion. He wore multi-storey gold rings that did double duty as knuckledusters, had a stubbled chin and black licks of hair pasted flat to a balding scalp. He crushed Black's hand in his own, grinning as the guard winced.

They sat in McAvoy's BMW so as not to be overheard. McAvoy could scare most people when he wanted to – it was a trick he had. He said nothing at first, just gave Black the house special stare. Black started to sweat: the interior of the BMW seemed to press in on him. Being near McAvoy was like being caged up with a dangerous animal – one that might turn on you without warning. The guard uttered some syllables that might have been 'All right?' and looked away. From that moment on the relationship between the two men was carved in stone – Black was the rabbit, McAvoy the fox. And they both knew it.

Robinson had recruited McAvoy to lead the proposed Brink's-Mat raid from a hard core of some 200 South London criminals ready and willing – make that spoiling – to be part of a major armed robbery at the time. Especially a blag organized by that renowned master of intelligence and planning, Brian 'The Colonel' Robinson.

There were so many willing criminals that The Colonel could pick and choose. The fact that he had fished Michael McAvoy from the murky pool was a tribute to the robber's reputation and record. Scotland Yard might suspect that McAvoy had led a series of successful armed raids and walked to spend the takings, but they couldn't prove it. Robinson knew damned well that he had, and respected him for it.

Where Black's gaze was liquid and doe-like, McAvoy's was like nothing so much as a rattlesnake's. He spoke in a grating near-monotone. 'Brian tells me you're willing to help us out again, Tony – that right?'

'Yeah, that's right, Mickey.' Black was already falling over himself to help, ready to do just about anything he was told. Seeing this – and not one to waste any time – McAvoy asked him there and then to describe the internal and external layout of the Brink's-Mat warehouse in sum and in detail; identify and point out any potential weak points; explain how all the alarm systems worked; detail the guards' shift patterns and work routines; itemize the door and window locks; describe the high-security vault; tell them who held the keys, the codes to the vaults and the safes inside it, and spill anything else he could think of that might be useful. Black told them everything he knew, chapter and verse.

The four men continued to meet at regular intervals: sometimes at Gibb's garage, other times at Hatton Cross Underground station, in The Bulldog public house in Ashford, Kent, or at the end of a randomly selected cul-de-sac. Each time they met Black gave more information, including details of the type and value of the shipments that had recently been through the warehouse, their method and time of arrival and departure, and the way they had been transported and guarded.

One day, in a repeat of their previous exploit, Robinson gave Black a self-winding auto-focus camera and asked him to photograph as much of Unit 7's interior as he could – if possible, all of it. It was a singular fact that at this stage of the proceedings, Black was taking all the risk in return for nothing more than a promise that the gang would, in the event of a successful robbery, 'sort him out' with some money in a numbered Swiss bank account. The real reward for Black was rubbing shoulders with the lawless: leading a secret double life, feeling he was part of something very big and very dangerous. He was a *gang member*, he *belonged*. While the world might still view him that way from the outside, on the inside he knew he was more than just a twopenny-ha'penny security guard. He was the kingpin – without his insider knowledge the robbers could do nothing. Armed with the expensive and beautifully made Minox camera, charged with a dangerous mission, he felt like James Bond.

Black's luck was in. During a lull in operations, he was asked to paint the inside of the security vault. It gave him the perfect opportunity to photograph it. Picking his times carefully to avoid detection, he photographed not only the vault but the stairs; all of the upstairs rooms including the crew rest-room and the radio room; the loading bay and the loading bay doors; the side-door the guards used for access and the lobby area inside it, and rounded off his photographic essay with close-ups of the side-door alarm box.

As well as being a bit of a practical joker, Black was a fair mechanic: he earned a little extra cash and made himself popular with his workmates by fixing any problems they had with their cars. So when he arrived at his sister's flat on the pretext of fixing a rattle in Robinson's Renault she thought nothing of it. Robinson drove to a house Black had never visited before, further east up the river in Greenwich. 'We went in through a bead curtain into the kitchen. Brian led the way through a second door into the sitting room. Mick and Tony were already there. They had the photographs out on the floor and a plan I had drawn to show the warehouse layout. They were big colour shots, professionally developed, not like snapshots. They kept asking me questions about the map and the photos, things like, "What does the Key Man do when he opens the door?" Or "What does the Key Man do when he opens the vault?"'

Black went through Unit 7's standard operating procedures for what felt to him like the hundredth time: when and how the alarms were set and deactivated; when the warehouse was likely to be quiet; when it was usually busy, and every little detail they could think to ask him.

A few days later they all met up again on the riverbank. McAvoy handed Black a thick wad of plasticine and a cuttlefish bone. Black stared down at the objects in bewilderment 'Take impressions of the keys to the side-door,' McAvoy told him impatiently, 'with these.' He took a Chubb key out of his pocket to demonstrate. 'All you have to do is lay the key in the plasticine, like this, and press down hard all round. Same with the cuttlefish – that's a fail-safe, in case the plasticine doesn't work.' He eyed Black narrowly. 'Can you do it?'

'Yeah, I reckon, Mickey.'

'All right. When are you next due on shift?'

'Thursday. Early.'

'Right. Be at The Bulldog pub in Ashford at one o'clock on Friday. Bring us an impression of the key to the side-door – nice and clean, mind. I'll get copies of it made while you wait in the pub. You take the copies in to work next time you're on duty. Try each of the duplicate keys in the lock until you find the one that works best.

When you've got the best key, mark it with something. Got that?'

'Yeah.'

McAvoy leaned slightly towards him. 'I said, have you got that?'

Black swallowed. 'I've got it, Mickey.'

'Good boy. We'll be seeing you Friday, then, at The Bulldog. And don't be late.'

The very next evening, on the late shift, Black got lucky again: the duty Key Man, who had a lot of paperwork to catch up on, loaned him his keys to let another guard in through the side-door. Black grabbed his chance. On the pretext of visiting the toilet, he took impressions of the door key in both the plasticine and the cuttlefish bone. When he'd handed the keys back and all was quiet again he made his way over to the warehouse payphone and called Robinson. His message was short, and, to his brother-in-law's ears at least, extremely sweet. 'I've got 'em.'

Black arrived at The Bulldog public house a few minutes early, but even so he found McAvoy, Robinson and 'Tony' waiting for him in the car park. McAvoy fixed Black with the viper stare. 'Did you get what we wanted?'

'Yeah – like I told Robbo.' He took out the block of plasticine: it held a good, clean impression of Unit 7's side-door key.

'And the cuttlefish?'

Black fumbled in his coat pockets, found the spongy cuttlefish skeleton and handed it over.

McAvoy studied the shape that had been pressed into the soft bone: it, too, was deep and clear and sharp-edged. He took out a fifty-pound note and shoved it into Black's top pocket. 'You done good, my son. Here, get yourself a drink and something to eat.' He turned and stepped into the car. 'Wait here,' he told them, 'I'll be back in an hour.'

He was as good as his word – fifty minutes later, Black was the proud owner of three brand-new keys to the front door of the very same Brink's-Mat stronghold he was being paid to guard.

Black went in to work the next day as scheduled, waited until all was quiet again and then paid another of his unnecessary visits to the toilet near Unit 7's side-door. He slid the first of the duplicate keys into the lock and tried to turn it.

The key stuck fast.

Anthony Black had never known the kind of panic that now seized him. He stood there, fingers locked around the handle of the key, prey to a succession of crystal-sharp, hyper-detailed images of disaster. The horrible reality of imminent discovery, arrest and humiliation flashed in front of his mind's eye, followed by hot waves of crushing shame at the thought that his wife Lynn, his sister Jennifer and his parents would learn he was a *thief*.

The prospect of prison, which had seemed glamorous when it happened to someone else, now struck him as terrifying in the extreme: he could almost hear the clang of the heavy metal cell door as it slammed shut, delivering him and his moustache up to the not very tender, but extremely insistent care of some hulking cellmate. A new realization hit him then, the worst one of all: he would have to explain to the police *why* he had a set of duplicate keys to the unit's side-door. They would want to know how he had come by the keys and what they were for. Black – now instantly demoted in his own estimation from super-cool professional *gangster* to hapless and tragic security guard led astray by *evil influences* – knew that the police would not believe he had intended robbing a Brink's-Mat warehouse unaided. They would want to know who he was working with. They would sweat him until he gave up the names of his accomplices.

The image of 'Mickey' came to Black – the implacable McAvoy, to whom violence was an everyday commodity, just another way of getting things done. As he heaved at the key with every ounce of strength he possessed, Black's tortured imagination sequenced through the worst possible outcomes, jumping from one to the next at lightning speed. What if the police found out Robbo was living with his sister Jennifer? There was no 'if' about it – they would discover the link straight away. Would he – Black – be able to resist their interrogation? Keep the identities of the other gang members secret?

In the tiny corner of his mind where Black was still able to be honest with himself, he knew that he would not withstand prolonged and insistent police questioning: he would crack; he would tell the detectives everything they wanted to know. But if he did that, what would Mickey say? Even more frightening, when he found out Black had not only failed the gang but dragged them all down into the dungeons with him, what would Mickey *do*?

Black thought he knew the answer – and it did not bear thinking about.

As these nightmares assaulted his fevered brain, he kept working furiously at the key. It would not budge a hair's breadth. It was as if the lock had been filled with cement and the key had set fast in the mix. The sweat was pouring off him now, his thumb and fingers slithering on the metal as he tried to keep a steady grip. He could hear a loud knocking sound from very close by, and glanced round fearfully: it was the sound of his own heart battering at his ribs. He rubbed his fingers furiously up and down his trousers in an effort to dry them, but the sweat kept leaking out: it seeped from his fingertips, ran down his forehead, pricked across his shoulders, leached into his eyes and trickled down the back of his uniform shirt. He heard a voice from upstairs and gave the key one last despairing wrench.

It came free. It was a miracle: almost enough to make him get religion, give all his worldly goods to charity and take holy orders. For a moment Black stood there, overwhelmed by the flood of relief that washed through him. Then reality hit. What if he'd damaged the lock? What if it didn't work when the Key Man tried to let them all out at the end of the shift? Would a forensic examination find some trace of the failed attempt? What if they searched all the guards, and found the duplicate keys in his pocket, or wherever else he tried to hide them? What about fingerprints?

The shift came to an end, and Black went downstairs with the rest of the duty crew. On any other day, he would have been leading the kind of banter that usually marked home time. But now he was silent and downcast, his fearful gaze intent on the Key Man. He watched as the supervisor stepped up to the side-door, inserted the key, and turned it.

The tumblers slid smoothly in the lock and the door swung open.

Seconds later, Black was a free man. A new wave of relief flooded back through him, the force so great that it was all he could do to keep walking. He wanted to kneel down and kiss the ground, do handsprings round the car park, anything to burn off the coursing nervous energy. He reached the Opel, got inside, put his hands on the steering wheel and rested his forehead against them.

That was as close as it came. He did not ever want to come that close again.

The second he got back home, Black called his brother-in-law. Robinson came straight round. He listened to the story, tutted a few tuts and tried to soothe Black. 'Don't worry, Tony – these things happen. Look, what if we forget about the side-door? How about we get in through one of the ground-floor windows? Maybe use bolt-cutters? That way, you won't have to do nothing more.'

It was no use – Black's nerves had been shredded by the ordeal of the key. He sat in silence, with a set face, barely responding to Robinson's questions, and then only with a monosyllabic 'Yes' or 'No'. Bottom line, Tony Black wasn't cut out to be a master criminal – he didn't have the bottle and they both knew it.

By chance, Black and his wife were due to go on holiday to Corfu, where his parents had a mobile home. The complete change of scenery and routine, the sunshine and fresh air – and the welcome freedom from the attentions of the gang – helped to calm him, so that by the time he returned a fortnight later he felt better about the fiasco of the key. The horror of those agonizing minutes had faded from his memory; he was ready to tough it out again with the lads.

Just as well – he had no sooner reached home than the telephone rang. It was Robinson, summoning him to an urgent meeting at The Bulldog. Black hurried over to find McAvoy, Robinson and 'Tony' waiting for him. Something in their eyes unnerved him. Not impatience – expectation.

It was McAvoy who broke the silence. 'Saturday,' he said in a flat tone. 'This Saturday.'

Black looked from face to face. 'What?'

'That's when we do it – Saturday morning.' McAvoy switched on the headlamp stare. 'The raid, Tony – that's when we're doing it. Are you working that day?'

'I don't know – they don't tell us if we're working until the night before.'

'Call Robbo Friday. Let him know if you're working. If you are, then we're coming in Saturday morning. Six-thirty sharp.' He leaned slightly. 'You might need to let us in. Got it?'

Black nodded. 'I'll call.' It was one thing play-acting the great, fearless robber. It was something else entirely now that the time had come to do the job.

6

That Friday, the duty crew chief asked Black if he'd be prepared to work overtime the next day as there was a shipment coming through. Black agreed to do the Saturday morning 'early'. As soon as the crew chief had gone, he walked – it was an effort not to run – over to the payphone on the warehouse wall. Slipping the agreed code words into the conversation as if they were innocent, he told his brother-in-law, 'I'm going fishing tomorrow.'

Next morning, at work, he surprised his colleagues by remaining unusually quiet, failing to respond to their jokes and generally behaving in a remote, distracted manner. On the inside, Black was wire taut: he was expecting an armed break-in at any moment. With no key to the side-door, he knew the gang had still not resolved the problem of how to get into the warehouse. He also knew that as a matter of routine the Key Man and the crew chief – or for that matter one or more of the other guards – could hit one of the panic buttons hidden around the building the moment anything untoward happened. The alarms were connected by direct radio link to Brink's-Mat security, and one was linked to Heathrow central police station. Unless he could find some way of letting Robbo and the boys in without attracting attention, the warehouse would be swarming with police officers and guards in minutes.

The seconds ticked by. Seven o'clock arrived and nothing happened. Lunchtime approached, and still there was no sign of action. Black was confused and disconcerted – what was going on? Had the whole thing been a set-up, a dry run designed to test him? Had something gone wrong at the last moment? He sweated, imagining that one or all of his fellow conspirators had been arrested and were telling the police about his vital role. But when he met the others later in the pub, they shrugged: there had been too little time to prepare the raid properly. Why didn't he calm down? There was no problem – in fact, as a result of the false start they were keener than ever to get at it. From now on, Black had to call Robbo every single Friday without fail and give details of his upcoming weekend schedule.

Three weeks passed without event, and then Black called Robinson with what, on the face of it, looked like bad news: David Stickland, the warehouse manager, had decided that the long-running refurbishments then going on at the depot should include a complete upgrade and renewal of the alarm systems, the introduction of an extra CCTV security camera to cover the side-door, and an array of new and better locks, including a replacement for the one in the side-door.

Robinson cursed – and then, with a flash of his usual cunning, saw the opportunity the changes might present. 'You say he's ordered new locks? What about the side-door – has that been changed?'

'Yeah – the new lock's just been fitted.'

'So there must be a set of new keys to it somewhere?'

'Yeah – he's got them: Stickland.'

'Can you get hold of one? I mean, borrow the actual key? Then we can get a proper copy cut.' He gave a grim little smile. 'One that works.'

The horror of that lifetime spent wrestling with the stuck key flooded through Black again. But there was no backing out now – the gang wouldn't let him. The fact was, by now they were all in too deep.

Fortune sometimes favours the stupid, and Black now struck lucky for the third time. The next day Stickland reported sick, leaving three shiny new copies of the side-door key lying in a bunch on his desk. As soon as he spotted them, Black called Robinson. 'They're lying there on his desk,' he gabbled excitedly. 'There's no one around right now. I reckon I can take one, borrow it and put it back.'

There was genuine warmth in his brother-in-law's reply. 'Good one, Tony. Where do you want to meet up?'

'At The Beaver, in the car park – about half-twelve.'

Replacing the wall phone, Black slithered back up to the

warehouse manager's office, skulking along the corridors like a modern-day Gollum. He glanced back out of the door to make sure no one was coming, sidled up to Stickland's desk and, heart racing, wrestled a key off the ring.

The Beaver was a pub near the Brink's-Mat depot, set in the middle of an outer-city shopping 'arcade' that was, even by the dismal standards of late twentieth-century suburban Britain, ugly, bleak and anonymous to a fault. Perfect for a clandestine meeting of armed robbers.

On arrival, Black found the whole gang waiting with the same air of eager – and quietly menacing – anticipation that had unnerved him before. Resembling nothing so much as a psychopathic undertaker in the badly cut charcoal suit and black tie he had chosen to wear for the occasion, Robinson heaved his large frame into Black's Opel. At once, like some particularly malicious imp, McAvoy's face appeared at the driver's side window. Black's fingers trembled as he handed over the key. McAvoy palmed it without a word and walked quickly back to the waiting Hillman. Nervously, Black watched them drive away. 'Where are they going?'

'Don't worry – there's a place in Hounslow two minutes from here does a proper job. I've had a couple of my own keys cut there.' Sure enough, McAvoy was back a few minutes later with three shiny copies of the purloined key. 'Cost me £4.50,' he quipped, as he handed Black the copies and the original. 'Try these, and mark the one that's the best fit.'

Later that afternoon, in Unit 7, it fell quiet. Even so, it took all of Black's courage to go down to the side entrance. With shaking hands, he slid the first key into the lock and tried it. The key did not work. But it came out again when he pulled which was something. Something like the most enormous feeling of relief he had experienced since the last time he'd tried this. He inserted the next key. That didn't work either, nor the third. Black cocked a nervous ear and listened intently. The warehouse was dead quiet – it was that lost hour of the afternoon when everything slides to a stop. Holding the new keys up to the light, he examined each one carefully in turn. All of the copies, he now saw, had tiny burrs of metal along their edges

– swarf that the lazy machinist had failed to remove. Black had the solution in his pocket – the small piece of emery cloth Robinson had suggested he take with him. He took it out, selected the key that looked best finished, and polished at the rough edges until the minute irregularities were gone.

With his heart in his mouth, he put the key back in the lock. Glancing back up the stairs and out through the window to make sure no one was coming, he turned it. The deadlock slid back with a chunky, reassuring *thunk*! Black padded back up to the crew-room, ripped a piece of Sellotape off the roll on the nearest desk and wrapped it round the shank of the working key. He then walked along to the manager's office and replaced the original on Stickland's bunch. He stood for a moment, his feelings brimming, flights of swallows swooping overhead. Success. He had done it. He was the main man.

With a working key to the side-door the gang was set to go. But Black's long run of luck now deserted him. Fridays came and went, without the call to work Saturday overtime that usually signalled a high-value shipment passing through the depot. As the weeks went by without a break the robbers grew increasingly nervous and irritable. October passed, and then the first three weeks of November. On the morning of Friday, 25 November, Black rang Robinson to give him the – by now customary – bad news. 'I'm not going fishing tomorrow.'

Then, at around 3 o'clock that afternoon, the duty supervisor called Black up to his office.

'All right for a bit of overtime tomorrow, Tony?'

Black's heart began to pound, but he kept his body language under tight control, giving no outward sign of the turmoil the request had set going. 'Yeah, I could use a bit of extra dosh. What shift is it?'

'It's an early – the usual – six-thirty in the morning. You will be there on time, won't you, Tony?' The manager smiled. Black's occasional lateness was a standing joke.

'I'll be there at six-thirty on the dot. Thanks.'

Black left the office, went back downstairs and picked up the payphone. 'Robbo, there's been a change – I can go fishing tomorrow after all as it turns out. Can you change your arrangements?'

There was a pause on the other end, and then Robinson said, 'Possibly, Tony, possibly. It's a bit short notice, but I'll see what I can do. What time do you finish today?'

'About four-thirty, after I do a run up Heathrow.'

'Let's meet up after that, shall we? Say The Bulldog, at half-five?'

'I'll be there.'

Black rang off. He was as good as his word – but when he reached The Bulldog, Robinson was not there. Worried in case something had gone wrong, Black rushed back home and sat by the telephone. At a quarter past seven, it rang. It was his brother-in-law.

'All right, Tony? I'm just round the corner. Can I have a word?'

Making hurried excuses to his wife, Black shot out of the house like a cat with its tail on fire. He skidded round the corner and saw a black Ford Escort sitting by the kerb about twenty metres away. McAvoy was in the driving seat; Robinson and 'Tony' were in the back.

As Black drew near, McAvoy leaned across and opened the passenger door with a gloved hand. 'Get in. Don't touch the inside of the motor. Use this.' He shoved a paper tissue into Black's hand. The car was stolen; they didn't want him leaving any fingerprints.

Black climbed in gingerly and closed the door with the tissue. His heart was in his mouth, and every nerve in his slight frame was stretched taut. They didn't need to tell him. He could see it in every face – the job was on.

'What have we got?' Robinson asked.

'I don't know for certain – but I know there's some gold in the vault. I seen some boxes come in.'

The three men watched him intently, hanging on his every word. 'Tony' said softly, 'Gold.' Black felt good about himself again, about what he was doing. Without him, these guys were nothing. When you got right down to it, he was the real player. These guys were just the muscle.

'How many boxes?' McAvoy demanded.

'Just a few so far – but I know there's more stuff clearing through Customs tonight.'

'What about cash? Any cash?' Robinson's eyes glinted at the thought of *ready money* – fat wedges of it, ready to be stolen and spent.

'Like I said, I don't really know. But it's never been less than around £2 million.'

'Ought to keep us going for a couple of weeks,' McAvoy growled.

In what was a departure for him, Black had been thinking ahead. 'Who's going to be on the raid?'

'Why?' McAvoy's head snapped up and the headlight stare came on.

'It's just, if Robbo comes on it, then it ties me in – through Jenny, like.'

'Robbo isn't coming. Me and Tony can handle it.' McAvoy's smile held not the least trace of humour. 'Robbo's going to be at his dear old mum's getting himself an alibi. Isn't that right, Robbo?'

Robinson grinned. 'That's right, Mickey. No need for me to be there. I might pay a visit to my brother, too, while I'm at it. Make sure I'm well alibied up.'

'Matter of fact, we're all going to have alibis,' McAvoy said.

'Tony' chimed in. 'Anyone gives us any trouble, me and Mick here will stick a nice hot poker up his arse – right, Mickey?'

'Fucking right we will.' McAvoy rested his gaze on Black. 'Business before pleasure – who's the duty Key Man?'

'Scouse.'

McAvoy glared. 'I asked you for his name, not his fucking nickname.'

Black quailed. 'That is his real name, Mickey – straight up: Michael Scouse.'

'And the crew chief? What's he called?'

'Riseley. Robin Riseley.'

'Stupid fucking names.'

Robinson intervened. 'We know where those two live – we been watching them for months.' Black was looking a little green around the gills.

'I'm not going to kill them,' McAvoy snarled. 'Not unless I have to.'

'Let's go through it one last time,' Robinson said hurriedly.

'Alarms, keys, procedures, access to the vault, the safes, the lot.' They sat in the car for the next hour or so going through the planned robbery over and over again in exhaustive detail. Black would be hooded and trussed like the other guards. They would rough him up a bit in the process the same as everyone else. Black said that was right, he wanted to be treated the same as everyone else, otherwise he would stand out, the police would know he was the inside man. They got down to the fine details, all of them familiar to the point of tedium by now. 'When we need to get the motor into the loading bay, Mickey here will come back up from the vault and order you to open the loading bay doors. We'll take your hood off, and leave it off, but your hands will still be tied. Just do as Mickey says and stand in the corner, OK?'

'OK. The only thing is, you'll need to be quick when you come in. If Scouse or Riseley get time to hit one of the panic buttons . . .'

'Don't worry about that,' McAvoy cut in. 'Those two fucking wankers won't know what's hit them.'

Robinson was worried now. 'This Scouse and Riseley – they're not going to come over all heroic, are they? Try and have a go, or anything?' While they would all be carrying firearms, Robinson didn't want any shooting if it could possibly be avoided. Black shook his head. 'Nah – they'll be shitting themselves, they won't do nothing.'

'Timing,' Robinson got back down to business. 'We want to be in there at 0630 and out again by 0730. That means we need to be inside as early as possible after the guards arrive – before they get time to settle down. We'll be waiting over the road in the Transit. The second you give us the nod, we're coming in. Tony?'

'I'll go in with the others as usual,' Black said. 'The first thing they'll do is start making tea. While they're doing that, I'll come back down to the side-door and give you the wave through the glass to say it's all clear. Then I'll leave the inner door on the latch and go back up to the crew-room and join the rest of the lads. Give me a couple of minutes after that to make it look like everything's normal, and then you come in.'

'What about the outer door alarm?' Robinson already knew about this, but he wanted to hear it again. 'Won't that go off?'

'It might go off, depends how he sets it, but like I said, it's not connected to the police station or nothing. No one will hear it, or know it's gone off. You can hardly hear it where we are, upstairs in the crew-room.'

The air went out of the meeting. From this moment on it was action, not words, that would decide the day.

'Right then.' Robinson drew things to a close. 'We're set. See you tomorrow, bright and early.' His gaze steadied on Black. 'You will be there, won't you, Tony? Bright and early?'

Black did his best to look pained, and at the same time treat the question as a joke. ''Course I will, Brian. Wouldn't want to miss it for the world.'

He went home and tried to carry on as usual. He shared a take-away with his wife, and then suggested they have an early night. But *tomorrow* would not let him sleep, there was always *tomorrow* forcing its way into his thoughts, tormenting him. 'What's the matter, Tony?' Lynn Black asked, after he had been tossing and turning for some time. 'Can't you sleep?'

'Reckon all this overtime's getting to me,' Black muttered. But it was his imagination that was working overtime, grinding on what might happen in the most minute detail – now projecting the worst result in all its horrible reality of arrest, humiliation and imprisonment, now the best outcome in a sunny, sparkling shower of gold. As he drifted on the edge of sleep, the imaginary scenarios grew more and more improbable. By the time he finally did begin to nod off, a silver strand of dawn was sliding its way in through the bedroom curtains.

Black woke with a start. He sat bolt upright in bed and stared at the clock: it showed 0620. Fuck! He had slept right through the alarm! He was late for work. No, he was late for his own armed robbery! He was supposed to be at Unit 7 in ten minutes! He was supposed to be letting an armed gang into the warehouse in ten minutes! They would kill him if he didn't get there. Slowly. Take him to a derelict warehouse and nail his hands to the floor.

He leapt out of bed, threw on his clothes and ran for the car.

Ripping through the sleeping suburbs at more than twice the legal speed, he threw the protesting Opel into the corners like a man with the demons of hell chasing him. He screeched up outside Unit 7 at 0640 – ten minutes late. The rest of the crew were already inside. Racing for the side-door in a muck sweat of fear, he glanced across the road. It was still barely light, but he saw it: a blue Ford Transit, parked up and waiting. He leaned on the doorbell. Scouse let him in.

7

'Mick Scouse came downstairs to let me in and locked the door behind me. I went upstairs and took my coat off in the radio room. There was a conversation about vehicle weights. I made an excuse about going to the toilet and went downstairs. I had a look round and then went to the door. I couldn't see anything outside and the light was on inside. I just put up my arm and waved. I had no way of knowing whether they'd seen me or not. Then I went back upstairs and into the rest room. I rolled myself a fag.

'A couple of minutes later they came upstairs. I saw one directly in front of me and another pass behind him. The one in front was Mick, I think, because he had a yellow balaclava on and later he pulled it up when I was lying on the floor and whispered, "It's all right – we've got the lot."'

It had taken the Flying Squad's DS Nicholas Benwell eight hours to write down Black's statement. When he'd finished, at 10.12 p.m., he caught the guard's eye. 'What was in it for you, Tony? What did you stand to get?'

Like his interrogator, Black was exhausted. He shrugged his shoulders. 'There was never any discussion about how much I would get. Nothing was said about percentage or cut, just that I would have to go on working for Brink's-Mat for another five years or so before I collected it. They were to make the arrangements. It could go in a Swiss bank account, they said.' Black leaned back in the unforgiving interview room chair. He looked grey with fatigue. 'Would it be possible for me to see Mr Cater now?'

Detective Sergeant Alan Branch, who had assisted with the interrogation, got to his feet. 'I'll go and find out.'

While they were waiting to see if Cater wanted to talk to him, detectives showed Black covert C11 surveillance photographs of McAvoy, a man named Anthony White and Robinson, mixed in with mug shots of a couple of dozen other well-known criminals. In each case Black picked the appropriate face from the rogues' gallery: 'That's Mick McAvoy. That's Tony – I'm pretty sure his last name's White; and that's Brian Robinson.' His interrogators closed the books, well pleased with the identifications confirming their own intelligence-based suspicions.

To say that Black was anxious to cut a deal with the police would be putting it mildly. He was prepared to tell them everything he knew; willing to attend identity parades and ID the robbers; happy to give evidence for the prosecution and do whatever else was required so long as the cooperation earned him a lighter sentence.

Cater breezed into the room, pulled up a chair and looked at the guard inquiringly. 'You wanted to see me?'

Black launched into a coy rigmarole that boiled down to his wish to horse-trade. Cater listened with mounting impatience while Black made this feeble attempt at playing hard to get. When Black had petered to an end, Cater told him straight out that full cooperation with the police was his only option. If Black played ball with the prosecution it would count in his favour with the judge when it came to sentencing. But as Flying Squad commander, Cater could not – and would not – give any assurances about a reduction in sentence. With that, he left. At midnight on Tuesday, 6 December 1983, Anthony Black was led down to spend the first of the many nights he would pass in a police cell.

Quite why McAvoy, 'Tony' and Robinson failed to make a run for it when they heard that Black had been arrested is a mystery. It might be they believed that Black's fear of what they would do to him if he 'grassed them up' would be enough to guarantee his silence. It could hardly be that they had confidence in his ability to withstand police interrogation. The false alibis the gang members had concocted with the aid of willing relatives may have lulled them into a false sense of security. They also knew that if they did make a run for it, then the police would take their flight as a sign of guilt. Whatever their reasoning or lack of it, and despite the very strong risk that Black would finger them, the alleged robbers decided to sit tight and sweat it out.

It was a bad decision. After less than twenty-four hours in the kind of basic accommodation to which he had not been used and never wanted to become accustomed, Black was singing like a one-man opera.

At 0630 on the morning of Wednesday, 7 December, Cater sent Flying Squad teams in to arrest McAvoy, Robinson and White on suspicion of armed robbery; McAvoy's wife Jacqueline and White's wife Margaret on suspicion of conspiring to provide a false alibi; and Mrs Patricia Dalligan, the tenant of 7 Tarves Way, and her two sons, Stephen, 23, and Mark, 17, on suspicion of aiding and abetting an armed robbery and aiding a criminal conspiracy. (According to Black, Patricia Dalligan's Deptford house was the place he had been taken to view the enlarged Unit 7 surveillance photographs.)

They started with Anthony White. Detective Sergeant John Redgrave arrested him as he stood in the doorway of his second-floor flat at 45 Redlaw Way on the rough old Bonamy Estate in Bermondsey, East London. Wearing only his pyjamas and feigning complete surprise, White put on his best outraged innocence act. Ignoring the tirade, arresting officers led him back inside the house and spent two hours taking it apart, in the vain hope of finding some of the missing gold.

Next on the list was Michael McAvoy. Led by Detective Inspector Tom Glendinning, a team of more than two dozen armed officers surrounded the Edwardian house at 51B Beckwith Road, Herne Hill, Kent, that McAvoy occupied with his wife, Jacqueline. Glendinning was taking no chances: the police had strong evidence to suggest that McAvoy was an 'armourer' – someone who made money renting weapons by the job, or sometimes by the hour, to violent criminals. On top of that, he was known to have a violent and unstable temper – there was no knowing how he might react when they tried to arrest him. In the event, confronted with overwhelming force and literally looking down the barrel, McAvoy went quietly, professing the same hurt and bewilderment as White.

Less than one minute later, Detective Chief Inspector Kenneth John rapped on the door of 7 Chilham House, a range of bleak flats thrown up by the local council in Rollins Street, Rotherhithe, East London. Clad only in his underwear, Robinson took one look at the police officers standing on his doorstep and said, 'Come on in. Look around, I've been half expecting you.' The search squad turned the ground-floor flat inside out, but found no heavy, shiny, yellow bars. Arresting officers then drove Robinson to West Drayton police station, where he was locked in a cell and left to mull things over.

The first to be arrested, White was also the first to be questioned, in his case by Detective Sergeant Robert Suckling and Detective Constable Michael Charman. According to the police account, the first interview ran like this: 'Like I told you this morning, that's bollocks. You've got no evidence, nothing; you just come round to me on the off-chance of hoping to find something. Now you've turned up a blank you're fucked. Don't waste my time.'

Suckling told off the points on his fingertips: 'You had your suitcases packed in the bedroom; there were groceries in the boot of your car; your son is away from home and the dust bag from your vacuum cleaner is missing.'

White laughed scornfully. 'So my missus can't go shopping? Or clean the house?'

'You cleaned the house and disposed of the dust bag to get rid of any forensic evidence linking you to the Brink's-Mat robbery – at least, that's what you hoped to achieve.'

'Bollocks. I want to see my solicitor. Now.'

'Where were you early last Friday morning, Tony? At 0630?'

'In bed, of course – ask my wife, she'll tell you. You haven't got fuck all, I know that. All I have to do is keep my mouth shut and you're fucked.'

'Listen, Tony: Anthony Black has made a full and frank confession about this robbery and the build-up to it. He has told us about your part in it – and Mick McAvoy's and Brian Robinson's.'

White's face adopted a pantomime expression of disbelief. 'What's he said, for fuck's sake? I don't believe it!'

'He's written it all down, Tony, in black and white.'

Busy devouring the first page, White missed the pun. Then he caught himself and stopped reading. 'What do you think I am, another Tony Black? You've got your grass. I'd die for my mates before I'd shit on them.' There was silence for some moments, and then White asked, 'Have you nicked the rest?' He meant McAvoy,

Robinson and the other as yet unidentified gang members. Suckling said they were all in custody. Visibly taken aback, White said, 'I need time to think about it. Downstairs.'

Suckling put the statement back in the folder and shut it. Then he showed White a contemporaneous account the second police officer had been making of their own interview. 'Here, read this and sign it. It's a record of the interview we just concluded.' He held out a pen, but the armed robber brushed it away.

'I'm not signing nothing without my brief. You get my brief, and we can talk again.' Still muttering and shaking his head, White was led down to his cell.

If White had allegedly given Suckling a small amount of encouragement, the same could not be said of Brian Robinson. At least, not at first. Interviewed at West Drayton police station by DCI John, Robinson refused point-blank to answer any questions whatsoever unless his solicitor was present. John eventually gave up and had Robinson sent back to his cell. Some three hours later, John tried again. This time he played hard ball. 'Tony Black has told us some things that incriminate you.' It was an obvious gambit, but Robinson had played the game before: he did not fall into the yawning trap of denying a specific crime, thereby revealing his prior knowledge of it.

'I don't know what he's saying. What's he saying?'

'You don't deny you know Anthony Black?'

'How can I? He's my brother-in-law.'

'How do you get on with him? Have you ever fallen out with him? Have you ever asked him about his work?'

'No. I don't smack his sister about or anything.' (This denial was interesting because unnecessary.) 'I don't owe him any money, and I never asked him about his work.'

'But you did help him find a flat some years ago?'

'Yeah, I helped him – like I said, he's my brother-in-law.'

'You get on well with him, then: you go fishing together sometimes?'

Robinson checked for a moment, and then shrugged his shoulders. 'We've been fishing together once or twice. So what?'

'Do you know a man named Michael McAvoy?'

'Mickey's a friend of mine – what about it?'

'What about Tony White – do you know him?'

'He's another mate of mine. What is this, "Twenty Questions"?' (He meant the hoary BBC radio show by that name.)

'Where were you last Saturday morning at around 0600?'

Robinson made a show of trying to remember his movements. 'Last Saturday? Wait – I was playing golf on the Friday. Let's see – Saturday: yes, I got up early that day – about 0610. Had to go and visit me mum, she's been a bit unwell, trouble with her glands.'

'Where does your mother live?'

'On the Isle of Sheppey.'

'Did you drive there?'

'Drove all the way. Stopped at a Little Chef, as it goes, on the motorway. They might remember me.'

'On the M2? What time did you get there? Roughly?'

'Must have been about 0650.'

'Why did you stop? For breakfast?'

'Nah – had to fill up the Renault. And I bought Mum a bunch of flowers to cheer her up.'

'What time did you reach your mother's home?'

'About 0800. Vic was there – Victor, my brother. He lives with Mum. He came downstairs and we had a cup of tea. Mum told me off for not bringing my boy with me, she wanted to see him. Then I told Vic my radiator was overheating. He said he'd drain it and fill it up with antifreeze for me.'

'What time did you leave your mother's house?'

'I dunno – later on in the afternoon, I suppose – around tea-time.'

John picked up an evidence bag with a roll of masking tape inside it. 'We found this in your flat. It's masking tape. Of a kind identical to that used in the Brink's-Mat robbery.'

Robinson's expression had all the innocence of a cornered tarantula. 'That tape? I use that when I'm decorating – painting skirting boards. Keeps the paint off the carpet.'

'How about this? Can you explain this?' Inside the second evidence bag was a Polaroid camera. 'Anthony Black says you loaned him this camera along with another, self-winding model. Asked him to take photographs with it inside the Brink's-Mat warehouse. We found it in your bedroom wardrobe.'

'I don't know what you're talking about. Or him.'

'Let's be clear – are you telling me you never lent Black these cameras?'

'Of course I didn't – nor any others, neither. That's rubbish.'

'And this – is this yours?'

Robinson peered at the object inside the third bag. It was a diver's knife. 'Yeah, that looks like my knife. Where did you get it?'

'From your bedside drawer. According to the guards, knives identical to this one were used in the Brink's-Mat robbery.'

'Loads of people have divers' knives. What about it?'

In common with many police officers, John was not averse to the odd spot of dryness. 'Have you ever *been* diving, Brian?'

'Not as such, no.'

'Did you take part in the Brink's-Mat robbery on Saturday November 26th, in which a large quantity of gold was stolen?'

'"Large quantity"? Fucking truckload, more like.'

'Did you take part in the robbery?'

'No. How could I? I told you, I was visiting my dear old mum on the Isle of Sheppey.'

DCI John motioned for his colleague to join them at the desk. He showed Robinson the notes the other officer had been writing while they talked. 'This is a contemporaneous account of the interview I just conducted with you. I'd like you to read through the notes and then sign them if you agree they are true.'

Robinson shied back from the pages as if they were contaminated with anthrax. 'I'm not signing nothing. Not without my brief. I asked for him – where is he?'

'All right,' John said, 'take him down.'

Over in Chiswick, DI Glendinning was making even less progress with Michael McAvoy. However banal or commonplace the question put to him, McAvoy refused to answer it. He would not even attempt to provide an alibi when invited to do so; all he did was keep on demanding to see his solicitor. When this had been going on for more than two hours with only a short break in between, McAvoy finally did speak, but only to say, 'I am completely innocent of these allegations put to me. I've had nothing to do with the Brink's-Mat job, and I would like my solicitor present during these interviews.'

Glendinning sent McAvoy back to his cell.

Flying Squad detectives now interviewed White, for the second time. 'Well, Tony – you asked for time to think things over – have you done that?'

According to the police record, White said, 'I'm facing the next twenty years away. My boy will be in his twenties by the time I come out. Be reasonable. I need more time. I know I've got choices. What I've got to do is pick the right one. Firstly, if I do do my bird, the biggest problem I've got ain't you people – it's what the animals on the outside will do to my family to get their hands on the gold.' There was a pause while everyone waited for his thoughts to catch up. 'So do I give it up, or keep it? I don't want to do thirty years – I done twelve the last time. If I give you the gold, the chances are I will do less. If I do, then my mates will think I've grassed, and I'm not prepared to risk it – I'm not prepared to do it to my mates. Robbo has been my buddy for years, we went to school together for fuck's sake, and Mickey is my best mate. If I do a day's bird less than them, then they'll know I've grassed and I'd rather do the whole thirty years than have them think that. My biggest problem is my wife and boy. I've got to take care of them. What if my wife told you where the gold is? Would she get the reward?'

The interviewing detective shook his head. 'I'm not in a position to discuss that – but if you give back the gold it's bound to stand well with you in court, isn't it? Tell me about the robbery – about your part in it.'

White's big, broad face closed like a trap. 'And give you ammunition to shoot me down? I've never pleaded guilty in my life and I don't intend to start now. I've got to sort out what's best for my family. I can't do that in an hour, you'll have to give me more time.'

According to the police record, White refused to sign the interview notes and was taken back to his cell.

8

Frank Cater and his Flying Squad team could feel some satisfaction about the way things were going. They were certain they had four members of the Brink's-Mat gang in custody. One of them, Anthony Black, was singing like the proverbial canary, while another, Anthony White, was, he believed, also beginning to show signs of cracking. But the prosecution was unlikely to stand up on Black's unsupported confession. And there was little hard forensic evidence from the crime scene or from the suspects' homes to back it up. That left identity parades and further confessions.

As a way of pressuring the suspects to admit what they had done, Cater told his officers to show them Black's written confession, stress how thoroughgoing, detailed and damning it was, and therefore how serious it was going to be for them when the case came to trial.

Bright and early next morning, DS Suckling had another go at White. DC Charman took notes as before. 'We left you last night on the understanding that you wanted time to think. Have you any more to tell us about the whereabouts of the gold?'

'I've thought about it – I've still got the same choices.'

'You've got to make your mind up which way you go about it.'

'You said last night I might be able to see Black's statement. Have you got it?'

Suckling slid a copy of the confession across the table and asked, 'Do you agree with the contents?'

'Yeah, it's more or less right.'

'Has it changed your mind about giving more details about the robbery and, in particular, your part in it?'

'All I'm saying is that it's about right. Don't expect me to put anyone in the frame or give any other details.'

'But you do know Michael McAvoy and Brian Robinson?'

'You know I know them.'

'Is it right that you met with Black on a number of occasions in the company of Robinson to plan the robbery at Brink's-Mat?'

'Yeah.'

'And was McAvoy present on those occasions?'

'Yeah.'

'Tell us about the robbery in your own words, Tony. Talk us through it.'

'Look mates, sorry for interrupting, but what you're saying to me goes back some time. I've told you I agree with the fucking thing.' A picture of truculence, he prodded a thick finger at Black's statement. 'Now I can't remember who done what, or where. Can't we leave it at that?'

Now that he saw light in the darkness, Suckling was not to be denied. 'Let's go back to the evening before the robbery. You, Black, Robinson and McAvoy meet up in the car park of The Bulldog pub in Ashford. Is that correct?'

'Yeah, we met up. But that's all I'm going to say.'

'Then what happened?'

'How many times are we going to go over this? What do you want me to say? Yes, it is fucking right and yes, I went on it but that's it. I've told you, no more fucking questions about that thing. What I want to talk about is that gold and what can be done for me, all right?'

'OK,' Suckling agreed. 'What do you want to say?'

'I've thought and I've thought but in the end I'm going mad. I want to give you where the gold is but I don't want to grass anyone up. I'm in a right Catch-22 situation. Can we do a deal?'

Suckling decided to play along. 'What kind of deal did you have in mind?'

'I'm not interested in the reward money. What I want is the best deal for me, Mickey and Robbo. If we can all get off with a lighter sentence, then I might be able to get the gold back.'

'How do you mean, "might"?'

'We haven't got it. It's being looked after.'

'Someone's looking after it for you? Who?'

'I can't tell you that.'

'In which case, I can't guarantee you a lighter sentence.'

'Right, that's it: I'm saying no more. Come back when you've made your minds up.'

Suckling asked White to sign the record of this, their third interview, but he again refused.

Confronted with the evidence of his brother-in-law's confession, Robinson, too, began making more conciliatory noises. At the end of the first page he stopped and looked up at DCI John.

'OK, guv, I can see he's done the business on me. Is he turning supergrass?' The 'supergrass' system had worked well for the police in Northern Ireland: in return for a guaranteed reduction in sentence, the supergrass gave the authorities chapter and verse on the structure, membership and activities of an Irish Republican Army cell or unit, usually when a bombing had been committed or was planned. The Maze prison was full of IRA members caught in this judicially controversial way.

'He [Black] will be giving evidence against you, McAvoy and White in court. Read the rest of it. It's interesting.'

Robinson read a few more lines, but he seemed to be having trouble keeping his attention on the page. 'What about the other two – have they said anything about this?' He glanced down at the statement.

'I am not sure,' John stalled. 'I believe one has put his hands up, but I don't know about the other.'

'Who is it? Who's talked?'

'Sorry, I can't help you.'

Robinson started reading again. One section of the statement made him sit upright in the chair and brighten. 'Look, I never intended to go into the place, not even through the window. See, he's got it here,' he tapped the paper. 'I told you I didn't go on the job, he confirms my story. All I did was introduce Tony Black to some bloke.' He went back to the document, but stopped reading again when he came to the details of the guards' treatment. 'I had nothing to do with the petrol, that was someone else's idea, not mine.' Finally, he reached the end. 'I can't say anything about that Saturday, guv: believe me, I wasn't there. The vans and all that, I can't help you with. Look, guv, if I could get the gold back I would help you. I'm looking at a thirty-year stretch. Do you think I wouldn't help you if I could? It all adds up against me, but honestly, I was only helping some others who were hard up. They never expected to get all that gold. We expected a good haul, but nothing like that gold. My share was just going to be a drink for the introduction, that's all.' The sudden switch in pronouns from 'they' to 'we' was telling.

'You don't honestly expect us to believe that, do you, Brian?' John said. 'The only reason you were not on the actual job – if that is true – is you knew you would be seen because of your family ties with Black. You therefore had to have a cast-iron alibi, which you appear to have. Tell me what you did on Thursday, 24th November.'

Robinson thought for a moment. 'Can't remember.'

'You see what I mean, Brian? You know your precise movements for Saturday, the 26th, but you don't remember Thursday.'

'I've told you my part. If you don't believe me, forget it. You told me you can't do me any favours, only I can help myself. So that's what I'm going to do. I don't want to discuss this any more until I've seen my solicitor.' He refused point-blank to sign the interview record. They locked him back up in his cell.

If his partners in crime had either already cracked or at least developed serious internal fault lines, over at Chiswick police station Michael McAvoy remained unshakeable. When DI Glendinning threatened him with an identity parade attended by all the Brink's-Mat guards including Anthony Black, McAvoy's only response was, 'Get on with it, then.' Told that Black had made a detailed statement naming him as the gang's leader, McAvoy was even more dismissive: 'Downstairs, I'm reading Harold Robbins – Black should start writing stories like that.'

Glendinning let McAvoy stew for the afternoon, hauling him back up for questioning later that evening. He pushed Black's signed confession in front of him. McAvoy stared. 'I'm not reading that – you read it.'

Taking him at his word, Glendinning read the whole statement out loud. He stopped at the end, and waited for McAvoy's comment, pleased to note that despite the gang leader's best efforts, some signs of underlying tension had crept into his shoulders and face. 'He's got some memory, he has,' McAvoy said finally.

'Is it true then? Were you involved in the robbery?'

'What are the others saying?' McAvoy was hedging; much better than refusing to talk at all, so far as Glendinning was concerned. 'Have they seen this?'

Glendinning kept his expression still – maybe he was gaining an edge, at last. But it was essential not to give McAvoy any sign he was thinking that. He said evenly, 'Tony White's accepted his part in the robbery, but he has indicated that he wants to have a meeting with you and Robinson to discuss the job and the recovery of the gold. I understand he doesn't want to break any loyalties between you.'

'If Tony's been talking, you must have offered him something?'

'I'm not aware of any such offer having been made.'

'Can I see Mr Cater?'

'How do you know Mr Cater?'

'I met him four years ago.'

'Why are you interested in Mr Cater?'

'Well, if White has seen him, then I want to see him.'

'So you are admitting, then, that you were involved in the robbery?'

'Can I see Mr Cater?'

'There's no point getting Mr Cater along until we know why.'

'You know why. If White's done this, then I might help myself as well.'

'Do you mean you were on the robbery?'

'It looks like it or I wouldn't be here, would I?'

'Mick: were you on the robbery?'

'Yes.'

Glendinning breathed a long sigh of relief. It had taken him two days of relentless questioning during which time he had been forced to rein his impatience in tight. McAvoy's dogged stonewalling had been infuriating, but the effort was worth it. The game wasn't over yet, though: McAvoy's direct admission that he'd been on the raid did not guarantee his conviction. In those days, stupidly, interviews were not generally tape recorded or documented other than in written form by a police note taker, and they certainly weren't videotaped. This left many prosecutions vulnerable to the frequently used defence ploy of claiming that the written account had been altered or even wholly invented by the police. Unfortunately this sometimes happened for real, as corrupt or misguided police officers became frustrated with what they took to be the inadequate machinery of the law – or simply decided it was time a villain who 'had it coming' went to jail. The practice had come to be known colloquially as 'verballing'. In the bad days of the 1970s, it became harder and harder to persuade British juries that verballing had not taken place – with the result that some police officers became convinced that they might as well verbal the accused – the defence would assume they had anyway. The whole thing became a ludicrous – and very counter-productive – vicious circle. It took the introduction of audio taping and video cameras to correct it.

They didn't have McAvoy behind bars yet. But his one-word confession was a breakthrough. Glendinning tried to get McAvoy to tell him in detail about the raid, but the gang leader clammed up again. In an effort to keep things going, Glendinning asked, 'How well do you know Mr Cater?'

'I trust him. I don't trust any of you lot.'

At midnight, Commander Cater arrived with one of his staff officers. 'Well, Mr McAvoy,' Cater said, 'what was it you wanted to see me about?'

'I want to know what Tony White's told you. I want to know what kind of deal you offered him. And I want a meet with him and Brian Robinson.'

'Anything else?' Cater asked drily. He pulled up a chair and leaned his arms on the back of it. 'Listen,' he said, 'you are not in a position to dictate terms. The evidence against you is overwhelming, and we're not going to offer you any deals. Don't waste my time: if you want to tell us where the gold is, then do so. All I can say is that whatever you say about the gold will be dealt with at the highest level. It's up to you.'

All of the truculence flooded back into McAvoy's face. He stood and walked to the door. 'I can't help you,' he told Cater. 'Take me back down.'

9

Although he would not help the police on the inside, on the outside
someone was trying to help Michael McAvoy: White's lawyer, Henry
Milner, had obtained a High Court writ of habeas corpus for Michael
and Jacqueline McAvoy, Anthony and Margaret White, and Patricia,
Stephen and Mark Dalligan. Since the law was changed in 1984,
suspects can only be held for twenty-four hours without charge.
This can be extended for 'serious arrestable offences' like murder or
suspicion of terrorism. But in December 1983 the Brink's-Mat suspects
were just the wrong side of the change: there was no hard-and-fast time
limit. When the application for habeas corpus came before Mr Justice
Taylor, counsel for Scotland Yard told him that the police would defend
the action. Justice Taylor adjourned the case until the next morning.

Their hands forced by the impending hearing, at 2130 on the
evening of Wednesday, 7 December, the police charged Robinson,
White and McAvoy with armed robbery and conspiracy to commit
armed robbery. Next morning, the three men were remanded in
custody at Feltham Magistrates Court. The Dalligan family and the
two wives were released without charge.

The next step in building the prosecution was to try and bolster Black's
confession by arranging identity parades. The five other Brink's-Mat
guards would pick out McAvoy, White and Robinson – or at least that
was the idea. The police had to deal with attempts by the accused men's
lawyers to make the identification procedure as difficult as possible.
Robinson's solicitor claimed that, since his client had attended a
wedding-reception and a football match at which some of the Brink's-
Mat guards had also been present, any identification was certain to be
a result of that coincidental prior sighting, and not because they had

plainly seen Robinson's face when he pulled his mask up to shout at them.

White's solicitor objected to his client's line-up on the grounds that the eight men the police had managed to find in no way resembled White in terms of build or appearance. It was quite true: the police were having the devil of a job finding men who were simply big enough, and menacing enough, to give White a fair chance.

After a lot of legal argy-bargy, the first line-up – Robinson's – went ahead at Ealing police station on Friday, 9 December. Robinson stood fourth from the left. The first guard, Holliday, came in. Identity parades, where accused and witness come face to face at very close quarters, are always highly charged affairs. With huge public interest in the case, the pressure on the security guards was redoubled. There was also the plain fact that they had only very recently been terrorized by the very men they were now being asked to identify. Looking nervous, Holliday walked up and down the line of eleven men. When he'd had a good long look at them, he asked each man to shout the phrase, 'Shut it!' repeatedly. Instructed that he must only make the identification if he was absolutely sure, Holliday listened to each man in turn, thought for a moment and then shook his head. 'I can't be certain,' he said.

Next up was Peter Bentley. He took a long look at the men, and then asked each of them to repeat the words, 'Get down on the fucking floor!' He listened to all eleven men and then took another long, hard look at them. Crestfallen, he turned to the waiting Inspector Hughes: 'No, sorry.'

Clarke tried next. But he, too, was confused about which of the robbers had said what, or what they had looked like. The apologetic expression on his face made his formal admission redundant. 'No, I can't identify anyone.'

So far, so bad for the police.

Riseley came next, and if the other guards had disappointed, Riseley did not: he was hardly in through the door before he turned to Hughes and said, 'I think one of them is here.'

'Who are you referring to?' Hughes asked ungrammatically. 'Touch the person.'

Riseley strode across to Robinson and touched him on the shoulder. 'This one.'

The police made a note of the identification, thanked Riseley and brought in Scouse.

The Key Man asked each member of the line-up to say, 'Are you all right, Mick?' But when they had done so, to the further dismay of the police, he touched a volunteer standing two places away from Robinson.

With the police still trying to find enough men who resembled White and McAvoy, their line-ups did not take place until the following day. In the meantime, his solicitor asked if White could be allowed to exercise in the courtyard behind the police station. DI Glendinning, the presiding officer, refused this apparently innocuous request point-blank: if White went outside into the exercise yard, it could subsequently be claimed in court that one or more of the Brink's-Mat guards might have caught sight of him through a window, and made a false identification based on that premature sighting. White remained unexercised.

The second line-up got under way at 1830 that evening. Dressed in a baggy red sweater, McAvoy did his best to look friendly and innocent. The effect was much the same as if a Komodo dragon had spotted you picnicking on his favourite stretch of beach. Holliday asked each of the men in turn to put on the trilby hat thoughtfully supplied by the police props department. Then he walked up to McAvoy and touched him on the shoulder. 'This is the man,' he said in a firm voice.

When it was his turn, Bentley asked everyone in the line-up to try on the hat, and also asked each man to shout the words, 'Get fucking down!' As soon as McAvoy had done so, Bentley walked up to the gang leader and touched him on the shoulder: 'This is the gentleman I heard on the day.'

Clarke and Scouse both failed to pick out McAvoy, but Riseley showed the same lack of hesitation as before. Walking straight up to the tow-headed gang leader and tapping him on the shoulder, he said, 'I am making a positive identification.'

When it was over, Glendinning asked McAvoy if he had any objections to the way in which the identity parade had been conducted. Keeping up his usual front, McAvoy replied, 'Only that the witnesses who have identified me have made a terrible mistake. I am completely innocent of this charge.'

With the police *still* struggling to find men built sufficiently like a brick outhouse to match White in the line-up, his parade did not take place until on 20 December. Even then, White's solicitor objected to the lack of any real resemblance between his client and the relatively puny volunteers. But Inspector Gareth Hughes, the police officer in charge, had had enough: he insisted the parade go ahead as scheduled, in the end agreeing to a so-called 'mingling' parade. In this, White and no fewer than fifteen other men stood in a loose, extended semicircle.

One by one, the Brink's-Mat guards came in; and one by one, they filed out again having failed to identify White. Even Riseley, who had been so solid until then, did not recognize the hulking prisoner, mixed in as he was with so many other rock-faced bruisers.

White went back to his cell well pleased with the day's work. But for McAvoy and Robinson, with three ominous taps on the shoulder between them, things were looking much less rosy.

Last but not least in the identification game was star witness Anthony Black. Black knew the alleged robbers inside out, and the process should have been a formality. And in the case of both Robinson and White, it was: a quick walk in, a wary tap on the shoulder, verbal confirmation of the ID to Inspector Hughes and out again. Then it came to Michael McAvoy.

Since 2001, witnesses do not have to touch the suspect to make a positive identification: the whole business can be conducted from behind a one-way glass screen, or, increasingly, by means of a virtual system called VIPER – the Video Identification Parade Electronic Recording System. VIPER's database of 7,000 images of male and female volunteers means that witnesses and victims of crime watch a video line-up which shows a 15-second head-and-shoulders moving shot of the suspect and eight or more similar-looking images from the database. This is a big improvement on the old system, not least in that it removes any risk of the witness being identified – and so put at physical risk – by the accused.

Lulled into a false sense of security by the trouble-free, almost casual ease with which he had made his first two positive identifications, Black and the armed police escort assigned to protect him walked into the charge room where McAvoy and his look-alikes were waiting. As soon as he had agreed to act as a witness for the prosecution, the police had issued Black with a bullet-proof vest. Everyone including Black knew that his fellow robbers were hopping mad at his decision to betray them. In fact, word was already out on the street that anyone able to guarantee his permanent discretion – the kind that results from a couple of 9mm bullets in the head – would earn themselves £50,000 in cash. On hearing about the body armour, which he kept on at all times during waking hours, and which some of the more imaginative journalists claimed he wore even in bed, elements of the press had dubbed Black 'Ironsides'. Black's wife, Lynn, was also under round-the-clock police protection, in case anyone had the idea of abducting her and holding her as a bargaining chip in return for his silence.

Black glanced along the line of men and spotted his old pal Michael McAvoy straight away. Ignoring the poisonous glare McAvoy fixed on him, he walked across the room, raised his right hand and laid it on McAvoy's shoulder. 'This is the man,' he said.

McAvoy had been waiting. Before anyone could move he dropped his right shoulder, swung his fist in a vicious, scything hook and smashed it into Black's face. Black reeled backwards, crying out in agony and clutching at his mouth and nose. If he had not staggered into the arms of a police officer who happened to be standing behind him, he would have hit the floor.

Black's police bodyguard hadn't exactly done their best. They sprang at McAvoy now, pulled his arms up behind his back, handcuffed him and then frogmarched him back down to his cell.

Everyone – including the police – seemed to have forgotten just who it was they were dealing with in Michael McAvoy. This wasn't someone who had made a career out of nicking milk bottles from old ladies' doorsteps. The blow had been rattlesnake-quick, and it had just about knocked Black into the middle of next week. He had been lucky not to have his nose broken or to lose any teeth. It wouldn't do McAvoy any good if the case came to court – but it must have given him some satisfaction.

10

While they were busy interrogating Black and the other suspects, the pressure on Frank Cater and his team to recover the missing gold was steadily increasing. It came from the news media, some sections of which always appeared curiously ready – even eager – to characterize the police as bungling incompetents. It came from the Brink's-Mat security company; from Johnson Matthey and the other banks that had lost an enormous amount of their customers' money; from the insurance companies that had indemnified the gold against loss; and from just about anyone else who felt like throwing in their two-pennyworth.

Bob McCunn, an insurance loss adjuster with the City law firm Shaw and Croft, was given the task of trying to recover the gold or its equivalent value in cash on behalf of the Brink's-Mat security company and its insurers. A qualified barrister with extensive financial training and experience, no one was more persistent or resourceful when it came to tracking – and unearthing – hidden accounts.

McCunn placed newspaper advertisements requesting information as to the gold's whereabouts. Driven by the insurance company's offer of a £2 million reward for information leading to its safe recovery, dozens of people telephoned or wrote in claiming to know where the proceeds of the heist had been hidden. All of the claims turned out to be false. It was as if the people making them believed they had entered a competition to make up the wildest and most outlandish story possible. One man even claimed that extraterrestrials had told him where the gold was buried. His kind offer to take the police – and McCunn – to the spot was declined.

If anyone had urgent reason for wanting to recover the bullion, it was the Flying Squad. This wasn't simply a matter of professional pride, or of damage limitation on the PR front. Discussions at the highest level, including those between then Home Secretary Leon Brittan and C11 Commander Brian Worth, all stressed the same point: £26 million could buy you enough guns and ammunition to equip a fair-sized private army; import an avalanche of hard drugs; or be used to fuel any number of crimes, from prostitution and large-scale racketeering to yet more armed robbery.

If that much money was allowed to enter the criminal food chain then the results for a Britain already plagued by serious crime could be disastrous. Pressured by the more vociferous elements of the media, Brittan made it clear to Met commanders that he would not be happy until the police had all of the robbers behind bars, and recovered every single ounce of the stolen gold. They'd better pull their fingers out and deliver, or some very senior heads would roll.

Without resorting to the kind of trade that Tony White had hinted the robbers might make in return for reduced prison time, the police still had one or two things going for them. First was the fact that, sooner or later, whoever held the gold had to convert it into cash. Gold is a difficult commodity to sell at the best of times. You need legal certification showing when, where and for what reason it has been bought; the bars bear markings that show its origin and more often than not establish proof of legal ownership; and there is usually some kind of assay mark certifying the metal's type and purity. Even on its own, this assay mark would be a worry for the robbers. The Brink's-Mat hoard bore the magic '99.99', or 'four nines', mark. It was bullion, the rarest and purest gold available, and each ingot was stamped with a serial number. As Johnson Matthey's property, many of the bars also bore the company's identification stamp: a crossed hammer and pick enclosed in an oval.

Then there was the sheer size of the heist: how exactly do you turn 2,670 kg of gold – the equivalent by weight of two medium-sized family cars – into ready cash without attracting attention? The only possible answer was to smelt it down; adulterate it to change the assay value; recast it into unmarked, unidentifiable ingots; come up with some legally viable reason for owning it, and then try and sell it back onto the open market.

The first and most important thing they would need, then, was a smelter. These were not easy to get hold of. The best place to buy a gold smelter in the UK – in fact, just about the only place, short of going directly to one of the country's very few manufacturers – was one of the larger jewellery shops in the Hatton Garden district of central London. Hatton Garden, which lies at the heart of the City, London's ancient commercial and financial district, is one of the world's foremost areas for the trade in gold, platinum, diamonds and jewellery. Anything you might want that is in any way connected to the trade is readily available – at a price.

The pieces were now in place on the chessboard. The first move Cater made was to dispatch a small team of detectives to warn all the Hatton Garden traders to be on the lookout for anyone attempting to buy an industrial gold smelter. They were to inform Scotland Yard at once if this should happen. There was nothing like getting proactive – doing a bit of leg work, setting the criminals up for a fall. The second thing he ordered was increased surveillance on those known and suspected armed robbers who figured on the Scotland Yard database so thoroughly and painstakingly acquired under the recently completed C11 intelligence-gathering exercise known as 'Operation Kate'.

The Kate in question was a C11 secretary, who not only gave her name to the operation, but also helped collate much of the intelligence gathered from it. Operation Kate was mounted at the beginning of 1981 in response to the massive increase in armed crime that began in the late 1970s.

Overseen by C11 Commander Brian Worth and one of his staff officers, a young, high-flying Detective Chief Inspector named Roy Ramm, Kate was one of the biggest undercover intelligence-gathering exercises ever mounted by the Metropolitan Police. It was also a striking success. Ramm had grown up in the very areas of South London where most of the capital's armed robbers had cut their teeth. He knew these 'manors' like the back of his hand, and as a result had a pretty good idea where to look when it came to spotting faces.

The C11 undercover surveillance teams sat and watched villains – both suspected and already convicted – for days and weeks and months on end. Some 200 strong and operating in shifts, they learned what worked best as they went along. They learned that a periscope fitted in the roof of a decoy builder's van disguised as an air vent was much better than a spyhole cut in the vehicle's side, which was easily spotted by the targets – on one occasion, a couple of wags had come up to a surveillance van and shouted abuse at the officers inside. They learned to mix it up – use black taxi cabs to move around anonymously, employ officers who had the knack of blending in with the street scene. They learned the importance of maintaining a technological edge on the criminals they were trying to catch, and a host of other tricks besides.

The result of all this top-secret and extremely expensive activity was a massive and detailed database containing information about and photographs of nearly all of the most active and dangerous robbers in the South London area. The task of compiling it was made marginally easier in that nearly two-thirds of the robberies carried out in the UK took place in London. A staggering three-quarters of those committed *outside* the capital were executed by the same South London faces now registered on the 'Kate' database.

By the end of 1982, 'Kate' had identified and filed information on a hard core of roughly 200 robbers who lived in and/or operated from bases south of the River Thames. Of this group, twenty or so were accorded special status. These men were considered the crème de la crème or, if you prefer, the dregs of the dregs, of Britain's armed robbers.

When investigators assigned to the Brink's-Mat case asked the database which of these super-villains were most likely to have taken part in the heist, the names Brian Robinson, Michael John McAvoy and Anthony White fairly leapt out at them. This did not prove their guilt. It also did not mean they would be easy to catch. All top-flight career criminals routinely behaved as if they were under surveillance, using as much wit and ingenuity in attempting to counter the police eyeball as the detectives employed in watching them. Standard tricks included: driving to the end of a cul-de-sac and then stopping to see who was following; making sudden U-turns in the middle of a busy road; buying the latest radio technology and keeping it tuned to the 'secret' C11 wavebands; slowing right down or even stopping in the middle lane of a motorway so that the police were forced, for reasons of simple safety, to overtake; and never, ever, referring to a criminal enterprise, past, present or future, in anything other than a prearranged code – especially over the telephone. But with all this, the three men Kate had put her finger on might have been surprised at the extent of the intelligence held on them.

Another name that popped up on the C11 screens was that of a fourth man who while he had no record of actually taking part in armed robberies was known to the police.

Having alerted Hatton Garden jewellers to let them know if any large men with Cockney accents wandered in off the street and asked to buy a gold smelter, the police decided to follow as many of the flagged-up names as they had officers to do it. The fourth man happened to be one of the nominated targets. We are not allowed to reveal his identity for legal reasons.

On the morning of 11 December 1983, fifteen days after the gold had been stolen, a man in his late thirties entered the premises of Charles Cooper Ltd, one of Hatton Garden's leading jewellers. A plump and affable middle-aged man with a pronounced Cockney accent, the customer, who gave what turned out to be a false name, asked if he could see the manager on important business. Company director Allan Duncan came down to the front desk. The stranger said he wanted to buy an industrial-sized gold smelter on the spot, for cash, and take it away with him there and then. Duncan was now confronted by a large Cockney gentleman with more 'front' than Brighton looking to buy a gold smelter of the exact same kind he had been asked to report. Curbing his desire to rush to the nearest telephone, dial '999' and shout, 'He's here!' down the line, Duncan took care not to let his suspicions show. With his charm setting on 'high', he said, 'The largest model we sell is the Alcosa GF080/2 WPG gas-and-air blasting smelter. It's capable of liquefying up to 36 kilograms of gold at a time. Is that the kind of thing you were looking for?'

'That sounds just the job,' the friendly customer replied. 'I'll take one of those, if I may.' Then, as if the question of cost had just struck him for the first time, he asked, 'How much is it?'

'It costs £1,047.71 – but I can't supply you with one right now.'

Some of the visitor's show of good humour vanished. 'Oh? Why not?'

Duncan held his hands out, palms upwards. 'This is a rather large item – I'm afraid we don't tend to keep them in stock.'

There was no hiding the disappointment in the visitor's face. 'Then I'll have to try elsewhere.'

Duncan tilted his head on one side. 'You can try – but I'm pretty sure you won't be able to buy a smelter that size off the shelf. They are especially made to order by a company in Worcestershire.'

'I bet I can find one somewhere round here,' rejoined the chirpy Cockney. But before leaving to find an alternative supplier, he bought a smelting pot, a set of heavy-duty scales and four large bottles of hydrochloric acid, a substance that – as well as in the manufacture of cocaine – can be used to test the purity of gold.

The very next morning, the customer was back again. 'You were right,' he told Duncan when the manager reappeared. 'Buggers won't sell me one for love nor money.' He took out a massive wad of £20 notes and placed it on the counter between them. 'You said you could order one?'

'That's right. From the manufacturers, William Allday and Company, in Stourport, Worcestershire. They trade under the name "Alcosa". The smelter is usually ready within seven to eleven working days, and then there is the delivery time on top of that.'

'I need one as soon as possible. Is there any way we can speed things up?'

Duncan smiled faintly. 'We could try and make it a priority order, if you like?'

'I do like – very much. Do I pay you now?'

'That would, as you suggest, speed things up. I'll need the address where you want the smelter delivered.'

'No need to worry about that – I'll pick it up myself from the factory as soon as it's ready.' He filled out the necessary paperwork, gave an address in London Road, Sidcup, and counted out the banknotes. In return, Duncan gave him Alcosa's address and telephone number along with a receipt, and they parted company.

When his customer had gone, Duncan walked around to the other side of the counter and stepped up to the side of the window where he could watch the man he had begun to call inwardly 'the Collector' walk away. As soon as he was out of sight, Duncan crossed the room, picked up the telephone and dialled the number written on the card DC Bill Miller of the Flying Squad had given him.

When Miller showed Duncan some mug shots at Scotland Yard a little later in the day, the manager recognized one of them at once as the Collector. Police knew he was a friend of Michael McAvoy's. The Sidcup address he had given proved false. And here he was trying to buy a heavy-duty gold smelter only a fortnight or so after the Brink's-Mat robbery.

Bingo!

For Cater, it was the most promising news he'd had since 26 November, when a colossal amount of bullion had been lifted from a Heathrow shed.

11

The Flying Squad's Bill Miller and his fellow detectives lost no time in asking the management of the Alcosa Works in Stourport to let them know when Mr Cooper's customer – or for that matter, anyone else – arranged to collect the smelter. The tip-off came nine days later: the Collector was so eager to get his hands on his new acquisition that he wanted to pick it up at the factory gates the second it rolled off the production line. He told Allday's he would come for it late in the afternoon of 21 December.

Come collection day, Miller and DS Daniel Conway were waiting in an unmarked Ford Escort police car parked a short distance from the Alcosa Works. But the Collector failed to show at the appointed time. Instead, a white Ford Escort van with the name of a local firm emblazoned on the side turned up. The driver was unknown to the police. It made no difference to the watching detectives, whose instructions were to keep the smelter in sight at all times until it reached its final destination. Staying well back, they tailed the van out through Stourport, south down the A449, across the M5 motorway at Junction 7, and on into the handsome Midlands town of Evesham, nestling in one of England's premier market garden areas and surrounded by rolling green hills.

At 1613, the van stopped at the rear of Manson Agricultural Finance, 107 High Street. The driver got out and went into the property – but the smelter stayed put. Miller and Conway reconciled themselves to the possibility of another long wait. They need not have worried – some fifteen minutes later, at around 1630, a Rolls-Royce drew up next to the Escort van. The arrival of such an exotic car – the stereotype buy for a certain class of crook – was like a trumpet blast in Miller's ear. He got busy on the horn again. A few minutes later, he found out that the car was registered to the Collector.

Could this be the same man who had bought the smelter under an assumed name and given a false address? It could, and was. The man disappeared in through the doors of Manson Agricultural Finance. About an hour and a half later, he came back out with the van driver. Together, they grappled the smelter from the back of the van and tried to put it into the boot of the Rolls-Royce. The crate was too big. The driver went back into the house and reappeared with a length of rope. The two men manoeuvred the smelter into position and tied down the boot lid.

The Collector sped away. He was driving a Rolls-Royce with a large packing case sticking out of the boot, and his average speed on the southerly route that he now took regularly exceeded 100 mph. Short of having flashing lights on the top of the car and a couple of sirens wailing, he could hardly have invited more attention. If the police hadn't already been tailing him, there was a good chance he might have been stopped by a random patrol. He travelled so fast that the two detectives trying to follow in their relatively underpowered Ford Escort had serious difficulty keeping up.

The Rolls-Royce rocketed south through the Cotswolds and on in the direction of London, with Miller and Conway straining every nerve and muscle – and every ounce of driving skill – to keep it in sight. The Collector drove to his home address. It was now just before 0200 on the morning of Friday, 23 December. The pretty village was fast asleep – only the mice and the owls were up and stirring. The Collector turned into the driveway of his house, which was detached and in darkness. Miller radioed in. The duty controller asked him if he and Conway would stay where they were and keep an eye on the smelter until 0730, when their relief was due to take over.

It arrived on time in the shape of four more unmarked Flying Squad cars, each manned by two detectives. All the new team had to do was observe the Rolls and the smelter, and wait to see what happened. There were two distinct possibilities: either someone else would drop round and collect the smelter, or the Collector would emerge and drive it on to its final destination.

Miller and Conway had mixed feelings about the handover. On the one hand, they were glad that their day-night vigil was coming to an end: they could drive off and treat themselves to a well-earned breakfast, followed by a long and equally well-deserved sleep. On the other, they were worried in case anything went wrong. They were very soon to wish they had stayed on duty.

The four surveillance vehicles took up position around the target's home in such a way that they had all the possible routes into and out of it covered. You might think that with four police cars now on the job instead of one, the chances of losing the target should have decreased in proportion. You might also think that a car as conspicuous as a Rolls-Royce with a gold smelter sticking out of its boot was impossible to lose. But in the dark arts of surveillance, anything that can go wrong generally will go wrong.

At around 0830 the subject came out of the house jangling his car keys and whistling cheerfully. He clambered into the Rolls-Royce and set off south once again at his usual breakneck speed. He crossed the A20 at Swanley moving at just over 80 mph, braked sharply just past the junction and turned down an overgrown country lane towards the nearby village. Just outside the village he hooked a sharp right into the driveway of a sizeable country house set back a little way from the lane.

In the nearest chase car, DS Chris Colbourne realized that he could not simply turn into the driveway after his quarry – the Collector would realize that he was being followed. Thinking fast, Colbourne floored the gas pedal, shot past the entrance to the house, screeched into a farmyard that came up almost at once on his right and did a handbrake turn. He roared back up the lane towards the house intending to make sure the Rolls-Royce was still outside. Then he would take up a strategic position, call in its whereabouts to the rest of the pursuit team, and wait until the vehicle set off again.

As he drew level with the driveway, Colbourne glanced at the house. What he saw – or rather, did not see – made his stomach pleat: the Rolls had vanished. Colbourne again flattened the accelerator. The specially tuned surveillance car rocketed forward, hitting the junction of the A20 seconds later at more than 100 mph. He was just in time to see the Collector disappear around a corner on the opposite side of the junction moving at roughly the same speed. Scattering terrified and angry commuters in his wake, Colbourne speared across the interchange, trying desperately to keep his quarry in sight. But when he reached the spot where he had last seen the Rolls-Royce, it had disappeared.

Trying to avert complete disaster, Colbourne and the other three Flying Squad vehicles fanned out and searched the immediate area, leaving no byway or driveway unturned. It was no good – it was as if the Collector, the Rolls-Royce and its extremely precious cargo had vanished from the face of the earth.

To say that Bill Miller was furious when he heard the news would understate it. The small but élite Met Police Special Surveillance Unit (SSU) he was part of had been trained in close target reconnaissance and surveillance techniques by the Special Air Service (SAS). With its years of experience in theatres like Northern Ireland to draw on, training did not come any better: the Met's SSU at that time was probably the world's best specialist police surveillance unit. Its members did not take kindly to any mishaps fouling up their diligent and painstaking work.

The second thing that angered Miller was the high-level decision that had been taken not to 'intonate' or place a tracking device in the smelter while it was still on the factory assembly line. Having worked with them at first hand, Miller was well aware that the Regiment's undercover teams frequently tracked down and captured or killed IRA members by 'intonating' or bugging a weapon in an illegal arms cache.

The technique was simple enough: watch, wait and be patient. A technical specialist hid the bug inside the relevant weapons or explosives. Mounted in one or more of the pursuit vehicles, a tracking device tuned to the bug produced a tone whose varying strength indicated its location. Covert Special Forces surveillance teams – or their Royal Ulster Constabulary (RUC) counterparts – would follow the cache to its final destination. Once it came to rest, SAS gun teams would wait until the bad guys moved in to collect the concealed weapons, and then pounce. The bugging device used at that time was crude, in terms of current technology, but more often than not it worked.

Miller had lobbied his superiors long and hard to get a bug placed inside the smelter. Among other things, he pointed out that the machine's mechanical and electrical complexity would make the bug all but impossible to detect, even to the trained eye. But the bugging system was expensive, both in terms of money and the personnel required to operate it. Nowadays, £3,000 buys you a GPS tracking device that will call you on your mobile phone when the subject starts to move. Less than the size of a pound coin, the bug is very easy to conceal. But in 1983, the bugs were so big they had to be screwed into place. There weren't many available because of the overwhelming demand for them in Northern Ireland, and they were very resource-intensive: as soon as the target moved, the pursuit units had to move with it. The specially fitted vehicles then used by C11 were always in extremely high demand. The signal would disappear in tunnels, or sometimes even when the target rounded a corner. The bug could be tracked from the air, but in that mode it was even less reliable.

What with all of this, senior officers were very choosy about where and when they used the 'lumps' as they were called. (In police slang, bugging was known as 'lumping up'.) Even so, it was surprising that Miller's request to have the smelter bugged was turned down flat.

It was also a terrible mistake – just how great a misjudgement the police would only come to realize many months later, when the cost of the decision would catch up with them not just in terms of loss of face, but in the loss of a colleague's life.

Desperate to get back on the trail of the missing smelter, Scotland Yard broadcast an all-units region-wide alert. The next few hours were a frantic all-out scramble to track down the missing Rolls. Twelve hours later, when it was clear that they really had lost it, DCI Glendinning marched up to the front door of the Collector's house and rapped hard on the oak panelling.

The Collector came to the door. He affected surprise at the intrusion, but Glendinning was having none of it. The suspect was bundled into a police car and driven to Bexleyheath police station. Under questioning, he claimed he had 'bought the smelter for a black man who didn't give me his name'. He said that on his way to deliver the smelter he had stopped off to call on a friend. Finding the friend was out he had driven on to the prearranged rendezvous in a lay-by near the M25, where he had handed over the goods. Questioned further, he insisted it had been a Turk, and not a black man, who had paid him the £1,500 in cash to buy and transport the smelter. Pressed as to why the 'Turk' had commissioned him in the first place, the Collector said all he knew was that the man – whom he described as a complete stranger – wanted to take the smelter abroad. He said he thought it might be something to do with one of the VAT-evasion gold-smuggling schemes that were then all the rage.

Naturally, Glendinning did not swallow one word of this rigmarole. But try as he might, he could not shake the truth out of his suspect. Since he had committed no actual crime, Glendinning had no choice but to let him go.

The trail of the missing Brink's-Mat millions was cooling fast. With no obvious leads now left to follow, the operation to find the bullion – and with it, the rest of the gang – was gradually scaled back.

Luckily for the Yard's reputation, one or two of the detectives asked to keep working on the case now came up with some creative ideas.

12

Anthony Black's dreams of getting accepted by his gangster friends and making himself rich in the process had ended in abject failure. He had taken a smack from the very face he most feared and admired; he had lost his job and the respect of his family and friends; and he had turned traitor to save his own skin. As if this weren't enough to teach him better, he now became the first person to be convicted in connection with the robbery. With armed officers stationed at strategic vantage points around the court for his protection, a high-speed police convoy whisked Black to the Old Bailey for trial on 17 February 1984.

Prosecuting counsel Timothy Cassell gave brief details of the robbery, describing it as 'highly organized, ruthless and enormously lucrative', and asked that the court make an example of Black. Without asking for any judicial concessions, Commander Cater then stood up and told the court what everyone already knew – that Black had both confessed to his own part in the crime and agreed to give evidence against the other alleged gang members. Inside the hour, it was all over: Judge David Tudor-Price sentenced Black to six years in prison. This meant he would serve a maximum of four, and might, with good behaviour, be released on parole after two.

The light sentence reflected Black's full cooperation with the CPS – but, as Tudor-Price made clear in his closing statement, Black's real punishment would be a lifetime spent looking over his shoulder: 'Never again will your life be safe. In custody you will be segregated at all times, and you and your family will for ever be fugitives from those you so stupidly – and so wickedly – helped.'

The threat to Black, whose armoured vest had by now become like a second skin, was considered so great that Cater asked that he serve his entire sentence in police custody. In an ordinary prison he would be much easier to kill. The request was immediately granted. Since his arrest, Black had been spending his time in a bomb-proof cell at Paddington Green police station. It looked as if he might be enjoying the high-security lifestyle for some time to come.

The joint committal hearing against White, McAvoy and Robinson began on 1 May 1984. As with almost all major terrorist incidents and most serious crimes of violence, it was held at the top-security Lambeth Magistrates' Court. Feltham, the magistrates court nearest Heathrow, was considered too vulnerable to attack. The risk was very real: C11 had picked up word that one of Michael McAvoy's friends, a man named Brian Perry, was trying to organize McAvoy's escape from Brixton prison.

A friend of McAvoy's from the early 1970s when the gang leader ran a neighbouring greengrocer's shop, 46-year-old Perry had convictions for burglary and robbery, and was known to pimp prostitutes at the same time as running Blue Cars (the choice of name was no accident), a minicab firm based near his home in Peckham, South London. Perry had started his criminal career as a gofer for a South London Anglo-Turkish crime family whose speciality was importing and distributing hard drugs, especially heroin. He also ran a 'drinker' or illegal drinking den in the upstairs office of Blue Cars. He would later claim that he had fallen into the prostitution racket when a female fare asked him to drive her to an escort agency in Conduit Street. The manager of the agency had come outside and asked Perry to take the woman on to the Hilton Hotel, and make sure she met the client who had booked her. In the several years since they had met, McAvoy had been employing Perry to ferry him around in one or other of the cabs, lie for him when he needed an alibi, and run all manner of other errands essential to the smooth running of a criminal lifestyle. Now it was payback time.

The decrepit blue Ford Transit used in the Brink's-Mat robbery had been found abandoned on 1 January 1984 – directly opposite the offices of Blue Cars. As soon as the police charged McAvoy with armed robbery, Perry set out to provide him with an alibi. Round-faced, of average height, with dark-brown hair and a chunky build, the brash and forceful Perry, who usually had a trademark Havana on the go, assured the police that very early on the day of the robbery, McAvoy had hired a Blue Cars cab to take him on a long-haul trip. This blatant attempt to pervert the course of justice – together with the Transit's proximity to his office – saw Perry promoted smartly to the top of the police investigation. Placing him under round-the-clock surveillance, C11 also put an intercept on his telephone calls.

The bugging paid off: Perry was setting up an escape attempt. Not just any old attempt, either, but a full-scale, Hollywood-style extravaganza. The plan was to smuggle a pistol in to McAvoy. A chartered helicopter would then swoop down and pluck him from the prison yard. If anyone tried to stop him on the way out, McAvoy would deter them with the pistol.

Perry and his fellow conspirators tried a dry run. They did not succeed in smuggling a weapon into Brixton prison, but they did hire a helicopter. Forewarned by the phone tap, a police helicopter intercepted the intruding aircraft and forced it away.

Strongly suspecting that he had been on the Brink's-Mat raid and might now lead them to the gold, the police decided that instead of arresting him, they would let Perry run and follow wherever he might lead them. But given the boldness and determination of the thwarted escape attempt, in which money was clearly no object, both McAvoy and Robinson were now moved to Winchester maximum-security prison. Banged up with a couple of IRA men in a unit that contained only six cells, this kind of porridge was no fun at all: no association, no workshops, very little to do, minimal visiting rights, endless cell and body searches, just you and the prison officers and the ceiling and the four white walls, twenty-four hours a day, seven days a week.

Outraged by this treatment, which, he complained, breached his basic human right to see family and friends – especially his girlfriend, Kathleen Meacock – McAvoy went on hunger strike. His brother Anthony complained that McAvoy's visits had been reduced from fifteen to ten minutes daily; that he was being held in solitary confinement; and that not just his conversation but his every movement was monitored by prison officers.

The prison governor retorted that McAvoy was one of Winchester's highest-risk prisoners, who had recently been the subject of an organized escape attempt; that he was on remand for Britain's biggest-ever armed robbery, in which two guards had been injured and five traumatized; and that on Sundays, McAvoy was allowed to see his sister, his wife and Meacock alone and unsupervised. The gang leader stayed where he was. His attempt to starve himself to death continued.

Committal hearings give the defence an opportunity to probe the prosecution's evidence for weaknesses. John Mathew QC, Anthony White's counsel and one of Britain's foremost defence lawyers, now set about doing this in formidable style. Mathew, who had defended one of the Great Train Robbers, immediately discovered that the police had mislaid a vital piece of prosecution evidence. During his interrogation of Anthony White, DS Suckling said he had given the prisoner a copy of Black's statement to read. According to Suckling, White had read the 26-page statement through twice and commented, 'Yeah, it's more or less right.' A note of this admission had supposedly been taken by the police. Together with the written record of the interview, the statement had been bagged as a prosecution exhibit and labelled with the reference 'RS/1'.

Mathew asked to see the original of RS/1, and have it checked for his client's fingerprints – a routine means of establishing whether or not an interviewee had in fact touched a police statement, and therefore was likely to have read it. The Yard was caught with its pants down: the bag, with White's crucial statement inside, had vanished. No one could find it. In terms of a successful prosecution, this was a disaster. For White it presented a great big gap in the legal barbed wire through which he now fully intended to wriggle. None of the Brink's-Mat guards had identified White at his line-up. Unless the detectives involved found the vital piece of corroborating evidence before his case went to trial, it would be White's word against theirs and Anthony Black's.

Some time later, Commander Carter told the court that statement RS/1 had been 'purposely destroyed in an abundance of caution in case it fell into the wrong hands'.

From the outset, White denied that he had ever set eyes on Black's statement, let alone had the opportunity to read and comment on it.

In order to demonstrate the absurdity of this, Henry Milner,

The door to Aladdin's cave
– Unit 7's side entrance
(Rex Features)

Anyone seen £26 million in gold bullion?
(Mirrorpix)

Heavy metal: getting on for three tons of fine gold. The problem was shifting it
(*Empics*)

Despite a £2m reward, Brink's-Mat never recovered all the gold bars

The insider: security guard Anthony Black
(*Mirrorpix*)

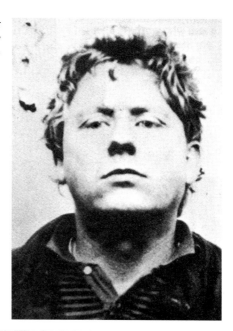

Gang leader
Mickey McAvoy
(Metropolitan Police)

... and much later,
after his release from
prison
(Mirrorpix)

'The Colonel' – Brian Robinson, who planned and took part in the raid
(Metropolitan Police)

He 'ain't heavy ... not half. Tony White, not someone you'd want to meet in a dark alley
(Rex Features)

Young, successful and on the make – a dapper Kenneth Noye (left).
'Gentleman' John Fordham, the undercover detective he stabbed to death
(right)
(Topfoto)

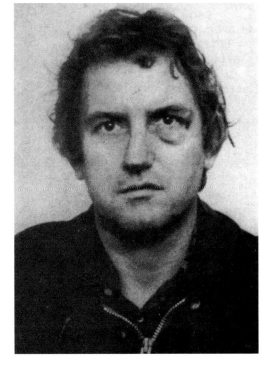

Kenneth Noye, hardly
recognizable as the same
man, directly after killing
Fordham
(Metropolitan Police)

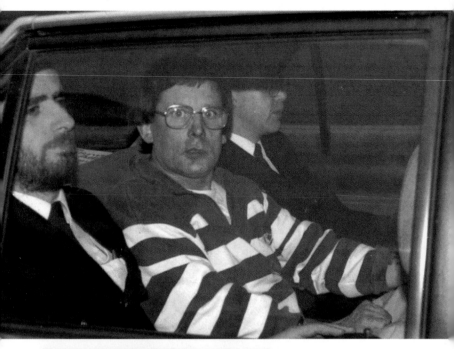

Garth Chappell liked
nothing better than to
tip huge piles of £50 notes
onto his office floor, get
down, and wallow in them
(South West News Service.com)

Are you looking at me?
Noye's chief accomplice
and near neighbour, Brian
Reader
(Topfoto)

Squeaky clean? Brian
Perry's right-hand laundry
man, Gordon Parry
(Topfoto)

Champagne Perry – or
should that be Dom
Perignon? Brian Perry took
the gang leader's gold –
and the gang leader's wife
(Rex Features)

Lifestyle of the rich and famous: John Palmer, convicted timeshare fraudster and wife Marnie after he was cleared of handling the Brink's-Mat bullion
(Rex Features)

McAvoy's solicitor, asked Harold Squires, the recently retired head of Scotland Yard's own Fingerprint Branch, to carry out an experiment. Milner asked an assistant to type 26 pages of random script on to virgin, untouched paper. He and Squires then paid Tony White a visit in Wormwood Scrubs prison, and got him to read through the pages – the same number as Anthony Black's 26-page confession 'RS/1' – twice. Careful not to contaminate the pages with his own prints, Squires then fingerprinted them. He found 41 clear impressions of White's fingerprint. Milner had the test pages sealed on the spot in front of witnesses.

In court, Milner was then able to show that RS/1's 'destruction as an abundance of caution in case it fell into the wrong hands' made little or no sense. Nor did the police claim that White's fingerprints might have faded with time stand up. Squires stated simply that fingerprints on clean typing pages last for forty years, at least.

After six weeks on hunger strike, McAvoy had lost more than 15 kilograms in weight and was said to be losing the sight of one eye. His brother Tony claimed, 'He is prepared to die rather than remain in Winchester jail.' Henry Milner applied for a judicial review of the conditions under which his client was being held. Whether or not this influenced the decision to return McAvoy to London is a moot point, but return he did at the beginning of July, ready to stand trial in the last week in October.

White's barrister might have discovered a hole in the prosecution's evidence, but the outlook for McAvoy and Robinson remained grim. Fingered by Black and identified by the other Brink's-Mat guards, it looked as if a Brian Perry special might be their only hope of escaping justice. The joint trial of McAvoy, Robinson and White on charges of armed robbery and conspiracy to commit armed robbery got under way at the end of October 1984, amidst some of the heaviest security ever seen at the Old Bailey. Prosecution exhibit RS/1 was still missing. Right on cue, Perry now decided to have another stab at getting McAvoy and Robinson off the hook.

Bill Miller recalls what happened next: 'He [Riseley] was giving his evidence one day. The court rose at four o'clock. He was supposed to be back in the witness box the next morning. At about seven o'clock I got a telephone call: he wanted me to go and see him urgently at home. When I got there he was in a terrible state.'

Riseley's upset was hardly surprising. Overnight, hate mail had been pushed through the letterboxes of his mother's home in Sheerness and the home of his girlfriend, Deirdre, in Gravesend. Made up of words cut from newspapers and pasted onto white card, the notes carried the same chilling message: 'If Robin doesn't tell the truth tomorrow Oscar will leave him.'

Riseley's mother had no idea what the message meant, but Riseley and his girlfriend understood only too well. 'Oscar' was their pet name for Riseley's penis. Like any man, he was pretty attached to it.

Riseley was already upset about the fact that he had been refused police protection for the trial. Now, just as he'd predicted, a real threat had come through the door. Why, if the police did not care about his personal safety, should he give any further evidence? Miller pointed out that if he did back out then the whole trial would collapse – and the gang would walk free. What then for the safety of those – not least Riseley himself – who had tried to help convict them? It was a good point. To back it up, and, he hoped, convince the newly terrorized shift leader, Miller told Riseley that from now on he and his family would enjoy round-the-clock police protection. Even so, it took every ounce of Miller's experience and persuasive power to coax Riseley back into the witness box.

Perry lost his temper when he heard that his new plot had failed. He sent a couple of his henchmen round to Riseley's home address, with instructions to leave Riseley in no doubt where his best interests lay. It was too late: the house was under heavy police guard.

White was the first of the defendants to give evidence. On the advice of his solicitor, Henry Milner, White had written down everything that had happened to him since his arrest. He now read this out.

'The officer said, "Look, I am not going to insult your intelligence: I know you will not tell us anything, nor will the other two. You've never nicked Old Bill before so I know you won't nick your own. We want that gold back and we don't care how we get it. It can be left on a motor or anywhere, or even on a rubbish tip or anything. We don't care if we don't nick anyone else, as long as we get it back we don't care." I said, "I've told you, I don't know nothing about it." He said,

"Let me tell you: you three will be nicked for this and fitted up – we'll make sure you get a long sentence. That's why we're not making any notes at all. Because if we get any help from you or the other two, we can write this up any way we like. You know what we can do; you know the power we've got.'"

It sounded like something out of *The Sweeney*, the hugely popular TV show based on the activities of the Flying Squad – warts and all. But White's statement had a visible impact on the jury. Noting this, when it came to his turn in the dock, McAvoy insisted that he, too, had been verballed.

Mindful of the threat to a key prosecution witness's safety, Judge Tudor-Price asked the Archbishop of Canterbury for permission to sit in session on a Sunday. Permission was granted, the first time in history it had happened. This was something that not even the wily Perry could have foreseen. The trial went ahead – and Riseley gave his evidence.

For Robinson and McAvoy, it was the last roll of the dice. They were found guilty. Tudor-Price sentenced each of them to twenty-five years. The severity of the sentence – 'ladles and ladles of porridge' as DCI Ramm put it – shook both robbers to the core.

13

The sentence also had a profound effect on the man who had done his best to help them escape it: Brian Perry. It started him thinking. He thought that the boys had done a magnificent job on the Brink's-Mat heist, grabbing more loot than anyone had ever dreamed possible. But at the same time, in using Anthony Black, whose connection to Robinson had been so easy to establish, they had made a terrible mistake. One that had cost his old mates Brian and Mickey twenty-five years apiece.

Without parole.

In a maximum security prison.

This meant that for twenty-five years, the gang's two leading members would be unable to do anything with their share of the stolen gold – a sum in the region of £13 million.

Perry knew all about maximum security – he knew you couldn't just pick up the blower and issue instructions to a third party on the outside when you felt like it. Everything an inmate did was monitored and watched. Contact with anyone and anything outside the prison was kept to an absolute minimum, to thwart any further law-breaking; or, in the particular case of armed robbers, to stop them profiting from the proceeds of the crime.

McAvoy and Robinson might be going away to a place where they would be assured of shelter, board and lodging in perpetuity, but their families and other dependants on the outside would not. They would need money. Life went on and bills had to be paid. What were Mrs and young Master Robinson supposed to do, with their breadwinner absent from the domestic hearth? What about Mrs McAvoy and the little McAvoys? Or Kathleen Meacock, McAvoy's girlfriend? They had made all of that effort to get all of that money, and now they had no means of ensuring that their friends and families were taken care of.

All very sad. But then, like a bolt from the blue, Perry had a Very Big Idea: why not steal the gold all over again? Why not *nick it from his own mates*? They were hardly in a position to go to the police. Perry was confident the two men in prison would not talk – unlike him, they believed in honour among thieves. From this point of view the wheeze was almost risk-free.

It was true that Mickey and Robbo had done most of the work planning and executing the robbery. It was also true they had trusted him to take care of their shares in the event that they were caught and sent to prison. But that was then and this was now: they *had* been caught and they *were* in prison. At a time when the Strategic Arms Limitation Talks between the US and the Soviet Union were showing signs of bearing fruit, Perry was indulging in his own spot of realpolitik. Did they really expect him to just sit there and watch over that great stack of gold until they were released? It was unreasonable – really too much to ask of a crook. It had to be used. It had to be turned into folding cash money and spent.

Of course, he would look after everyone's interests: had he not tried to do this already, in his – admittedly thwarted – attempts to help Mick escape? Had he not tried his best – at real personal risk – to stop Riseley from giving evidence? And would he not continue to look out for Mickey's interests once he had taken control of the gold? Of course he would. He would see Kathy Meacock right: make sure she had a roof over her head, and a good one at that. He would do the same for Jackie, Mickey's wife, and sort something out for Robinson's family.

The more Perry thought about it, the more excited he became. It was a simple plan. He could launder the gold. Use it to make even *more* money and then, when Mick and Brian came back out . . . Perry wasn't really sure what would happen when Mick and Brian came back out. What would he do if they took a dim view of his behaviour? Skip the country? Pay for plastic surgery? Have the two of them killed? Killing wasn't really his style. But, assuming all went well, maybe he would give them back the *value* of the gold they had entrusted to him – perhaps even with a little interest. But then, why worry? It was going to be at least twenty-five years before he would have to deal with the problem. Anything could happen in the meantime – either or both men might die of disease, or in a prison fight. He would cross that particular bridge when he came to it. The main thing was to keep Mickey sweet, make him think the gold was safe and convince him that his interests were being properly looked after.

While Perry was mulling all this over, Jacqueline McAvoy came round to see him. She was distraught. She had just found out that Mickey had been having a long-term affair with a woman named Kathleen Meacock. And as if that wasn't bad enough, she had two young children to care for and a husband in prison. What was she going to do? As an old friend, Perry put a commiserating arm round her shoulder and took her for a drink. 'She was in a bit of a state – I just took her for a drink and we got chatting and it went on from there; logical, really.' One commiseration led to another, until they were commiserating so vigorously they both achieved a certain relief.

That decided it.

Perry knew he had to be careful: no one knew better how dangerous Michael McAvoy could be. But still, all that gold! A mountain of it, right there at his fingertips. And now he had Jacqueline into the bargain. In for a penny, in for a pound.

Faced with the prospect of half a lifetime in prison, McAvoy and Robinson had entirely different ideas about what should happen to 'their' gold. They began making overtures to the police. They wanted to trade their shares of the bullion in return for a reduced sentence. Newly promoted C11 Commander Brian Worth and his senior staff officer, DCI Roy Ramm, agreed to a meeting. If any deal was to go ahead, then it would have to be sanctioned at the highest level and conducted through one or more – most likely criminal – intermediaries. Under such circumstances, the chances of something going seriously wrong – and the Home Secretary ending up with egg on his face – were high.

Ramm was circumspect going into the negotiations, with low expectation of success.

'We started this lengthy process whereby Brian Worth and I travelled up to Leicester to negotiate with Robinson and McAvoy. It was bizarre. Even as senior police officers we were searched on the way in. There were endless doors and locks to get through; there was the horrible smell of the place, the hygiene in there wasn't exactly what you were used to. You'd find yourself sitting across the table from two guys who have scratched, bitten and fought with the police their entire lives, been convicted bang to rights, and yet here they are pleading "not guilty" and claiming that the whole thing was a police fit-up.

'McAvoy is a very hard character, very steely-eyed – he was never comfortable with the situation. He hated the police and hated having to deal with us. Robinson seemed a little bit more at ease. He and I were roughly the same age – in our early thirties. I'd sit there looking at him, thinking, "I'll get back tonight, maybe have a beer with the boys, take my wife out for dinner or whatever, and he's going to go back into his little box and stare at the same four walls he'll be looking at for the next twenty-five years." It was an extraordinary feeling.

'We had some very strange conversations: we would ask them to tell us who else had been involved in the robbery, drop a few likely names, say we'd seen so and so out on the town flashing a wedge of fifties, having a good time with a couple of dolly birds. We were teasing them, of course: as far as we were concerned they were fair game. But they would not even hint at the identities of the other gang members. Honour among thieves.

'The problem we faced with these two was that they had nothing to do all day except think about a possible deal. As a result they were very well prepared coming into the negotiations with us and very, very careful about what they said. There would be a gap of at least two or three weeks between our visits, which gave them a lot of time to come up with a game plan: they would have mapped out word for word what they were going to say. After a lot of toing and froing, we reached an agreement whereby Robinson and McAvoy would return fifty per cent of the Brink's-Mat bullion in return for a police letter stating that they would not be benefiting from the crime. The letter could then be lodged as part of their appeal against sentence.

'We got down to talking the nitty-gritty of how we would get the gold back – physically make the exchange. The main stumbling block was the fact that these two thought that instead of returning the gold to the authorities, we, the police, were going to nick it for ourselves. "We're going to deliver it," McAvoy complained, "and you're 'not going to be able to find it'. We'll have given up our gold and you'll keep it." That was the way their minds worked: everyone was always out to do you down; no one could ever be trusted.

'We gently pointed out to them that this was an outrageous suggestion – but you get used to that kind of thing in the police, as long as we got the gold back it was no skin off our nose. We said, "Look, let's find a way of doing this that works for both sides." We suggested the gold should be put in a van by their own agents and associates – people they could trust. These intermediaries would then tell us when and where to collect the bullion and the whole thing could be overseen by independent observers, the media, lawyers or whoever. At a certain time we would find a van in a certain street. The observers would verify the exchange, they would get their letter and that would be the end of it.

'McAvoy's Achilles heel was his girlfriend, Kathy Meacock. He was always looking to get extra visits from her – they were the only thing that kept him from going mad inside. A slim, attractive brunette, for her part Meacock seemed to be entirely in McAvoy's thrall. She would only ever say what he told her to say. Even when I had busted a gut to fix up an extra visit for her she was cagey with me. The only person in the whole world McAvoy really trusted, Meacock was the only person he allowed to carry messages for him. At one point, he was even caught trying to kiss a message to her as a way of getting it out of jail unscrutinized.

'Along with the official letter stating that he and Brian Robinson had returned the gold, McAvoy wanted an increase in the number of visits he was allowed for the remainder of his time inside. This might seem like a tall order. But if the deal for recovering one-and-a-half tons of gold meant fixing Michael McAvoy up with a few more visits from his girlfriend and deducting a couple of years from his sentence, we were comfortable.

'The next thing that happened is that someone tried to turn me over personally. Using our own tactics against us, one of McAvoy's associates – we strongly suspected it was Brian Perry – managed to place a bug on Meacock's phone. The plan was to do a "cut and shut"

– record my conversations with her from my office at Scotland Yard, and doctor these with Meacock's help in an effort to show that I was corrupt: trying to get Meacock to do things she shouldn't be doing, like sleep with me or whatever. We never quite got to the bottom of what it was they were hoping to achieve. Naturally, I had my own taped copies of all the conversations in question. But it was an indication of just how far they were prepared to go.

'Despite his absolute faith in Meacock, McAvoy did not want her to act as his intermediary in the deal we were trying to thrash out. This wasn't a criticism of Meacock's abilities; it was just that he didn't want her mixed up with the police. Instead, he asked Tony White to act for him. It wasn't his best choice. We all knew White was no rocket scientist. Tony White was a robber: thick-set, heavily muscled, a wild, heavy, dangerous robber, nothing more and nothing less. But Tony got the job of negotiating on their behalf, so we arranged for him to visit McAvoy and Robinson in prison. They talked about the deal for a while – with the prison service listening in – and eventually White came back to us.

'From the outset it was obvious that he was extremely uncomfortable in the role of go-between, not least because he could hardly string together a coherent sentence. He would do things like arrange to meet us and then not turn up; be drunk when he did show, absolutely slaughtered when we tried to phone him and so on. What he actually did, instead of negotiate, was obfuscate. Whenever he referred to the gold, it was always as "it". He would say, "It's gone away," or, "It can't be done right now, there are reasons why." To which we could only respond, "Well, if *it* ever does come back, Tony, the door is never closed."'

14

Despite the successful prosecutions of McAvoy, Robinson and Black, some detectives on the Brink's-Mat inquiry were still unhappy about the embarrassing, Keystone Cops-style failure to track the gold smelter to its final destination. They decided to take a 'drains-up' look at the elusive Rolls-Royce owner – the man whose super-fast driving had caused them so much trouble.

One detective now thought he had evidence that the Collector was a member of a Freemasons' lodge, and that several of its members traded legitimately in gold bullion. The detective also concluded that the Collector had tried to help another man, whom he met frequently and who appeared to be a close friend, to join the same lodge. This second man lived at a place called Hollywood Cottage, in School Lane, West Kingsdown, Kent. The 'cottage' was in fact a substantial modern house with six bedrooms, an 'apple-drying barn' that was in actual fact a warehouse large enough to conceal a truck and other outbuildings standing in extensive private grounds.

What interested the police, besides the association with the Collector and his gold-dealing Masonic cronies, was the fact that Hollywood Cottage lay within five miles of the spot where they had lost track of the gold smelter. It was also within ten miles of the Collector's own address.

They decided to take a closer look at West Kingsdown man, and the closer they looked, the less the police liked what they saw. On the face of it a successful and legitimate self-made businessman, who among other interests ran a road haulage company from his home address, the new suspect had a long list of previous convictions. These included time served in a young offenders' institution for handling stolen cars; two convictions for assault on a police officer; a fine for possession of a shotgun without a licence; a suspended sentence for handling and receiving stolen goods; and, the latest in a long list, a conviction and fine for attempting to smuggle a pistol into the UK when returning from a business trip to Miami, Florida.

Here, then, was a 36-year-old man with a substantial criminal record involving firearms and receiving stolen goods, who was possibly a member of a Freemasons' lodge that included bullion dealers and police officers. A man who was a close friend of the same man who had picked up the gold smelter, and whose home was within spitting distance of the place where police had lost track of it. If anyone in the gradually expanding web of the Brink's-Mat robbery was worth keeping under observation, it had to be this new player in the game.

Every single detective still on the case developed a sudden and burning desire to know everything about this square-jawed, stockily built suspect. Worth decided to place him under round-the-clock surveillance. Around five feet six inches tall, with a broken nose and freezing blue eyes, they were soon to discover that he had the most extraordinary, chameleon-like personality: utterly charming one moment, utterly poisonous the next.

His name was Kenneth Noye.

Asking central London jewellers to alert them if anyone tried to buy a gold smelter in the weeks following the raid was a piece of good, old-fashioned detective work that should have paid off more handsomely than it had for the Flying Squad. Luckily, the Brink's-Mat squad now came up with another good idea. This was to fax a list of top suspects identified by the Operation Kate database to the police forces of the UK's main offshore banking centres. Given their readiness to go for the obvious – as in rushing out to buy a gold smelter about ten minutes after a major bullion robbery – there was always a chance that someone in the criminal community might get the sudden and equally unwise urge to open an offshore account.

The Jersey police duly received a list of more than a dozen names from Scotland Yard. It included Michael McAvoy, Brian Robinson and Tony White. It also included the Collector and his newly identified associate, Kenneth Noye.

*

On the morning of 24 May 1984, Brink's-Mat detectives watched Noye board a flight to Jersey. The best-known of the UK's offshore banking centres, the island handled billions of pounds every year deposited by people anxious to take advantage of its multifaceted and – in comparison with the UK mainland's extortionate rates of income tax – relatively generous financial system.

When Noye's plane landed, officers from Jersey's Special Branch were waiting. Provided with a full description of the visitor by Scotland Yard, they had no trouble in identifying Noye, who was travelling light with a briefcase. Jersey authorities let him carry it through unchallenged.

Looking impatient, Noye hailed a taxi outside the airport and asked the driver to take him to Charterhouse Japhet Bank, 22b St Helier Street, St Helier – the island's capital. Jersey Special Branch officers followed at a discreet distance. Noye went into the bank and asked to see the manager. The conversation ran along the following lines, with Noye getting straight down to business.

'I want to buy one hundred thousand pounds' worth of fine gold bars. It's an investment, for my son.'

Noting his visitor's strong South London accent, the diamond-studded Rolex glinting on the left wrist and the flashy suit, the manager took a swift mental step backwards. 'I'm sorry, sir,' he said, 'but I'm afraid certain formalities have to be observed before we can sell gold to individual customers.'

'Such as?'

'Well, in the first place, you would have to open an account at this bank in your own name.'

'No problem,' said Noye, 'I'll open it right now – only I want it to be a joint account, in my name and the name of my wife, Brenda.'

'And then we would have to take up references from your own bank.'

'That won't be a problem either.' Noye gave details of his mainland account.

'I also need to make you aware that the bank requires a cash deposit of at least half the value of the proposed transaction before we can proceed,' the manager said, assuming this would put an immediate end to the conversation.

Noye opened the smart new briefcase on his lap, took out £50,000 in new £50 notes and plonked them on the desk. 'Here's the first half,' he told the now astonished manager. 'I'll get my bank to transfer the rest when we've closed the deal.'

The manager looked at the pile of cash, and then back up at the stranger. It wasn't illegal for an individual customer to buy gold for cash – it was just very, very unusual. When he spoke, there was a new note of respect in his voice. 'An investment, you say – for your son?'

'That's right – now, how many kilos of gold does a hundred grand buy me?' The manager checked the price of gold, reached for his calculator and did the sum. 'It comes to eleven, one-kilogram bars – almost to the penny.'

'Good. When can I come and pick them up?'

'It usually takes us about a week to take up references. If you are able to leave me your contact telephone numbers, we can let you know.'

Noye watched as the bank manager counted out the money. 'Couple of other things,' he said casually.

'Sir?'

'When I come back to collect the gold I want to take it with me.'

The manager stared at him in renewed astonishment. 'You mean, you intend taking the actual ingots out of the bank? On your own? Without professional security?'

'That's right.'

The manager shook his head. 'But – that's highly inadvisable: what if anything untoward should happen? Even on Jersey.'

'Don't you worry about that – I'll take care of any problems if I have to. It's not as if they are going very far, anyway.' He paused. 'When I buy these bars – they come with a certificate, don't they?'

'That's right, sir – each bar comes with a certificate to prove you are the legal owner.'

'And these certificates – do they have the serial numbers of the gold written on them?'

'No, sir, they are simply a proof of purchase.'

'Even better.' Noye snapped shut the now empty briefcase, said goodbye to the mystified bank manager, quit the bank and hailed another taxi. The many other attractions of the island did not interest him.

Jersey Special Branch tailed him back to the airport and watched him board a return flight for London. In the meantime DCI Charles Quinn, head of Jersey Special Branch, went in to have a word with the Charterhouse Japhet manager. Half an hour later, Quinn was back in his office, briefing an appreciative DCI Glendinning in London about the visitor's busy day.

Once word got round that Noye had been in Jersey to buy eleven bars of gold, the Flying Squad's interest redoubled. A known fence with direct links to the man who had collected the smelter buying fine gold in the wake of Britain's biggest-ever bullion robbery? That would do nicely.

Brink's-Mat detectives started digging further into Noye's past, and kept digging until they had unearthed every last scrap of information on him they could find. They discovered that Noye had been born on 24 May 1947 at Maternity House, Lavernock Road, Bexleyheath, Kent – an address long since flattened in the name of progress. All kinds of stories about the suspect now cropped up: at the age of three, challenged in the act of scrumping apples from a neighbour's orchard, he had supposedly fallen from the tree and broken his nose. This shaky start to his criminal career was not improved when, according to another interviewee, his scandalized mother, Edith, caught him trying to steal a ten-shilling note from the till in a branch of Woolworth's while she stood chatting to the shop assistant.

Noye's school record showed that he had bullied and extorted money from the other pupils, once even allegedly breaking the nose of a boy eating his lunchtime sandwiches for no other reason than because he could. Later, Noye had moved on to receiving, stripping down and selling stolen bikes.

In his last year at school, aged fifteen, Noye had gained five O level passes and enrolled in a commercial art course at the London College of Printing. Through the influence of a cousin, he got an apprenticeship as a printer, and on completing this started working nights at Swaines Ltd, a reprographic company with offices near Fleet Street, then the hub of London's newspaper trade. Dissatisfied with the money he made from his full-time job, Noye took a second, Saturday job at Harrods, the Knightsbridge department store. Here, in the men's clothing department, he developed his lifelong love of fine clothes. Still not content with his income, on Sundays he sold newspapers stolen from a nearby print works.

One way or another, the young Noye was earning good money – but nowhere near enough to keep him in the style he aspired to. He began fencing stolen car parts, jewellery and other valuables for local burglars. Caught in the act and convicted, these activities earned him a year in Borstal, as young offenders' institutions were then called.

Around this time he met his future wife, Brenda Tremain, in a solicitor's office where she worked as a secretary. When Noye, facing new charges of shoplifting and assaulting a policeman, went in to see his solicitor, he and the law firm's attractive blonde secretary hit it off and became an item.

The Tremain family lived in Bridge Road, Slade Green, Kent. A friend of theirs ran a local pub, The Harrow, where the family liked to go for a Sunday lunchtime drink and where Noye would occasionally join them. It was in The Harrow that he had met and befriended the Collector. Operating on the margins of the law, the Collector introduced Noye to some of the hardest and most feared South London gangsters of the day. One of these took Noye under his wing, alerting him to the gaps in the criminal market then opening up. Top faces like Charlie Richardson and his associates had recently been put away. There was plenty of opportunity for a new kid on the block to make his mark.

His criminal mentor also reminded Noye – if he did not already know it – that the smarter criminal operates at one remove from the burglar and the robber. The profit margins fencing stolen goods are generally much better and involve less risk.

Noye learned to play it cool – stay in the shadows, give every appearance of running a legitimate business, and exploit the work of those dull-witted or unlucky enough to be operating further down the criminal food chain. There was only one problem: Noye's Force 10 temper. Drinking alone in a Peckham pub one day, he fell into an argument with a man who had accidentally knocked over his drink. Backed up by his two friends, the stranger refused to buy Noye a replacement. Noye left the pub to the catcalls of the watching crowd, who assumed he was too scared to fight. They could not have been more wrong. In a pattern that would repeat itself over the years, Noye went to his car, took out a weapon – in this case, a double-barrelled shotgun – and marched back into the pub.

The place went quiet. All of a sudden, no one felt like making any more jokes about 'buying the twerp a Campari and soda'. Levelling the shotgun, Noye took aim at his three tormentors. 'Do you,' he asked in a cool tone, 'want some of this?'

There were no takers. Noye's finger tightened on the trigger. At the last moment, he whipped the barrel skywards. Shotgun pellets blasted into the ceiling, raining plaster and dust on the terrified men. Noye had made his point – word got round fast that crossing him could seriously damage your health.

In 1971, Noye bought a truck and began running a road haulage company based in a caravan behind a garage in West Kingsdown, Kent. On the face of it the company was respectable. In fact, along with the legitimate loads Noye was running contraband and stolen alcohol and cigarettes, and fencing jewellery and other goods on the side. A naturally good businessman, he started to make serious money. Moving into the property market over the next few years he made even more, not least the £300,000 profit (more than £2 million at today's prices) realized from the acquisition and sale of a US trailer park, a deal made possible, it was said, by Noye's contacts with elements of the Florida Cosa Nostra.

With his new-found wealth Noye had a bungalow built in Hever Avenue, West Kingsdown. Brenda and he married and had two sons: Kevin, born in 1972, and Brett, born two years later. In 1979, looking to move upmarket, Noye paid £50,000 in cash for a 20-acre plot of land in School Lane on the outskirts of the village. By now he was smuggling South African Krugerrands into the UK, melting them down and selling the gold – by law taxable – on to legal traders and pocketing the VAT.

Noye wanted to demolish the existing bungalow on the School Lane plot and build a large new Mock Tudor home to his own specifications, but the local authority refused him planning permission. A month or two later, an unexplained electrical fault sparked a fire that razed the problem property to the ground. Noye claimed on the insurance. The many-bedroomed mansion went up. Built in the shape of an 'L', the main house had a jettied half-timbered upper storey and red-tiled roofs. Adjoining it was a large, heated indoor swimming pool complex in the shape of a second 'L', complete with jacuzzi and extensive outdoor patio area. Standing at the end of a long, straight paved driveway, the house, which also had a snooker room, was surrounded by semi-tamed scrub and broken woodland. Not bad going for a man who had started out with nothing.

Moving up to date, detectives discovered that Noye enjoyed playing squash – a sport his wife had indulged to the extent of buying him a local club for a cool £110,000 in the winter of 1983. Noye's other main leisure interest was shooting – he had qualified as a marksman at a local club.

Detectives discovered that, as well as breaking the law himself, Noye had been regularly passing information to the police about other villains. On his arrest in 1977 for receiving stolen goods and possessing a shotgun without a licence, the record also showed he had offered bribes to the arresting officers.

Noye's apparent links with members of his local police force, and the strong possibility of Masonic involvement, caused DCI Glendinning great concern. This man, he decided, must be carefully watched. But even Glendinning had not yet understood the full significance of Noye's trip to Jersey.

On 31 May, 1984, unaware of the bulging dossier on him that now existed at Scotland Yard, Noye flew back to Jersey using a ticket made out in the name of 'K. Swan'. Keen to see what he would do next, Quinn set a watch on the suspect and let him run. Noye breezed back into the manager's office at Charterhouse Japhet bank and asked if everything was in order. The manager – now even more wary of this customer following an official visit from the head of the island's Special Branch – replied that it was.

The outstanding balance on the gold, £47,322, had been transferred from Noye's mainland account: eleven 1-kilo bars were ready for collection. Noye asked if he could have them. For the second time the manager warned Noye against taking the gold off the premises without professional security, urging him to keep it safe within the banking system. Even in the relatively crime-free haven of Jersey, something untoward might still happen. Noye waved away all objections. 'The thing is,' he said in a confidential tone, 'I want to put a cut-out between me and your bank. Keep the income tax bill down, if you know what I mean?'

The manager agreed faintly that he did know. In the offshore banking industry, tax evasion of one kind or another was among the most common reasons for depositing money. Growing visibly impatient, Noye repeated, 'Can I have the gold, now?'

The manager pushed a certificate across the desk, together with a fountain pen, and asked Noye to sign it. Noye did so with a flourish. There was a moment of silence. Then, like a magician performing a trick, the bank manager whisked away a cloth: the gold had been sitting on his desk the whole time. Noye eyed it hungrily.

'Got a bag?'

The manager lifted the phone on his desk and asked if anyone had a shopping bag. A few minutes later, a secretary arrived carrying two plastic bags emblazoned with the name of a major supermarket chain. 'Will these do?' she asked brightly.

Thanking her, the manager turned back to his visitor. 'I'm afraid this is all we have.'

'Nothing to be afraid of,' Noye quipped, 'makes it like I've been doing the weekly shop.' He placed the ingots in the bags – which threatened to split under the weight – hefted them in both hands and walked out.

Jersey Special Branch watched Noye take the gold a couple of hundred metres up the street to the local branch of the Trustee Savings Bank (TSB). He went inside, rented a safe deposit box to which both he and his wife had both sole and joint withdrawal rights, placed the eleven bars of gold in the box and left. The watchers followed, but managed to lose their target somewhere in central St Helier. An hour or so later, surveillance officers staking out the airport spotted Noye as he strolled into 'Departures'.

Noye checked in for the return flight to Gatwick and passed through security. As he was about to board the aircraft, a burly man stepped forward and blocked his path. A second man appeared at

Noye's shoulder. Both were Special Branch officers. Some of Noye's jauntiness deserted him. The first detective asked him to fill in an embarkation form. Noye completed it in his own name. The detective then asked Noye to confirm his identity. Noye replied that except for his airline ticket he had nothing on him. The police asked him if they might see it.

'This ticket – it's made out in the name of a Mr K. Swan,' said the first detective. 'But according to this embarkation form, which you have just completed in your own handwriting, your real name is Kenneth Noye. Can you explain that?'

Noye blustered, 'There's this mate of mine, works for the airlines – he gets tickets on the cheap. He bought it for me, but it was already in this other geezer's name.'

The detectives stared at him. It was evident that the longer they detained Noye, the more nervous he grew. The second detective said, 'Would you mind telling us what you were doing in Jersey, sir?'

'Business,' Noye replied curtly.

'Any particular kind?'

'You know, bit of this, bit of that – nothing special.' The detectives, who knew perfectly well that Noye had been on the island to buy gold to the value of £110,000, kept him standing there until the last call for his flight, and then let him go. The problem was that Noye had not done anything illegal. But the fact that he had a criminal record and was being watched in connection with a major Scotland Yard investigation led Jersey police to ask the TSB branch where Noye had taken the gold to label his safe deposit box with the words: 'CARE: DO NOT ALERT THE CUSTOMER'. If he or his wife ever showed up to collect the gold, the bank's staff would behave as if there were some red tape to be gone through in order to effect a delay and immediately alert senior managers to what was happening. They, in turn, would call DCI Quinn, on his home number if necessary.

This was all very well and good, but it was passive, not active, police work, and not in itself enough to move the investigation forward. What mystified police on both sides of the Channel was why, if he was in some way connected to £26 million pounds' worth of stolen Brink's-Mat gold, Kenneth Noye was out there buying more of the stuff.

Although they had not yet realized it, for the second time in six months the police were within touching distance of the missing bullion. If, on his return from Jersey, the Yard had kept Noye under twenty-four-hour surveillance, there was a better than even chance that they might have recovered some of the gold, rounded up many of the people involved in handling it, and stopped a flourishing laundry business dead in its tracks. But hindsight doesn't catch thieves.

15

The hot London summer of 1984 slid into the lazy days of August, and the silly season came in. The investigation into the robbery was certainly looking silly, in that the gold trail had once again gone cold. Detectives knew about the smelter and the identity of its collector; they knew about Noye and his newly acquired gold bars. All the evidence seemed to suggest that somewhere out there in the boondocks a cleverly concealed and well-established network was busy converting the Heathrow heist into ready cash. But this was speculation: it brought the police no closer to the missing millions.

Frustrating. And not an outcome that the Brink's-Mat detectives could allow to prevail. And so it was ears to the ground time again, especially in the South London pubs, clubs, bars and massage parlours frequented by the likes of their quarry. They needed to find someone who might have picked up a rumour, and be prepared to share it either as a result of police persuasion, or in return for hard cash.

That year, London's Metropolitan Police force had another major problem to deal with. In March, more than half of Britain's 190,000 coal miners had gone on strike in protest at the proposed closure of twenty pits labelled 'uneconomic'. The Thatcher government brought in repressive anti-strike legislation, and the strike turned nasty. With widespread violence between police and miners, as well as between striking and non-striking miners, Britain's police resources – including the Met's – were stretched to the limit. But with the manpower that was left to it, the Yard did its best to keep an eye on Kenneth Noye, who still looked by far the most promising lead. Detectives also watched other South London criminals with a record for armed robbery.

In December 1984, all of this activity bore fruit when a C11 detective inspector working the South London beat heard a whisper: the informant said Kenneth Noye, along with a second man named Brian Reader, were the kingpins laundering the stolen Brink's-Mat bullion. A separate piece of intelligence backed up this information, but insisted there was a whole network of people, and not just Reader and Noye, busy turning the gold into cash.

It was now the best part of a year since the Flying Squad had discovered and targeted Noye. During the early months of 1984, they had put a lot of time, money and effort into watching him; had him bang in their sights, but been unable to prove any direct connection between him and the stolen bullion. With new intelligence marking him out as one of the main conduits for the gold, it now looked as though detectives would have done better to keep Noye permanently under the microscope.

With Commander Cater nearing retirement, a new man, Acting Detective Chief Superintendent (ADCS) Brian Boyce, was asked to take up the Flying Squad reins. One of his first actions was to reinstate the twenty-four-hour surveillance on Kenneth Noye, and to start it from scratch in the case of Brian Reader. Watching the pair of them round the clock was expensive, but Boyce had a hunch it might pay off.

Reader had only one prior conviction – for handling stolen goods. But he was wanted for a string of sophisticated burglaries he had allegedly committed in 1982. In each of these the target had been a manufacturing and/or wholesale jewellery firm; and in each case, the thieves had exclusively targeted gold. Faced with the prospect of an Old Bailey trial, Reader had skipped bail and headed, like just about every other British criminal on the run at that time, for the extradition-free haven of the 'Costa del Crime' in southern Spain. Now, according to the C11 'snout' or informant, the fugitive was back in the UK helping Noye turn the bullion into ready money. He lived at an address in the same A20 triangle as Noye, in Winn Road, Grove Park, in the London borough of Lewisham. This, too, went under the C11 lens.

Tasked with the ticklish job of watching the highly surveillance-aware Noye on his home turf, the C11 team set up a temporary command post in the unlikely surroundings of the Stacklands Retreat House, a rest and retirement home for Anglican clergymen in School Lane, West Kingsdown, directly opposite Noye's house.

Stacklands was set back a couple of hundred metres from the lane. Detectives used one room in the house as a command post, and built a hide in the bushes next to Stacklands's main gate. From this vantage point they could watch Noye's driveway around the clock. Officers also set up a video camera in a bird box nailed to an oak tree overlooking Noye's elaborate wrought-iron gates. This CCTV feed would give them a continuous record of his comings and goings, and help them identify his many visitors.

The surveillance operation started early on the morning of Tuesday, 8 January 1985. Almost at once, it paid off. Shortly after 0900, Brian Reader came out of Noye's front door, climbed into a green Vauxhall Cavalier saloon registered in his own name and drove to his home in Winn Road. He left home again twenty minutes later and drove to Cowcross Street on the edge of Hatton Garden in central London. Watched by a detective who was so close he was able to see and memorize the number, Reader used a public telephone booth in Farringdon station to make a telephone call to a neighbouring jewellery shop. Reader then left the station, went into a café opposite and sat down at a table with two men.

The first was a well-established gold dealer named Christopher Weyman. He ran Lustretone, a gold and jewellery business in nearby Greville Street. The other man was Thomas Adams, who described himself as an asphalter, but who was in fact a member of the notorious 'Adams Family' crime gang based in Islington, North London.

As if aware he might be under observation – or perhaps as a matter of routine security – Reader wrote something down on a piece of paper and showed it to his companions. All three men then walked out of the café and crossed to Reader's car. Adams opened the rear door, took out a heavy oblong parcel about 30 by 15 centimetres, and put it in the boot of a white Mercedes sports car parked some little way up the street. Adams and Weyman then got into the Mercedes and drove away.

At the same time as this exchange was taking place, back in West

Kingsdown another, unidentified, man arrived at Hollywood Cottage driving a vehicle registered to the same man who had picked up the gold smelter. The unknown man went inside for a few minutes, came back out and then drove to Kenneth Noye's former address in Hever Avenue. This was now occupied by John 'Little Legs' Lloyd and his common-law wife Jean Savage.

A classic gangster's moll, the diminutive but ferocious Savage had close-cropped, dyed blonde hair, an expensive taste in clothes, and three children by a previous husband. Extremely fond of gold jewellery, she was a friend of George Davis's, the South London minicab driver sentenced to twenty years in prison in 1975 for his alleged role in a 1974 Ilford, Essex, payroll robbery in the course of which a police officer had been shot and injured. Convicted on the identification evidence of two detectives, and protesting his innocence to the last, Davis was sent to Albany Prison on the Isle of Wight. His supporters – Savage included – said he was the victim of mistaken identity and had not taken part in the robbery. They organized marches, petitions and fund-raising events to increase public awareness of the case. The campaign snowballed, with graffiti sprayed on railway bridges and walls proclaiming Davis's innocence.

When this had no effect, campaigners resorted to direct action: Jim and Colin Dean, Davis's brothers-in-law, carried out a seven-hour roof top protest at St Paul's cathedral in London. Four of his supporters vandalized Headingley cricket pitch in the middle of a vital match between England and Australia. They dug holes in the pitch, poured oil over one end of the wicket and daubed the familiar 'George Davis is Innocent' and 'Free George Davis' slogans on the walls surrounding the ground. The real damage was done when the Test Match – having been extended to six days – was drawn, robbing England of the chance to win back the Ashes.

Savage became a leading light in the campaign, which finally had its effect: Davis was released in May 1976 after Home Secretary Roy Jenkins decided that the original conviction was unsafe. But then, in July 1978, Davis was jailed for fifteen years after pleading guilty to taking part in a bank robbery. Freed in 1984, he was sentenced to a further eighteen months in prison three years later for attempting to steal mailbags.

Detectives watched Noye and a second unidentified man leave Hollywood Cottage in Noye's dark-blue Range Rover and drive along the A20 towards London. After about 12 miles the vehicle turned into the car park of the Beaverwood Club, a Spanish-style nightclub concealed from the road by a curtain of trees. A few minutes later, Noye left the club and drove back home alone.

Clandestine meetings involving gang members and gold dealers, heavy parcels transferred between cars, the interplay between Noye, the Collector and Reader – it was clear that something fishy was going on. And the pattern of activity suggested a strong connection to the stolen Brink's-Mat bullion.

Boyce decided there was enough evidence to intensify surveillance – especially on Reader. On 10 January at about noon, C11 officers followed Reader from his home address to the Crest Hotel in nearby Bexley. As he neared the hotel, Noye, who was waiting outside in his Range Rover, did a U-turn and set off towards London. Reader followed, as did Myrna Yates, a female constable in plain clothes who was part of the C11 surveillance team. After a short distance, Noye and Reader pulled into a secluded side road and stopped. Showing great courage and skill, Yates parked her car, crept up until she had eyeballs on the two men, and watched as Noye took a heavy black briefcase from the Range Rover's boot and handed it to Reader. The suspects then got back into their respective vehicles and drove away in different directions.

The next day, Noye again met Reader in the car park of the Beaverwood Club. Following a brief conversation, Reader continued on alone to the Royal National Hotel in Bedford Way, Bloomsbury, central London. Strolling into the reception area – and looking for all the world like an anonymous hotel guest – Yates spotted Reader talking to Christopher Weyman and Thomas Adams at a corner table. She sat down nearby, ordered a cup of coffee and did her best to eavesdrop on their conversation without appearing to do so.

A few minutes later, Weyman and Adams left the hotel, slid into the same white Mercedes as before and drove to Paddington railway station. Adams got out holding a heavy briefcase. He stood looking around nervously on the station concourse for some minutes while Weyman made two telephone calls. Both men then bought first-class tickets for Swindon, a busy commercial town in the English Midlands.

They would have been very surprised to learn just how many of their fellow passengers on the journey to Swindon were undercover surveillance officers. On arrival in Swindon, Weyman made several more phone calls, and then the two men acted out what looked to the watching detectives like some elaborate, prearranged pantomime. They shook hands as if parting company, and then, just in case anyone had failed to register the fact that they were separating, enthusiastically waved each other goodbye. Weyman strolled off down the road in one direction, followed after an interval of about two minutes by Adams, who went the other way. Apparently satisfied they were unobserved, the two turned sharp about, retraced their steps, met up again and went into a sidestreet fish-and-chip shop. They ordered some food and sat down to eat.

About an hour later, a Jaguar XJS with two more men in it rolled to a halt outside. Checking the licence plate, police discovered it was registered to a man named Garth Chappell. But neither man inside the vehicle could, for the moment, be positively identified. Further checks revealed that Garth Chappell was the 42-year-old managing director and co-owner of Scadlynn Ltd, a bullion and wholesale jewellery company located in North Street, Bedminster, then a scruffy area of Bristol. Until March 1984, detectives found, the firm had been co-owned by a man named John Palmer.

Adams came out of the fish-and-chip shop, glanced up and down the street, shoved the briefcase into the Jaguar's boot and slammed it shut. The car sped off, followed by detectives who tailed it all the way to Scadlynn's premises in Bedminster. The Jaguar's driver and passenger took the briefcase inside, after which the passenger came back out, climbed into a second car and drove to Bali-Hi, a grandiose detached bungalow complete with *arriviste* stone lions on the gate pillars in Bishopsworth, one of the more upmarket Bristol suburbs. Further investigations revealed that this man was almost certainly Terence Patch, aged forty-one, a self-made businessman who ran scrap metal and central heating businesses and who also owned a slice of a local country club. Patch turned out to own both the second car and Bali-Hi. That meant that the other man – the Jaguar's driver – had to be Garth Chappell.

Detectives now ran further checks on both men. Patch had a wife, Diane, who liked to go horse-riding, and two teenage sons. He also turned out to be the owner of a cosy country cottage in the village of Chew Magna a few miles distant.

The connections between Patch, Chappell, Weyman, Adams, Reader, Noye and a precious metals dealership were not lost on the Flying Squad, and the whole pack was kept under close watch.

Over the next few days, Brian Reader made several more trips to Cowcross Street in central London. On the first occasion he met Adams in the same café they had used before, playing out the same game of 'Pass the Parcel': Weyman and a second man arrived in a taxi carrying heavy boxes. Thomas Adams came out of the café, opened the boot of the white Mercedes and placed the boxes inside. Then they all trooped back inside and had a cup of tea. When they had recovered from their exertions, Reader and Adams transferred the boxes to the boot of Reader's Cavalier. Reader then drove directly to Hollywood Cottage for another rendezvous with Kenneth Noye.

On 21 January, Reader was back in the same Cowcross Street café, deep in conversation with a jeweller, antiques dealer, and, the police knew, major-league fence. Right on cue, Weyman drove up in the white Mercedes. He sat down opposite Reader, who pulled a green Marks & Spencer carrier bag from his coat pocket and placed it on the table between them. As they talked, Reader kept his right hand on top of the bag. Weyman took out a thick manila envelope and slid it over to Reader. At the same time, Reader pushed the carrier bag across the table to Weyman. Reader then drove back to Hollywood Cottage, but left after spending no longer than fifteen minutes inside. He drove on to the Royal National Hotel, where he met the fence. The two men sat at a table where they could watch the street until Thomas Adams arrived in the white Mercedes. Adams got out, Reader and the jeweller came out to meet him. Reader went to the boot of his Cavalier, reached in and handed Adams a large, heavy, brown paper package done up with masking tape. Adams put the parcel in the boot of the white Mercedes and drove away.

A well-oiled merry-go-round was in operation, that much was clear. But the police wanted to find out exactly how the machinery operated, and make sure they missed none of the people turning the wheels. To this end, C11 watchers now followed Thomas Adams west along the M4 motorway. Adams exited at Junction 15 for Swindon, and shortly after that turned into the car park of The Plough, an attractive country pub conveniently close to the M4. Garth Chappell's Jaguar was already there. Sliding the Mercedes neatly in behind the Jaguar, Adams went inside the pub. A short time later, a group of men came out and gathered around the two cars. Two of these men reached into the boot of the Mercedes, took out the same brown paper package police had watched Adams place there in London and transferred it to the boot of Chappell's Jaguar. Sauntering across the car park as this transfer took place, one of the C11 watchers clocked the action.

Chappell climbed into his Jaguar and set off, followed at a discreet distance by a team of surveillance officers. Trying to be a little too careful this time, they lost track of the Jaguar just outside the village of Litton, in Somerset. Had they only managed to keep on his tail for a few minutes longer, Chappell might have led them on to one of the men who was smelting the stolen gold, and with him to one end of the Brink's-Mat gold-into-cash-laundry.

Despite this setback, and for the time being blissfully unaware of it, the police were fairly satisfied with what they now knew. A pattern of activity had emerged which appeared to confirm Kenneth Noye as a key member of the network laundering the Brink's-Mat gold, and Brian Reader as his first lieutenant.

All they had to do now was catch them with their hands in the till.

16

Having spent the best part of a month bird-watching from the bushes outside Noye's home address, and observing the complex game of pass-the-parcel that he apparently end-stopped, senior police officers decided the time had come to make a move. At the end of January 1985, Acting DCS Boyce obtained warrants to raid thirty-six addresses in the London, Kent and Bristol areas. At the same time he called the team of Brink's-Mat detectives to an action meeting.

There were various options open to the police: they could hit Hollywood Cottage blind and hope to catch Noye, Reader and anyone else who might be there at the time in the act of handling gold; they could raid Scadlynn Ltd, in Bedminster, and hope for a similar result; they could intercept the chain of couriers in the hope of catching one or more of *them* in possession of stolen bullion; or they could whack the whole pack at all of these separate premises at the same time. There were dangers in each option. If the suspects got even the slightest hint they were about to be raided, a large amount of gold might vanish all over again. And if their luck was really out, detectives might hit them at the very time when there was no laundry activity taking place, and be unable to press charges then or at any time in the future.

In an attempt to avoid the various pitfalls, Boyce asked for – and got – the services of the Yard's Specialist Surveillance unit. On the face of it, the plan Boyce had come up with was straightforward: he would ask one of the SSU's most experienced teams to go into the grounds of Hollywood Cottage every evening under cover of darkness and carry out close target surveillance on Noye's home. The team would only go in when the best opportunity presented itself – that is, when the surveillance suggested, or better still confirmed that Reader and Noye, or Noye and one or more of the other suspects, were in the act of making an exchange.

The whole idea was to get eyes on Noye and any associates actually handling the gold. When they thought this was happening, the two-man undercover team would transmit a prearranged coded radio signal to the waiting back-up units. The hit squads would then crash in and arrest everyone in sight. Should the SSU team see nothing suspicious on any given night, they would withdraw from the grounds at daybreak and keep on trying until they saw suspicious activity.

Boyce sent a second SSU team to cover the areas in and around Hatton Garden and Bloomsbury that Adams, Reader, Weyman *et al*, had visited over the past weeks. He put a third unit on Brian Reader's home, dispatched a fourth to cover Swindon and the M4 corridor, and kept one last, mobile, team of watchers ready to provide back-up as and where necessary. This was the big one. There was no percentage in hanging back.

Any surveillance changeover inevitably brings with it an increased risk of discovery. Boyce therefore decided that seventy-two hours was the maximum length of time he could ask his watchers to remain on station and alert. If there was no movement along the gold chain during that three-day period, and no sign of Noye or his associates handling the gold, then the whole operation would be called off.

Bearing out the old saw that life is stranger than fiction, there were two further reasons why Boyce wanted his men to get right close up and catch the suspects red-handed. The first was that during World War Two, Britain's Special Operations Executive (SOE), which controlled pro-Allied resistance groups across Europe, had used the house then standing on the site of Hollywood Cottage, the primary school next door to it, and the grounds of both properties for storing secret equipment. There were thought to be numerous underground bunkers and tunnels where the bullion might be stashed. It would not do to go blundering in there mob-handed, and then be faced with a fireproof Noye while a couple of his mates clambered out of a rabbit hole half a mile away lugging boxes full of stolen bullion.

There was also the problem of Noye's obsessive security. He controlled the gates to Hollywood Cottage remotely from inside the house, while a gate-mounted CCTV camera enabled him to scrutinize his visitors. Mr Caution was unlikely to welcome a police surveillance team. Boyce did not want Noye and his associates having any more time than was absolutely necessary to flee the scene, hide the gold, or make any other defensive moves.

On the evening of Saturday, 26 January, the SSU teams moved quietly into position. The job of penetrating the grounds of Hollywood Cottage and trying to get eyes on Kenneth Noye 'at it' fell to Detective Constables Neil Murphy and John Fordham. DS Robert Gurr, a veteran surveillance sergeant, would act as forward controller from the hide opposite the gates.

John Fordham, a family man from Romford in Essex, was one of the most experienced – and best – police undercover surveillance officers in Britain. He had joined the Metropolitan Police service in his late twenties, following a slightly chequered career that had included employment as a merchant seaman and as a prison officer. In the dark arts of covert watching, Fordham had discovered both his métier and himself. Consistently refusing promotions so that he could stay on the operational duties he loved, Fordham had personally trained Neil Murphy, his partner, in surveillance techniques. The tutor-pupil relationship had blossomed into one of the SSU's most successful pairings. The two men were faced with a tall order – but it was the kind of challenge that Fordham, in particular, relished.

All the elements of the tragedy that was about to unfold were now in place.

Noye and his wife Brenda had returned home a few hours earlier. At around lunchtime that day, the police watched Reader miss a rendezvous with Noye at the Beaverwood Club. Noye turned up in the car park first, waited for some minutes, showed signs of clear frustration and annoyance, and then drove back home. Reader arrived at the club about forty minutes later. After hanging around looking puzzled and consulting his wristwatch several times, he too drove off. It was obvious that an exchange of some kind had been scheduled, but there had been a mix-up.

At 1812 that evening, Reader turned his Cavalier into the gateway of Hollywood Cottage. It was the moment the police had been waiting for. If Reader had missed the earlier rendezvous because of a blunder, there was every chance his arrival now signalled an exchange of the latest gold shipment. This was it. This was the moment when the Flying Squad broke the gold chain, recovered the bullion, caught the villains bang to rights, and sat back to bask in the plaudits.

Boyce ordered Fordham and Murphy in.

To obstruct surveillance of any kind, and in particular the kind now about to take place, Noye kept three Rottweiler dogs. Barely trained, these dogs were let loose in the grounds of Hollywood Cottage at night to give him early warning of any unwelcome visitors. Having watched the house for so long, the police were aware of these dogs. They also knew from the local force that Noye had several licensed firearms on the premises, including two shotguns. Boyce nevertheless decided not to arm his two-man surveillance team. At this stage, as far as anyone knew, Noye was just a middleman. Despite his previous convictions for assault, there was no reason to believe he would resort to violence if challenged.

But as they put together their meticulous plans for the operation, Fordham and Murphy were worried. Bred as a guard dog and known for its courage, ferocity and persistence in attack, the average Rottweiler weighs between 40 and 50 kg (90–110lb) – mostly hard muscle. The officers asked the Met's specialist dog-handling unit for advice on how to deal with the Rottweilers if they were surprised. The answer – 'Knock the dogs out' – did not strike them as feasible. There was a chance they might manage to knock out one dog – but three of them? It sounded like bad advice, and they said as much. The next suggestion was to stand perfectly still until the dogs calmed down. This again struck Fordham and Murphy as wildly optimistic, as well as operationally impractical: the dogs would be certain to bark, alerting Noye.

The SSU men went back to the dog-handlers a third time. The unit's final piece of advice – throw yeast tablets – was the last straw, as far as Fordham and Murphy were concerned. According to the experts, no dog could resist a tasty yeast tablet. But in the pitch dark, as they came bounding in to attack, was it really likely that the Rottweilers would skid to a halt, snaffle up some hurriedly scattered yeast tablets and then go contentedly about their business? Still uneasy as to what might happen if they went in, the two men nevertheless pocketed the yeast tablets and made ready.

Clad in wetsuits covered by two sets of clothing – the outermost layer standard British Army camouflage pattern – two balaclavas apiece, scarves, gloves and anything else they could think of to combat the bitter cold, Fordham and Murphy carried light-intensifying binoculars; miniaturized surveillance radio sets with earpieces for receiving messages; larger radios for sending them (officers had discovered that when they lay prone, the aerials on the smaller sets tended to garble transmission); military-style webbing harnesses for carrying the larger radios and other bulky items of equipment; infrared cameras; high-energy sweets to keep them going on watch; water; plastic bags in case they had to answer a call of nature, and various other tools of their arcane trade. The balaclavas were full face, with small holes cut for vision and breathing. The fact that they went into the garden masked would later prove crucial.

Naturally, Fordham and Murphy were part of a much bigger team that night, but only the two of them would actually penetrate the grounds of the house. Two more SSU officers would maintain a watch with DS Gurr from the hide in School Lane opposite Noye's gates, and, together with several pairs of officers patrolling the local area in cars, act as quick-reaction back-up if necessary. Suckling, now promoted acting DI and in another unmarked police car stationed nearby, would remain in overall control of the operation, while up in London, DI Brightwell and most other members of the Brink's-Mat squad would listen in on the radio traffic and hope for a result.

Despite all the back-up, once they were actually inside the grounds of Hollywood Cottage, Fordham and Murphy would take full operational control, and maintain it until they came out again: only the people at the sharp end can judge how best to react in a given circumstance.

Gurr gave the 'go' signal at 1815. With everything quiet up until Reader's sudden and unexpected arrival, Murphy had been lying flat on the ground reading and recording car number plates from the hide opposite Noye's gates. He left the heavily concealed position and joined Fordham 20 metres further down School Lane. The two men climbed onto the perimeter wall of Hollywood Cottage and sat there in silence for several minutes listening and watching, while their senses grew accustomed to the garden beyond. There was a light sprinkling of snow on the ground and the moon was obscured by a thick bank of cloud.

All was quiet.

To their right, by the light of the globe lamps strung along its length, they could make out the first section of the long driveway leading up to the house. Directly ahead of them on the far side of some low bushes, a second screen of denser shrubbery and trees concealed the remains of a derelict garage that stood in front of the apple-drying barn. If they could reach this second cover, they would be halfway to their objective. They could pause there, observe the house at close range and decide when and if it was safe to move right up to it. They watched and waited a few more minutes to be absolutely sure it was safe to go in. The garden was still as a graveyard. There was no sight or sound of the three dogs. The freezing January air hung heavy and still. They decided to move forward.

Fordham slipped over the wall and made for the first line of bushes. Murphy was right behind him. Reaching this first barrier they rested for a moment and then, in best SAS style, began 'pepper-potting' towards the apple barn: one man advanced low and slow while the other watched and listened; the first man stopped, got down, listened and watched in his turn; then, if the coast was clear, the second man moved past him and the wait/observe/move cycle started again. Fordham, who had point, reached the copse in front of the apple-drying barn and dropped to one knee. Murphy moved up to join him. They stared into the icy darkness, ears pricked for the slightest unusual noise.

They were now some 150 metres from the garden's perimeter wall – well inside the property. Through the trees, they could see their objective: the brightly lit rooms at the front of the big house. All was quiet. They made ready to move forward again.

There was an odd rushing sound. They looked up to see two huge shapes hurtling towards them, black against the snow. Murphy reared backwards and frantically keyed his radio: 'Dogs – hostile!' He yanked the yeast tablets out of his pocket and threw them to the ground. He might as well have sprinkled rose petals. The snarling Rottweilers leapt at him and Fordham, tearing and ripping at their clothes. The furious sound of barking on the still air was enough to wake the dead.

C11 rules stipulated that surveillance teams should always try to 'blow out, not show out' if compromised – that is, retreat before discovery. Realizing that people would come from the house to investigate at any moment, and assuming that Fordham would follow him, Murphy backed slowly away from the dogs, arms outstretched in an effort to protect himself. He headed for the nearest point of safety, the wooden fence to his left that separated the grounds of Hollywood Cottage from the neighbouring property. As he made for this boundary Murphy transmitted a second message timed at 1826: 'Neil out towards fence.'

One minute later, at 1827, Fordham transmitted, 'Somebody out – halfway down drive. Calling dogs.'

Reaching the fence, Murphy hauled himself up onto it with the aid of a branch and looked back to see what was happening. Peering through the shrubbery, he made out a dark figure coming towards him from the direction of the house. The shape was searching the underbrush with a torch. Murphy froze. He suddenly realized that Fordham had not retreated with him. Although he could not see exactly what was happening, Murphy had to assume that his partner was still under attack from the dogs – and at risk of immediate discovery by the figure heading his way. He started kicking the fence hard with his heels, shouting, 'Keep those dogs quiet!' His intention – by pretending to be an irate neighbour – was to distract the Rottweilers and the dark, searching figure long enough for Fordham to beat a tactical retreat.

Hearing the racket, the dark shape turned towards him and took two more steps. Murphy climbed over the wooden fence into the adjoining garden and began making his way along it towards School Lane. He now wanted to reach the back-up officers at the surveillance point and alert them to what was happening in time to save his partner from further compromise – or worse.

As he hurried back along the lane skirting the front wall of Hollywood Cottage, Murphy heard the sound of angry male voices coming from the grounds, followed by the shrill, penetrating screams of a woman. Crouching in a clump of cover near the main gates, Murphy looked back. He could see two men standing over something – or someone – lying on the ground at their feet. The men were shouting at the prone shape. One of them was brandishing what looked like a stick. Murphy later stated that he saw the other man draw back his leg and kick the figure – a claim both men subsequently denied. Then he heard the man with the stick shout, 'I'll blow your head off!' The blood like ice in his veins, Murphy realized that the 'stick' was in fact a shotgun. In a message timed at 1837 he transmitted, 'Man compromising John: stick/shotgun.'

As soon as they heard Murphy transmit, 'Dogs – hostile!' the nearest back-up officers on foot moved up to the perimeter wall. If necessary, they would try and draw the Rottweilers away from their colleagues. But for a few crucial minutes, unaware of exactly what was happening and not wanting to rush in and compromise the operation further, they stood off and awaited either instructions from above or a direct appeal for help from Murphy or Fordham.

Hearing Murphy's new message – that Fordham might be under threat from a shotgun – Suckling transmitted, 'All units AM.' It was the emergency assist code, ordering all available units into Hollywood Cottage – fast.

A short distance up the lane, moving slowly towards the house in an unmarked police car, Flying Squad Detective Constables John Childs and David Manning heard the call. Childs floored the accelerator. The car surged forward. They were in luck: the gates, which Noye had opened to admit Reader, were still standing wide – he had forgotten to close them again.

Childs spun the police car in through the gap, roared onto the apron beyond and stood on the brakes. Fordham was lying on his back to the left of the driveway. The car's headlights picked out three Rottweiler dogs ripping at the fallen man. (A third dog, slightly smaller than the first two, had by now joined in.) Two men, one armed with a shotgun, stood over Fordham. A woman standing next to the group was screaming at the top of her voice. As the police car skidded to a halt Manning leapt out, held up his warrant card, and shouted, 'I am a police officer!' The man holding the shotgun swivelled round, pointed it at him and shouted, 'Fuck off, or I will do you as well.' As the speaker's face caught the glare of the headlights, Manning recognized Kenneth Noye.

Manning shouted, 'Put the gun down and get those dogs away from the officer.' At the sound of this new voice, the Rottweilers went for him. The first dog worried at his legs while the second, larger animal leapt for his throat. Manning tore off his jacket, wrapped it round his arm and used it to try and beat back the leaping dogs. Childs radioed, 'All units stand by.' With one officer down, three ferocious dogs trying to savage them and at least one armed man threatening to shoot if they did not withdraw, they needed all the help they could get.

Fast.

Ignoring the shotgun, which was still trained on him, Manning, a 38-year-old, no-nonsense, former professional footballer walked across to Fordham and bent down. Peering at his fallen colleague, he felt a clamping sensation, as if his chest had been bound with an iron hoop. There were dark patches on Fordham's clothing. Black against the surrounding cloth they grew in size even as he watched. Manning ripped off a glove, reached out and touched one of the stains with his forefinger. The fingertip came away wet.

Fordham opened his eyes and looked up at him. 'He's done me,' he said softly. 'He's stabbed me.' Manning stood and whipped round. Childs was standing behind the police car trying to fend off the Rottweilers, which were now attacking him. Manning shouted, 'John! Call an ambulance!' Childs fought his way past the snapping dogs to the driver's seat, radioed for an ambulance and called: 'All units AM.' Manning looked up to see Noye, still levelling the shotgun at him, backing slowly away in the direction of the house. A moment later, Noye turned and ran off into the darkness.

Manning looked back down at Fordham. His clothing was now almost all black. Kneeling beside him, Manning tried to give his comrade first aid: cardiac massage and mouth-to-mouth resuscitation, compress the wounds with his hands to stem the bleeding, anything his training brought to mind. It was too late: stabbed eleven times through the chest, armpit, head and back, John Fordham was bleeding to death.

While Manning was trying to save his colleague's life, a second police car manned by DS Anthony Yeoman and DC Bruce Finlayson skidded into the driveway. Drawing their truncheons, the two officers leapt out and moved up in support of Manning. Spotting Noye running across the front of the house from left to right ahead of them, Yeoman shouted, 'Come here, you!' Noye ignored the call and kept running. He disappeared behind the new garage to the right and in front of the main building, and then, a short time later, came back into view. Finlayson ran forward, grabbed Noye by the left arm, and said, 'Police.'

Eyes staring wide in the half-darkness, Noye peered at him. 'I know.'

The ambulance arrived, a banshee wail of sirens and blue flashing lights. They got Fordham on board. Murphy got in with him. The paramedics had cut away the injured officer's clothing. Pleased to see his colleague's chest rising and falling, Murphy said, 'He's alive, he's still breathing!' The paramedic looked at him. 'No,' he said, 'that's the oxygen I'm giving him. He's not breathing by himself.'

Fordham died a few minutes later.

For Worth, Brightwell, Miller, Curtis, Ramm and all the other detectives who had already spent more than a year working on the case, the night's events were an utter disaster. Most terrible was that they had lost a well-liked, respected and highly professional colleague to an act of obscene violence. It did not get any worse than that. But they had also lost any chance they might have had of recovering the gold.

As soon as he realized there were police on the scene Reader ran out through the neighbouring back gardens until he reached the A20 trunk road. Standing on the London-bound side near a pub called The Gamecock, Reader stuck his thumb out in the hope of hitching a lift. At 1940, after dozens of cars had ignored him, one vehicle finally slowed down and came to a stop. Reader ran up to the car, leaned in and said, 'Is there any chance of a lift to London?' A man who had been sitting in the passenger seat of the car stepped out and took a close look at the hitchhiker. 'Yes,' he said. 'Get in.' Reader scrambled gratefully into the warm interior. As the car pulled away, the man turned to face him. 'I'm Detective Constable Paul Gladstone of the Kent police,' he said, 'and this' – he nodded at the driver – 'is Detective Sergeant McAllister.' His face a picture of shock and disbelief, Reader sat dumbstruck. 'Where have you come from?' Gladstone asked.

'The pub,' Reader said, jerking his thumb at The Gamecock.

'Where were you before that?'

Reader shook his head. He was trembling with shock and breathing heavily. 'What's all this about?'

'We're looking for a man in connection with a serious incident tonight. Where did you come from before The Gamecock?' Reader went as if to put his right hand in his pocket, but Gladstone caught it. 'Wait – what have you got there?' Reader showed him a handful of coins. 'Put your hands on the back of the seat in front of you,' Gladstone ordered. He took the handcuffs from his belt and snapped them around Reader's wrists. Staring into his passenger's eyes, he recited, 'Brian Reader, I'm arresting you on suspicion of assaulting a police officer. Anything you say may be written down and used in evidence against you. Have you anything to say?'

The look of shock on Reader's face was by now almost comical. 'What? You must be joking.'

Gladstone kept staring at his prisoner. 'No, Mr Reader,' he said, 'we are not joking.'

17

Back at Hollywood Cottage the police were swarming everywhere. They arrested Kenneth and Brenda Noye, handcuffed them and drove them to Swanley police station in separate vehicles. DS David Columbine, the desk sergeant on duty that night, was the first police officer to question Kenneth Noye. 'Do you know why you are being held?' he asked.

Noye shook his head. 'No idea.'

'You're here for the attempted murder of a police officer.' Columbine had not yet heard that Fordham was dead.

'Is that all?' Noye retorted.

A search of Noye's pockets revealed £850 in cash – all of it in crisp, new £50 notes. He refused to give his name and address. Asked to surrender his clothing for forensic examination Noye spat, 'You're not having my clothing until I've seen my brief.' He was escorted to a first-floor room to be photographed. As the photographer made ready, Noye pointed to his left eye. It was bruised and becoming discoloured. He also indicated a small cut on the bridge of his nose. 'I want these photographed,' he said. 'Make sure you get them.'

Back downstairs in his cell, Noye suddenly changed his mind about surrendering his clothes. 'All right,' he said, 'you can have my stuff.' He started to strip. 'Will I be taken to London?'

'No,' replied PC Fred Bird. 'The offence happened in Kent. You will be dealt with here.' (It was not until the Monday afternoon, once a substantive link to the Brink's-Mat inquiry had been made, that the Flying Squad took over the investigation.)

Duty police surgeon Dr Eugene Ganz examined Noye early on the Sunday morning. Insisting Ganz made a note of his bruised left eye and the small nick on his nose, Noye kept saying that Fordham had struck first and without warning, so that he, Noye, had been forced to defend himself. This was why he was so anxious to have the injuries documented.

From the outset Noye was at pains to cast himself, and not Fordham, in the role of victim. He refused point-blank to answer any of the questions Kent police put to him throughout the whole of that first weekend in custody, only repeating that he would 'tell my story to the judge and jury' when the time came. To anyone within earshot and prepared to listen, Noye complained loud and long that he was the innocent and aggrieved party, attacked in his own garden and obliged to act in legitimate self-defence. On the Sunday afternoon, he was allowed to see his lawyer, Raymond Burrough. Burrough then went on to counsel Brenda Noye.

Questioned separately, Brian Reader vehemently denied playing any part in the stabbing. So, too, did Brenda Noye, maintaining that not only had she not been anywhere near the incident, but she had stayed in the house throughout.

While the interrogations continued, a police forensic team started a fingertip search of the area where the killing had taken place. At the same time, scores of other officers began an exhaustive search of the house and its outbuildings. They also started digging anywhere and everywhere that looked as if it might be a good hiding place for 2,670 kg of gold bullion. As they searched, the police made an amazing discovery: despite all his wealth – or perhaps because of it – Noye was stealing electricity to heat his swimming pool and supply the house from the young offenders' institution next door.

Other little quirks came to light. When a young female constable named Helen Barnett who was accidentally locked out of the house pushed the doorbell, the stereo system in Noye's living room came to life and started belting out Shirley Bassey's version of 'Goldfinger'. Encouraged by this indicative example of criminal humour, the police kept on digging.

At around 4 o'clock on the Sunday afternoon, investigating a stretch of unfinished gutter running along the base of a garage wall, Kent police sergeant Peter Holloway came on a half-used tin of paint standing on a piece of old rubber matting. He lifted the tin and the matting and set them to one side. There was a dirty piece of red-and-white striped cotton cloth lying in the gutter below, with something wrapped inside it. Gingerly, Holloway lifted one corner of the material and pulled it clear.

Eleven bars of gold gleamed up at him.

Holloway stared at the cache for a moment. Then he started yelling for assistance.

Although it had been roughly smelted in what looked like a crude attempt to hide its origin, Boyce knew at once that the ingots had to be part of the Brink's-Mat hoard. He also now understood why Noye had bought eleven bars of gold from the bank in St Helier: if, by chance, the police should happen to stop any of the laundry syndicate and ask them to explain what they were doing in possession of fine gold, the Charterhouse Japhet purchase certificates would, on the face of it, show that the bars had been legitimately acquired. To be sure, the gang could only move eleven kilos at a time – but since their combined value was in the region of £110,000 every time they did, the restriction was a small price to pay.

When Boyce had it assayed, all eleven ingots turned out to be 99.99 per cent pure gold – the same quality as the stolen bullion. As far as he was concerned, it made a direct link between Noye, Reader, Adams, Weyman, Chappell, all the other couriers and the Brink's-Mat robbery.

As the search continued, police found globules of gold consistent with smelting in the boot of Noye's Ford Granada, along with fibres from the same piece of cloth that had been wrapped around the ingots found in the gutter. More gold debris was found near the apple-drying barn; on a pair of heavy-duty gloves and a leather apron found inside the building; on a second pair of gloves discovered in Noye's Range Rover; on the front floor mat of a Cadillac he also owned; on the gloves taken from him at Swanley police station; in the back of a pick-up truck parked near the house; on the boot mat of Reader's Vauxhall Cavalier; and in a briefcase discovered at Brian Reader's home.

Encouraged by the wealth of incriminating evidence coming to light, the police spent a further six weeks combing every inch of Hollywood Cottage and its extensive grounds. As well as a large number of officers searching on foot, they used a mechanical digger, dogs, and a helicopter equipped with a device that could supposedly detect buried metal. Their time was not wasted: in a cunningly hidden floor safe under one of the carpets they found £2,500 in brand-new £50 notes, all consecutively marked with the alphanumeric prefix 'A24'. They also discovered a large quantity of jewellery.

In the living room, detectives found a copy of the latest edition of the *Guinness Book of Records*. When they opened it, they saw that someone had drawn a circle in pencil around the entry citing the Brink's-Mat raid as Britain's biggest-ever robbery.

Conducting a detailed search of the apple-drying barn, detectives found an instruction booklet for an Alcosa GF080/2 WPG gas-and-air blasting smelter: they had last seen one of these not 10 miles distant in the boot of the Collector's speeding Rolls-Royce. In the woods behind the house a police dog unearthed a flick knife; a second flick knife was found in the driver's door pocket of Noye's Ford Granada. A white-handled kitchen knife, thrust blade-first into the earth at the base of a tree near one corner of the swimming pool, then came to light. Unfortunately for the police, forensic tests on all of these weapons – as well as on the soil adhering to the white-handled knife – produced no trace of human blood.

Two camouflage caps belonging to John Fordham were found in the shrubbery close to the spot where he had died.

Ripping the wood panelling from the walls, the search teams uncovered several secret compartments. Inside one, at the back of a bedroom cupboard, they found £3,000 worth of Meissen porcelain stolen from a country house some two years earlier.

Snap-searching Brian Reader's home in the hours immediately following his arrest, officers found a black briefcase. It held £66,000 in brand-new £50 notes. Marked in consecutive sequence, they bore the same A24 prefix as the ones found in the floor safe at Hollywood Cottage. A further £3,000 in A24-series £50 notes came to light in Reader's kitchen. Widening their search, detectives found £50,000 more of the same new A24-series £50s – wrapped in a bright orange blanket and partially buried – in the woods behind the homes of Kenneth Noye's parents and sister in West Kingsdown. When questioned about this buried money, Noye and his relatives denied all knowledge of it.

On the Tuesday following the death of John Fordham, Kenneth Noye, his wife Brenda and Brian Reader were jointly charged with his murder. Brenda Noye, who had simply gone out into the garden on hearing the noise, should not have been charged, and the charge was dropped at the subsequent committal hearing. All three were refused bail. The Flying Squad took formal charge of the case and interrogations continued in London.

When DI Anthony Brightwell entered the interview room, Kenneth Noye stood up and held out his hand. Brightwell took it. Noye pushed his right thumb hard into the space between the second and third knuckles of Brightwell's hand. Known as 'Tubalcain', this was a secret Masonic handshake. If he had been hoping for an assist, Noye was out of luck – Brightwell was not, and never had been, 'on the square'. Following this curious exchange, Brightwell did his best to get Noye to talk. But the prisoner fell back on his constant 'not without my brief' refrain.

Questioned by DI John Walsh, whose team had found the A24-series banknotes hidden in his home, Reader was more forthcoming. He strongly denied playing any part in Fordham's death. But when Walsh asked him whether the gold found at Hollywood Cottage formed part of the proceeds of the Brink's-Mat robbery, he replied, 'I can't understand you – of course it does.'

'Is the gold I showed you in the same shape as it was when it was stolen?'

Reader again looked puzzled. 'You know it's been smelted.'

'That's what I mean. Now, when it was smelted was anything added to reduce its gold content?'

'No, it's pure gold.'

'So the only purpose of smelting it was to change its appearance so it could not be identified? Really, it was just smelted, is that what you're saying?'

'Well, that's what I thought,' Reader nodded.

While Walsh kept at Reader, DI Suckling took a turn at trying to get Noye to open up. Like his colleagues, he had spent a lot of time getting nowhere with Noye: he needed to use anything and everything he could. With the discovery of the A24-series banknotes at Noye's and Reader's homes, Suckling felt he had a new lever. 'We found fifty brand-new £50 notes in serial number sequence beginning with the prefix A24 in your safe,' he told Noye.

Noye shrugged his shoulders. 'That's not much.'

'Where did the money come from?'

'I can't remember.'

'We found a further £50,000 hidden in the woods behind your father's and sister's homes.'

'What's that got to do with me?'

'The identification prefix on the banknotes is A24 – the same as on the notes discovered in your safe. Every single one of these notes is new, and forms part of the same numerical sequence.'

'So what? It's not mine.'

'The A24 prefix also corresponds with the serial numbers on a large sum of money found at Brian Reader's home. And with the serial numbers of notes found on other persons associated with the stolen bullion.' At this, Noye began to look a little less sure of himself. Suckling moved in for the kill. 'You must admit that the series of £50 notes, like our observations of you and the others, seems to link all of the people concerned in the disposal of the gold.'

Noye turned his face to the wall. 'I want to see my solicitor,' he intoned, 'it's gone far enough.'

Brenda Noye was questioned last, by DS Kenneth O'Rourke. 'Do you know why you are here?' he began.

'Yes – a man was killed.'

'Yes, we know that – but how?'

'I don't know anything.'

'You must know something. There were three people there, and you were one of them.'

Brenda Noye shook her head. 'I don't know about anyone else. I was in the house and I didn't see anything.'

'There was a green Cavalier outside your house. The driver of that was a visitor – who was that?'

'I don't know anything about a Cavalier or any visitor. I don't know what a Cavalier looks like.'

'It's a light-green saloon car.'

'I have never seen a light-green saloon car at my house.'

'Don't be silly, it was there when the police arrived, on your drive.'

'I didn't see it. Anyway, I know that I don't have to say anything to you – my solicitor told me.'

'That's correct – but is there any reason why you shouldn't answer the questions?'

'No reason.'

'Does the name Brian Reader mean anything to you?'

'No,' said Brenda Noye, 'I have never heard that name.'

'Before the incident – not long before it – you, your husband and Reader were seen standing near the boot of the Cavalier. What have you got to say about that?' (O'Rourke was misinformed – WPC Yates had only seen Reader and Noye.)

'I was in the house.'

'And you never saw anything regarding that incident where the man was murdered?'

'I told you, no.'

'You were heard to scream by officers nearby.'

'I don't want to answer.'

'You were seen to run from the area where it happened back to the house.'

'I went to get the phone.' This statement flatly contradicted her earlier insistence that she had never left the house and had consequently seen nothing. O'Rourke jumped on it. 'So you were out there. You did leave the house.' She refused to answer the question.

'You were a witness to a murder – do you want to sit there and say nothing about it?' She fell silent again. 'The man was stabbed nine times.' (In fact, there were eleven stab wounds, though some reports mentioned ten.) 'Did you stab him?'

'No.'

'There were only two other people there. Which one did it?'

'I love my husband.'

'Are you saying that he did it but you won't say so?' Brenda Noye made no reply. 'The green Cavalier has been seen at your house, with Reader driving, almost daily in the course of the past few weeks. This is the culmination of a year's work. We haven't just stumbled on you.'

'I realize that.'

O'Rourke decided to call a halt. 'I'm sure you know more than you are saying. We'll continue this interview later.'

Brenda Noye refused to sign the interview notes. An officer led her back to her cell.

Four hours later, O'Rourke had another go at getting his prisoner to talk. But before he could even put his first question, Brenda Noye interrupted. 'I can't help you.'

'Can't,' O'Rourke shot back, 'or won't? We believe your husband carried out the killing.'

'Look, I can't help you. My husband couldn't do such a thing.'

'Are you saying it was the other man – Reader?'

'I don't know his second name.'

'You won't know this,' O'Rourke told her, 'but we have found a large quantity of gold on your premises. Is that the reason your husband went to the extremes he did?'

'You will have to ask him if he did it, why he did it.'

'You did know he was dealing in stolen gold?'

'Why should I know?'

'He's your husband. You were seen at the boot of the green Cavalier that night. You live with him. You must have known. Why not tell us from the beginning what happened?'

She shook her head. 'I can't, I just can't.' She looked up. 'I'm not a hard bitch like you think. My stomach is knotted up. My life is destroyed.' O'Rourke gave her a chance to sign the interview notes, but once again she declined to do so. Brenda Noye was remanded in custody to Holloway prison, where she would spend the next two months.

18

In a series of coordinated raids carried out at dawn that same day, police targeted thirteen addresses in the London, Bath and Bristol areas. In the days immediately following Fordham's death, the number of police working on the Brink's-Mat case had multiplied tenfold, from around 20 to some 200. But numbers weren't everything: with their surveillance operation on the gold-laundering chain utterly compromised, all the Flying Squad officers could do was try and make what arrests they could as fast as they could, and in the process hope to find more of the gold.

Top of the hit list was Garth Chappell. Given what had happened to Fordham, the police were taking no chances: no fewer than fifty officers, some of them armed, sealed off the village of Litton, near Bath, where Chappell and his family lived. At 0800, as he was getting ready to take one of his sons to school, police pounced on the tubby, bespectacled Scadlynn director.

Led by DI James McGoohan of the Flying Squad, eight detectives burst into the house and grabbed Chappell. 'Is there any gold in the house?' McGoohan demanded.

Shocked at the suddenness and force of the raid, Chappell nodded. 'Upstairs.'

The detectives exchanged glances. At last they had run some of the heist to earth. Chappell led them up to the main bedroom and pointed to a black briefcase standing beside the bed. McGoohan bent and opened the case. Inside was £15,000 in cash, including £12,500 in new A24-series £50 notes. He asked Chappell the obvious question. 'Can you tell me what you are doing in possession of this large amount of cash?'

Chappell had begun to recover some of his composure. With the bluff pomposity the police would come to recognize as characteristic of him, he said, 'I'm a businessman – I always carry a large amount of cash. I don't have to answer your questions.' Another officer reached into the briefcase and took out a plastic bag. It held twelve gold Krugerrands. There were four more bags containing the same amount. There was also a Victorian crown coin, and a single, loose Krugerrand. McGoohan held up one of the bags. 'Can you tell me about these?'

'I deal in them. So what?'

'What do you mean, you deal in them?'

'I'm a businessman – I do deals of half a million pounds a day. That's all I'm saying.'

Detectives took him outside to his car. There was a pickaxe handle in the Jaguar's boot, and a sheath-knife in the glove compartment. Chappell explained that these were for his personal protection when he was transporting valuables.

'We're taking you in for questioning,' McGoohan told him.

Chappell shrugged. 'Do as you want.' He turned to his wife. 'They're taking me back to London. Don't worry. I might see you in a day or two; if not, you won't be seeing me for a long time.'

While McGoohan and his men were busy with Chappell, a second squad led by DS Michael Ruffles was raiding Bali-Hi, the luxury bungalow in nearby Bishopsworth owned by Terence Patch. Patch was in bed asleep when the detectives crashed in. Arresting and cautioning Patch to be getting on with, they searched the house. They found six new £50 notes, all bearing the same A24 prefix as the ones that had been discovered at Noye's, Reader's and Chappell's addresses; an accounts book in Patch's handwriting detailing Scadlynn's gold transactions for the preceding December, and various other interesting scraps. There was a Jaguar outside the house – the same one police had seen Chappell and Patch use at the rendezvous near Swindon station with Adams and Weyman. Asked if it was his, Patch explained he had borrowed it from Chappell in order to use the car's telephone – at the time a new and exotic invention. There was a pickaxe handle on the rear parcel shelf. 'That's for my protection,' Patch said.

Moving on to his garage, detectives found five crucibles and four metal trays of the type used in smelting gold. 'Why are these here?' Ruffles demanded.

'I brought them from the office to clean them,' Patch replied. 'You can't clean them when they're hot, so I brought them here to cool down.'

Ruffles shook his head. 'I don't understand that – surely it would have been better to let them cool down before moving them?' Patch had no answer to this piece of logic. He, too, was led away for further questioning.

At Patch's cottage in Chew Magna police found the number of the jeweller's shop in Hatton Garden the undercover police officer had seen Brian Reader dialling.

The raid on the premises of Scadlynn Ltd netted accounts and bank deposit books, invoice books and a large amount of paperwork. Detectives seized the lot.

Boyce thought his men had found a few interesting titbits, which might or might not bolster a prosecution of the gold-laundering syndicate. But they had not found what they wanted: the rest of the missing Brink's-Mat gold, along with incontrovertible evidence that the men now under arrest had been handling it. Even so, Boyce and his team had high hopes of their third major target. This was a man named John Palmer, who had a home in Battlefields, near Bath. He had been seen occasionally entering and leaving the Scadlynn offices with Garth Chappell. From the bearing and evident closeness of the two men, not least the fact that they had been business partners, police thought Palmer might be another major player.

At first light, thirty police officers, some of them armed, were in position surrounding The Coach House, Palmer's handsome Georgian home. A surveillance drive-by at 0700 reported, 'All quiet.' Cutting the mains electricity supply to the house to increase their advantage, the raiding party moved in.

Through the small window let into the front door, the detective sergeant leading the assault saw an unknown man standing in the hallway with a phone to his ear. The sergeant shouted, 'Open the door – armed police!' Instead of complying, the man dropped the telephone and ran up the stairs. 'Quick lads,' shouted the DS. He moved back. The two officers behind him stepped forward and buried an axe and a sledgehammer in the front door. It buckled but did not give. 'Faster!' yelled the DS. They smashed it again and the door flew open. Pistols at the ready, four armed officers poured into the hallway and started moving up the stairs. A second wave came in behind this advance guard. Outside, a third team smashed the downstairs windows to further confuse and distract the occupants.

A quick search of the ground floor proved it was clear. The four armed officers crept on up the stairs, straining to hear any sound. The house was silent. They reached the first-floor landing. To the right was a door. The C19 (Met Firearms Squad) sergeant leading the assault tried the handle: it was locked. He shouted, 'Armed police! Open the door!' There was a muffled cry from inside, followed by the sound of someone moving. The sergeant roared, 'Armed police! Open the door!' for the second time. Nothing happened. He nodded at Axe and Sledge. 'OK boys – make entry.'

The flimsy bedroom door flew clean off its hinges. The armed officers stormed in. They found three men hiding in the bedroom and a woman cowering in the bathroom beyond. 'Lie face down on the floor!' the sergeant shouted at the terrified men. 'Put your hands behind your backs and don't move!' The officers spread-eagled and searched the trio. They were all unarmed. Handcuffed, they were ordered to stand up and identify themselves.

'James Harvey,' said the first.

'John Thomas.'

'Lee Groves.'

'And you?' Frightened half out of her wits, the woman who had locked herself in the bathroom was shaking visibly. 'Carole Howe,' she gabbled. 'I'm John Palmer's groom.'

One of the back-up team led her downstairs to the kitchen to get her some tea and calm her down. The DS turned to Harvey. 'Where's John Palmer?'

'He's gone on holiday.'

'Where and when?'

'Three weeks in the Canaries, with his wife and kids. They left yesterday.' The DS relayed the news up the chain of command. They had missed Palmer by one day. It was a bitter blow. He turned back to Harvey. 'Why didn't you let us in, downstairs, when I shouted?'

Harvey looked sheepish. 'We thought you were villains,' he said. 'Why?'

'We saw a car in front of us this morning with two men in it. We thought they were robbers.'

'What time was this?'

'About a quarter past six.' The men Harvey and Groves had seen were C11 surveillance officers in an unmarked car.

'What were you doing out at that time of the morning?'

'We'd been smelting. Out the back.'

'Smelting?' This was more like what he wanted to hear. 'You mean gold?'

'Yes. We thought they – the two men we saw – were after it.'

'Show me.' Harvey led him downstairs to the living room. He walked up to the large settee set against the side wall, lifted one of the seat cushions and pointed. Two crudely smelted gold ingots lay on the sprung base, gleaming brightly in the strong early morning light. The sergeant picked them up. The gold was still warm to the touch. He rounded on Harvey. 'Where's the furnace?'

Harvey jerked a thumb. 'Outside.' He led the police out into the grounds behind the house and pointed to a shed standing in the middle of a copse. The shed, which had no fewer than three air vents, was concealed on three sides by earth embankments covered in shrubbery, and from in front by a strategically positioned horse box.

Keeping a wary eye out, the police moved up to the shed in best assault-team style and booted the door wide. Inside stood a large gold smelter. Like the ingots they had found under the sofa cushion, it was still warm to the touch. Harvey explained that he and Groves had been smelting gold two days previously, on the Sunday, and had started on a new batch of bullion at 0600 that same morning. He said the smelting had been going on for many months, and the routine was always the same: someone brought one or more packages of gold from Scadlynn to The Coach House. Palmer employed the 38-year-old Harvey, who was a partner in Palmer's building firm, and 18-year-old Groves, an assistant in Palmer's Bath jewellery shop, to smelt the gold on a casual and part-time basis. Palmer had told them that the gold was from a legitimate source. As far as they were concerned, they were doing nothing wrong, just earning themselves some useful extra cash.

The third man at the scene, 33-year-old green keeper John Thomas, was Carole Howe's boyfriend. Thomas just happened to be in the wrong place at the wrong time. Asked why he had tried to phone the police from the hallway, then dropped the phone, bolted upstairs and locked himself in with the others when he could see large numbers of police in full uniform outside the house, Thomas said, 'All I saw was the guns.'

A search of The Coach House revealed two shotguns; a rifle; a red wallet with three brand-new A24-series £50 notes, and, in the garage, three bags of copper coins. Harvey said Palmer had told them these coins should be added to the gold to change its purity. When officers looked in Harvey's pick-up truck they found a third shotgun and two large ingot moulds still so hot from the furnace they had caused a layer of condensation to form on the inside of the vehicle's windows.

Police removed the smelter and the gold bars for forensic analysis. The next day, they brought in pneumatic drills, diggers and a bulldozer, and started to dig up large areas around the swimming pool and in the grounds. They also lifted the floorboards in the main house. It was to no avail. Warm or cold, there was no more gold.

Thomas Adams was at home in Islington when the constables came to call. Spotting them from a ground-floor window, Adams ran out into the back yard, climbed onto a wall, walked along it and jumped down into a neighbouring garden. One of the officers lying in wait for that precise eventuality gave chase, and found Adams hiding in a clump of bushes. He collared the suspect and hauled him back into the house. DC Anthony Davis questioned him.

'Why did you run away?'

'You've got to take your chance and run, haven't you?'

'What have you got to run from, though?'

'I knew you were coming eventually.'

'What have you got to hide?'

Adams shook his head. If the police didn't know, he wasn't going to tell them.

Searching the flat, detectives found a roughly smelted gold ingot lying in the bottom of his bedroom wardrobe. They also unearthed a collection of nearly 200 gold wedding rings, seven Krugerrands, a large quantity of gold sovereigns and six gold watch chains. More gold rings and a set of jeweller's scales came to light in a next-door room. Davis asked, 'How do you account for all the jewellery I've found – and this gold bar?'

Adams smiled. 'If you'd done your homework, you'd know all about me.'

'Do you or does your wife own a car?'

'No.'

Davis held up a set of car keys. 'These were found in your basement. They fit the ignition of the BMW parked outside your house.' He brandished a black briefcase, of the type surveillance officers had watched Adams, Patch and the other couriers use in the transfers. 'We found this behind the driver's seat. Is the BMW yours?'

'What BMW?' Adams said.

'These keys are the keys for a BMW. It is your car.'

'No, I know nothing about it.'

Detectives took him in for further questioning.

19

The Flying Squad now had three of the Brink's-Mat gang behind bars. They had rounded up many of the people they suspected of laundering the gold. They had even recovered fourteen of the stolen ingots. Only another 6,826 still to go. But they still had no idea where all this remaining gold might be, or if it had already been turned into cash. Unless they could persuade at least one of the suspects to open up, they had little prospect of unravelling the conspiracy. Or, for that matter, of effecting any successful prosecutions. Not surprisingly, no one was talking: there was little or nothing to gain by cooperating with the police. But then, in one of those coincidences that can happen in law enforcement as in life, the cavalry arrived. In the course of a separate and unconnected investigation of more than six months' standing, HM Customs & Excise officers had stumbled across the trail of the missing Brink's-Mat millions.

Customs officers had started their inquiry in the summer of 1984 following a tip-off from a regular and reliable underworld 'snout'. The informant alleged that a man named Roger Feltham, using the alias 'Peter James' and trading from a false address, had been attempting to sell Krugerrands to the value of £31,350 using a false VAT number. In the first place this was illegal; secondly, experience had taught Customs that where there was one batch of Krugerrands being nudged around in a VAT-avoidance racket, there was usually another.

Undercover officers from the Customs Surveillance Unit (CSU) tailed Feltham to Farringdon station in the City of London, where he picked up a car. They then tracked him down the M4 motorway to the main Swindon junction. Feltham turned off here and drove into the car park of The Plough public house – the very same pub where C11 detectives would later witness other suspected members of the

Brink's-Mat laundry syndicate exchanging heavy packages, jokes, and rounds of beer.

Neither the Flying Squad nor Customs knew it yet, but they were holding separate ends of the same Brink's-Mat tether – and almost falling over one another in the process. Communication is a wonderful thing – when it happens. In 1984, unproductive rivalry between the two agencies often got in the way.

Leaving the first car in the pub car park, Feltham got into a Jaguar and set off west. In an exercise that was almost an exact replica of the police operation a few months later, Customs first traced the Jaguar to Garth Chappell, and then followed it out to Bali-Hi, the bungalow owned by Terence Patch. The next day, Patch got into his car and drove to Scadlynn Ltd.

A glance at Scadlynn's records on the national VAT computer brought the Customs investigators up short. For the preceding six months, this company – on the face of it a crummy little back street scrap precious metal merchants – had been trading vast quantities of gold. What made this all the more remarkable was that up until May 1984, Scadlynn's accounts showed a slight loss on a turnover of less than £100,000 per annum. One minute the company had been failing and apparently about to fold – the next it had shot into stratospheric profit.

When they took a snapshot of the period August 1984 to January 1985, CSU case officers could hardly believe their eyes. During that same six-month period, Scadlynn had banked more than £10 million – every single penny from the sale of gold. It was a staggering sum. And it set the whole Customs Investigation Division on fire. This was no longer some routine, piffling little exercise in swatting Krugerrand-smuggling/VAT racketeers. This had all the hallmarks of major-league villainy.

The phenomenal upturn in Scadlynn's fortunes dated from early in 1984, when company boss Garth Chappell had started selling 'scrap' gold onto the precious metals market. The gold went first to the Public Assay Office in Sheffield, where its purity was tested and verified. All gold – any gold – has what's known as an 'assay' – a unique chemical signature based on a gas spectrometer test. The Scadlynn gold reached the Assay Office in the form of ugly, misshapen lumps, which had to be resmelted, and which staff there jokingly nicknamed 'skull gold' from its frequent and disconcerting resemblance to a human head. Once it had been transformed into regular ingots, officially assayed and restamped, the gold became legitimate: there was nothing to stop Chappell selling it back onto the open market.

The big question was, how had Chappell come by such a mind-boggling quantity of gold?

Chappell had told the Assay Office it was 'scrap' gold – i.e., less than 10 per cent pure. He said he and his agents had bought it legally, at 'jewellery fairs' they had organized in pubs, clubs and hotels in the West of England. With no obvious reason to question this explanation – at least, to begin with – and bearing in mind the relative laxity of financial regulations at the time, Assay Office staff had never thought to run checks on either Scadlynn or the gold's provenance. But one thing did not add up – Assay Office staff consistently found that far from being 'scrap' and less than 10 per cent pure, Scadlynn's 'skull gold' was very nearly of bullion quality. Where was he getting it?

On examining the 'skull' ingots more closely, they found copper and other coins sticking out of the mix in what looked like a crude and deliberate attempt to adulterate it. Why was Chappell trying to reduce the purity of his gold by chucking old coins and dollops of cheap jewellery into it? And where was he getting gold of such extraordinary quality in the first place? It could not possibly be coming from cut-rate jewellery fairs. Assay officials called Chappell to a meeting and put him to the question. Chappell ducked and dived, giving anything but a straight answer. Whatever the real truth, his recent dealings had rocketed this small-time scrap dealer from near-bankruptcy to one of Britain's biggest private gold traders almost overnight.

The main front company behind the jewellery fairs was Shimmerbest Ltd, nominally owned by Matteo Constantino, a London-based jeweller and precious metals dealer. Customs officers now set about turning Scadlynn inside out. Like some kind of modern alchemist, Chappell seemed to have found the secret of transmuting base metal into gold – buckets of it. But fairy tales were not part of HM Customs' operational remit. An immediate check revealed that one of the companies to which Chappell was selling the assayed and, on the face of it, now legitimate gold was Dynasty Ltd, a Leeds-based dealer in precious metals.

Launching a special operation codenamed 'Operation Law Degree' after the initials of the three major cities involved: London, Leeds and Bristol, Customs investigators started to dig, determined to find out everything they could about Scadlynn, the people who owned it, and the source of the magical gold. Jim McGregor, Operation Law Degree's leader, set up a covert surveillance position opposite Scadlynn's offices to record the inward and outward movements of people and gold.

And so it was that many months before the Flying Squad came on the same information as a result of watching Noye and Reader, their own surveillance led Customs to note the close connection between Chappell and a frequent visitor to Scadlynn named John Palmer; to the discovery of Palmer's back-garden smelter; the jewellery fairs and to many links in the chain of couriers who were transporting regular heavy shipments of what Customs knew must be gold into and out of Scadlynn's offices.

As the Law Degree team looked more closely at Chappell's books, it became obvious that the company's accounts did not even begin to add up. The most glaring anomaly was the fact that, on the declared difference between the price he claimed he was paying for the 'scrap' gold and the price at which he was selling it on to Dynasty Ltd, Chappell could not possibly be making a profit – certainly not the £10 million he had made in the space of a single year. Questioned further, Chappell said he had bought the gold legitimately from International Precious Metals (IPM) and Shimmerbest Ltd – companies owned by Matteo Constantino. An inspection of IPM's accounts and VAT records revealed no evidence whatsoever that the company was trading gold with Scadlynn as Chappell claimed. The two sides of the equation simply did not add up.

Asked again to produce full and accurate accounts, Chappell again resorted to bluster: 'I am a dealer. I don't understand books – books are all Chinese to me.' This specious exercise in self-deprecation earned him an immediate fine for £80,000 in unpaid VAT. But

Customs realized the fraud ran much deeper. There was only one way Chappell could be banking millions and millions of pounds from marginal profits, and that was if both the jewellery fairs and the supposed trade with International Precious Metals amounted to a smokescreen – a rigmarole intended to disguise the real source of the bullion.

What could that source be?

In the autumn of 1984, McGregor told two senior Scotland Yard detectives that he suspected Garth Chappell and others working for Scadlynn Ltd of processing at least part of the stolen Brink's-Mat heist. It was one reason Boyce ordered his own surveillance of Noye, Reader, and the rest of the couriers.

Fordham had not died in vain. Coming as it did at a key moment in the whole case, his death revitalized the Brink's-Mat investigation; dynamited better cooperation between the police and HM Customs; and made Boyce and his team more determined than ever to nail every single person associated with the Brink's-Mat robbery and ensure they went to prison for a very long time.

Thanks to Operation Law Degree, they now had a very promising lead.

Comparing notes in the wake of Fordham's death, Customs investigators and their Flying Squad counterparts agreed that the stolen Brink's-Mat bullion was shipped eleven kilos at a time from an unknown place of concealment, possibly a shop or a rented flat in the Hatton Garden area, by couriers who they now believed included Adams, Weyman, Patch, Feltham and Reader. These men were suspected of ferrying the gold to Kenneth Noye in West Kingsdown, as well as to John Palmer's home address. Investigators also agreed the two smelting sites must have been operating in concert.

Roughly resmelted and adulterated, at least part of the gold went back to Scadlynn. Chappell paid the couriers for the consignments in cash. He then had the gold shipped to the Assay Office in Sheffield. The Assay Office made it legal. Chappell traded it on the open market; cashed the cheques he received in return for the gold; took the money home.

And wallowed in it.

The beauty of the whole operation lay in its simplicity – and in its sheer gall.

The two main customers for the Scadlynn gold were Johnson Matthey Bank and Engelhard Sales – the same companies from which almost all of the Brink's-Mat's bullion had been stolen in the first place. Not one to work when he could take the easy route, Chappell banked the cheques he received for the gold in an account at his local bank – the Bedminster branch of Barclays Ltd.

The first batch of gold traded provided Chappell with the cash to 'buy' more from the people controlling it; and the whole merry-go-round started in earnest. One of the most fantastic Mickey Mouse operations in the history of crime, it all held together on a wing and a prayer. Like the scene from Walt Disney's *The Sorcerer's Apprentice*, in which Mickey Mouse loses control of the buckets and brooms, the faster the carousel went, the less control anyone had of it.

The essence of the laundry business was speed. Everyone involved in the operation understood the enormous risks they were taking. They were all well aware that the long arm of the law could reach out and feel their sweaty collars at any time. But they were hoping they could turn enough of the gold around fast enough to make each and every one of them extremely rich – and shortly thereafter extremely invisible – on some distant and exotic foreign shore in a very short space of time. The maximum length of time they all thought it worthwhile to risk the laundry business was one year.

The money from the gold sales started to roll in – and it kept right on rolling. Using the alias 'Charles Cooper', Chappell cashed the cheques either in person or, more occasionally, by deputizing the job to one of the couriers. The choice of name was another example of whimsical gangster humour: Charles Cooper was the name of the perfectly legitimate Hatton Garden dealership that had sold the Collector the Alcosa gold smelter.

By the end of the second week in September 1984, the average *daily* cash withdrawal from Scadlynn's Barclays Bedminster account was £20,000. By October this had risen to £50,000; in November it went up again to an average of £120,000 per diem. On 4 December, an unidentified Scadlynn proxy presented himself at the bank's counter and coolly demanded £200,000 in cash. When the astonished cashier had verified the account and succeeded in scraping together the enormous number of banknotes, the unknown punter shovelled the money into a bin liner and sauntered out of the branch with a cheery wave.

As the weeks and months went by, this tiny branch of the mighty Barclays banking empire gradually adapted to the relentless demand, supplying ever greater cash sums to Chappell and his agents. By the end of 1984, the Scadlynn account was gobbling up so many banknotes that Barclays' Bedminster office manager Angus Leng had no choice but to set up a dedicated supply system: every Monday, Chappell told him how much money Scadlynn wanted to withdraw for the coming week. Leng then ordered the requisite amount from Barclays Bristol Cash Centre.

As the size of the withdrawals increased exponentially through the autumn and winter of 1984, Barclays Bristol Cash Centre managers in turn had to ask the Bank of England for help. The Old Lady of Threadneedle Street duly obliged, sending millions of pounds in new £50 notes – the denomination Chappell preferred – to the apparently insatiable West Country customer.

The Bank of England notes were not only new – they were all in consecutive numbered sequence, and they all carried the A24 identification prefix.

On 6 December 1984, a Scadlynn gofer withdrew £270,000 in new A24-series £50 notes, on this occasion scooping the banknotes into a large cardboard box. For the boys with the Midas touch, Christmas had come early. In mid-December, Scadlynn made three further cash withdrawals from the trading account, each to the tune of more than £200,000. And so it went on, with huge cash sums leaving Barclays Bedminster.

In January 1985, when the average withdrawal had leapt to more than £300,000 a day, Chappell warned the branch that he would shortly be looking to withdraw even larger sums, perhaps as much as £1 million at a time. At this, Leng and his team decided they had no option but to recruit more staff. Even with the help of a counting machine, simply processing that much money every day was taking up most of his employees' time.

Appalled by the scale – and success – of the operation they now saw laid bare, in March 1985, Flying Squad detectives demanded – and gained access to – the whole history of the Scadlynn account. The figures, when they examined them, showed things were even worse than Customs had realized. Between 14 March 1984 and 7 February 1985, Barclays Bedminster had received and placed to the credit of the Scadlynn account the perfectly astonishing total of £14,234,894.91.

£10,315,500 had been withdrawn in cash, the bulk of it by Garth Chappell. Other people were known to have collected the odd sports bag or two filled with cash, but when questioned and shown photographs, bank staff were unable to identify or name any of these proxies. This now seems hard to believe – but as Leng subsequently pointed out, before the stringent anti-laundering and anti-terrorism regulations that nowadays affect all financial transactions in the developed world came into force, customer privacy was sacrosanct. And business was business.

The police now knew they had no chance of recovering the stolen gold. In the sixteen months since the robbery had taken place, the horse had well and truly bolted.

There had been one or two minor setbacks for the launderers. In August 1984, Chappell had dispatched five of his resmelted, Assay Office-approved 'skull' ingots to Engelhard Sales. But despite reprocessing, the gold still had a reddish tinge. On examining the shipment, company managers smelled a rat. Unfortunately, it was the wrong rat: Engelhard thought the red tint derived from copper, which crooks frequently added in an attempt to disguise the origin of smuggled Krugerrands. The red colour of the Scadlynn gold was indeed the result of copper adulteration, but it had nothing to do with Krugerrands. The boys in the back garden of The Coach House were simply chucking pennies into the mix.

A senior Engelhard manager contacted Chappell to voice the company's suspicions. Chappell fell back on his habitual blasé charm; he perfectly understood Engelhard's worries – indeed, he had had the same concerns himself. If Engelhard would kindly return the suspect ingots to Scadlynn, he would check back with his suppliers and make sure there was nothing illegal going on. Naturally, if he did discover wrongdoing then he would inform the police at once. And so on. Engelhard duly returned the gold; Chappell fell about laughing at the idea of conducting an investigation; and that was the end of the Scadlynn trading account with one company.

In December 1984, Chappell lost his second main customer when Dynasty Ltd also became suspicious of the gold's provenance. Dynasty had been selling the 'clean' assayed gold it bought from Scadlynn on to a Staffordshire-based firm by the name of TVA Noble Metals Ltd. But Dynasty managers had also noticed the gold's odd colour. They, too, wanted to know where Chappell was getting the ever-increasing quantities he was sending them.

Following a brief exchange that did nothing to allay their suspicions, Dynasty, in turn, pulled the Scadlynn plug. Undeterred, Chappell started trading directly with TVA Noble. Then there was Johnson Matthey Ltd, which had owned the bulk of the Brink's-Mat gold to begin with. Between July 1984 and January 1985, Johnson Matthey bought gold to the value of £13,605,440 from TVA Noble. Every single ounce of it came from the Brink's-Mat robbery: all unsuspecting, the company was buying back its own gold.

On 17 December 1984, Roger Feltham, the suspect who had led HM Customs to Scadlynn, was found blindfolded and tied hand and foot in the back of a Ford Transit van. The van, with £250,000 of gold on board, had been hijacked on the outskirts of Bristol. The robbers had bound Feltham, grabbed the gold and then dumped the vehicle at a motorway service station with Feltham inside.

To most other businesses this would have come as a crushing blow. But Chappell didn't want to answer too many difficult questions. He told the police that he had 'only lost gold to the value of £97,000'. The real amount lost only came out at his trial. But from then on he paid a professional security firm to transport his shipments of gold and cash.

By now, the extended criminal enterprise that had grown up around the Brink's-Mat heist had so much money to play with, its architects hardly noticed if a quarter of a million went missing. More than once, Chappell asked the security guards he had hired to tip the cash consignments they were delivering out onto his office floor so he could 'count it more easily'. The startled guards did as he asked. On the first occasion, Chappell squatted down and counted out £320,000. The second time it came to a cool half a million.

Chappell had always known that at some point Customs or the police might turn up and start asking awkward questions. This was where Matteo Constantino came in. The Sweeney had lifted Constantino from his home address at 0630 on what the laundrymen had started calling 'Black Tuesday'. Detectives drove the elderly jeweller – who was still half-asleep – directly to the offices of International Precious Metals Ltd, his business in Greville Street. DC Anthony Purdie found an up-to-date account book in a desk drawer. He showed it to Constantino.

'Does this book contain your current business transactions?'

Tall and angular, with a shock of white hair, Constantino, who was short-sighted, squinted at the ledger. 'Yes.'

'I've had a brief look. It seems that you have not done any selling or buying since October 1984? More than a year ago?'

'That's right.'

'Are you really telling me that you have done no business whatsoever since October 1984? In either of your companies?'

'I haven't done any business at all.' This was sweet music to Purdie's ears: if neither of Constantino's companies had done business for a year, then he could not have sold Scadlynn the gold Chappell claimed to have bought from him. Purdie arrested Constantino, locked him up in a sweaty little cell in the basement of West End Central police station and left him to stew for a few hours. Whether it was his age (he was in his seventies), fear, or simply his conscience getting the better of him, Constantino decided to break the vow of silence that up until now had been observed by the rest of the gang.

Sitting him down on a hard chair and staring him hard in the eye, Purdie said, 'Have you any idea what our inquiry is about?'

'Well, I've been doing a bit of fiddling, yes,' replied Constantino. The frankness of this admission surprised Purdie. 'You say "a bit of fiddling" – I consider it to be a lot.'

'Yes, the amounts are, but I've not made that much.' Constantino explained that Chappell had offered him between £2,000 and £3,000 a week in return for making it look as if Shimmerbest and IPM were selling Scadlynn large quantities of gold. Asked how he was supposed to make it look as if Scadlynn had paid for the gold, Constantino said that Chappell wired the money from the Scadlynn account to his, Constantino's, bank account in London. The next day, Chappell arrived in a taxi, waited outside the bank while Constantino withdrew the exact same amount in cash, took it from him, stuffed it into his briefcase, got back into the waiting taxi and returned with it to Bath. The record of Constantino's IPM account showed this had happened eight times and involved a total of £600,000. Shimmerbest had further taken receipt of fraudulently intended wire transfers to the tune of £250,000. When Constantino's bank eventually began refusing to clear the funds for the huge cash sums inside the required twenty-four-hour period, the pair came up with a new arrangement, whereby Constantino travelled down to Bristol to collect his weekly 'fee' from Chappell in person.

Good old folding money. Much less visible. Much less traceable. Or so Chappell thought.

Chappell gave Constantino counterfeit sales invoices for the fictitious gold purchases, but, not wishing to get caught with anything incriminating on paper, the elderly jeweller flushed these receipts down the train lavatory on the return journey. He had personally made no more than some £30,000 by the time the Flying Squad caught up with him, but over the weeks and months they had been working together, Constantino had provided Chappell with a false alibi for some £9 million worth of gold. Told that it was stolen Brink's-Mat bullion, Constantino expressed disbelief. He said Chappell had told him it was the proceeds of smuggled Krugerrands.

The whole false enterprise had been set up in a way that was amateurish and did not stand up to more than the most cursory inspection. Chappell had assured Constantino their dealings would be over by the time the police caught up with them. Constantino believed him. His faith had been misplaced.

Over at City Road police station, Chappell was clinging hard to his story that Constantino had sold him the gold legally. Flying Squad detectives David Ryan and Daniel Conway kept at the Scadlynn boss at intervals throughout the night. 'Did you ever ask Constantino where he was getting the gold?' Ryan asked.

'No,' Chappell said. 'It seemed impertinent, almost, to ask a man with such a well-established business something like that.' He admitted that he and others had sometimes driven to London to collect batches of gold, and that exchanges had also taken place at Bristol Parkway station and at a service station on the M4. Asked why the gold was always resmelted, Chappell said, 'It was to do away with any foreign bodies and to stop pilfering.' He specialized in illogical, irrelevant answers to straightforward questions.

By this time it was 4 o'clock in the morning. Conway and Ryan let Chappell sleep for a couple of hours, waking him again at 0600. 'HM Customs had your offices in Bristol under observation for a number of weeks. During that time they saw couriers bringing gold to Scadlynn. Is that correct?'

Even Chappell found this hard to deny. 'Yes.'

'Who were those couriers? What are their names?'

'I can't tell you that, because of security reasons.'

'What do you mean?' Conway asked in disbelief.

'I mean I'm not prepared to add anything to what I've already said.'

'I am a police officer. What do you mean, "security reasons"? Do you not trust me?'

'I will, with respect, just repeat what I have said,' Chappell intoned. 'I am not prepared to make any further comment before seeing my solicitor, whom I tried to contact when first arrested and so far have not been allowed to.' He then flatly denied knowing Kenneth Noye, Brian Reader, Thomas Adams, Black, Weyman, Patch, Robinson, Palmer, McAvoy, or White.

'The thing we keep coming back to,' Ryan said, 'is that, however much you might say you've been buying all this gold from Matteo Constantino, he's told us he never sold you an ounce. It was all a setup.'

Chappell's bluff façade failed him for a moment. 'That is untrue – it is untrue, I tell you.'

Conway held up a copy of the jeweller's signed statement. 'Would you like to read what he says? It's all here in his own handwriting?'

'No,' Chappell said, sitting back as if he had just been asked to swallow poison. 'No.'

'No?' Conway affected mild surprise. 'Then let me read you some of what Mr Constantino has placed on the record. Referring to your claim that he supplied you with the bullion he says, "That's stupid, ain't it? I can assure you that I have never supplied him with one ounce of gold, no gold whatsoever."'

Chappell stared at the detectives like a rabbit cornered by a couple of particularly efficient stoats. Portly and bespectacled, he began to sweat as if he had eaten one too many of his favourite Cotswold sausages. The detectives asked him a few more questions, which Chappell once again blanked, and then Conway hit him with the quick, sucker punch: 'The gold you've been getting in large bulk recently is stolen, isn't it?'

'If it is, it is without my knowledge. I have never thought of it as anything but completely legitimate.'

'Mr Constantino is a one-man show,' Ryan countered. 'He is elderly. How can he suddenly afford to produce £10 million worth of gold?'

'He didn't suddenly produce it. It was done over a period of time in relatively small amounts.'

'Three million pounds' worth in one week is not relatively small.'

Chappell had a ready answer. 'I hadn't finished. I was about to say that Mr Constantino has a reputation among the trade for being a wealthy man, made rich by his knowledge of uncut diamonds. I also believed Mr Constantino to be a businessman of substance and dealt with him along those lines.'

One of the great things about being a policeman has to be that, when you get fed up listening to the brass-necked criminal sitting across from you lying out of both sides of his mouth at the same time – and expecting you to believe him – you can always lock him up again. It was back down to the dingy dungeon for Chappell, still vociferously protesting his innocence.

Detectives got nothing worth their time and trouble out of Adams or Patch – but when they questioned the Collector, who had also been picked up in the sweep, they had better luck. The Collector admitted that he and Noye were friends of long standing: their wives played squash together and their children were friends. But he insisted he could not remember when he had last seen Noye. Interrogating officer DS Cam Burnell reminded him, citing chapter and verse from the surveillance team that had logged him going into and coming out of Hollywood Cottage time and again. The Collector looked shaken. But when Burnell asked him about the Alcosa smelter, he stuck to the story he had given before: he had bought it in a lay-by, from a man named 'Benny', for a third man he had known only as 'The Turk'.

Burnell nodded. 'Can you explain how the operating instructions for the smelter you bought were found in Kenneth Noye's barn?'

'No, I can't.'

'We've charged Noye with handling stolen gold – the Brink's-Mat bullion. Did you know that?'

Visibly taken aback, the Collector said that he had not known. They took him down to his cell and left him to think things over for the night. The next morning, it was a different suspect who responded to their questioning. 'I've been thinking about this all night,' he said.

'And what have you decided?' Burnell asked.

'It's difficult. I've been friends with Kenneth Noye for a long time. I just don't know what to do.'

'The best way is just to tell the truth.'

'I want to but, like I say, it's difficult.'

'You got that smelter for Noye, didn't you?' Burnell asked quietly.

'Not exactly.'

'What do you mean?'

'I knew where it was going.'

'To Noye?'

The Collector drew a long breath. 'Yes.'

20

At the five-star hotel on the Playa de las Americas, Tenerife, where he and his family were holidaying, John Palmer was fielding questions from an even more ferocious pack of interrogators – the ladies and gentlemen of the British press. Looking either relaxed and pleased with himself, or cornered and angry, according to whichever newspaper report you happened to read, Palmer presented himself as an innocent abroad. 'I've got nothing to hide,' he told a television news reporter. 'The first thing I knew was that I had an urgent telephone call to ring home. They told me it was connected with some bullion robbery and the murder of a policeman. I was astonished and amazed when I heard what had happened. I rang my solicitor, who was astounded. I can categorically deny I was involved in the bullion raid, and I have nothing to do with the gold from it.'

Pressed further by the ITN news crew, he said, 'I have in the grounds of my house a smelting works, which was put there approximately two-and-a-half to three years ago. This was connected with my former business, which was a bullion company.' (He had been a director of Scadlynn until 1982, when he had officially resigned.) 'It's hidden only because of the valuable materials processed there. The police have found gold at my house. Some jewellery would have been mine, and the gold belonged to another dealer who often used my furnace. But it was legitimate gold. If someone came to me with a lot of gold which they wanted me to melt down, I would inform the police at once.'

Asked again why he had not returned home to face inquiries, the outraged and puzzled expression on his face deepened. 'The police could have found me here if they wanted to. We never made any secret of where we were going. Now I am considering action against them. They smashed down doors and have damaged the swimming pool and living-room floor. There is thousands of pounds' worth of damage. They overreacted. It would have been quite easy to knock on the door.

'My wife is very upset,' Palmer went on. 'She has a six-month-old child to cope with and we have all been devastated by this.' Asked whether he would return to the UK to clear his name, Palmer replied, 'I don't think I could achieve anything by going back early. I think once I touch England I will be arrested.'

That much was true.

Once they were formally charged with the murder of John Fordham, Judges' Rules meant that Reader and Noye could not be questioned further about the killing until the case came to trial. But nothing said they could not be interrogated about the Brink's-Mat robbery. Despite the lack of success in interviewing him so far, DI Suckling and DC Charman had another go at Noye on Tuesday, 3 December 1985.

Noye blocked and stonewalled as before, until Charman said, 'We've arrested you with what I'm pretty sure is some of the Brink's-Mat gold. Our interest is to recover what's left of the £26 million worth that was stolen. You can help us, I'm convinced.'

Noye replied coolly, 'I can help get myself killed as well. I'm a businessman: if I thought there was any way I could put things in my favour, I'd tell you as much as I know. But this is a pretty one-sided sort of deal, from what I can see.' The detectives outlined a little of what they knew about the gold-laundering chain, and put it to Noye that he was its main hub. 'The activity around you tends to indicate that you are the trusted middleman who has got the contacts and the money to get what's necessary done,' Charman said.

'I know what you want from me, but any business I do with you will get me done in.'

'Aren't you exaggerating a bit?' Suckling suggested.

Noye shot him a look. 'I know enough about the people involved to know that if I say what I know, and anything happens after that, they'll know it can only have come from me. If I do anything to get you back that gold which they think belongs to them, then that's me done.'

'Well, two of them can't bother you – they are locked up for twenty-five years,' Charman responded.

'What can you tell us about Tony Black?' Suckling asked.

'I can tell you he's as good as dead,' Noye said flatly. 'I know all about false identities and all that, and I know that won't help him at all. They'll find him and they'll have him.'

'Who's going to have him, then?'

'There's enough money from this to get anyone to do it. They don't have to get their own hands dirty.'

'Do you know if anyone has been hired or propositioned to do it?'

'No, but they'll get that sorted out – it's easy enough.'

'What were the instructions for an Alcosa gold smelter doing in your apple barn where we found them?'

Noye refused to answer.

'Where did you get your money from – the money to build your house?'

'I'm a businessman. I told you what I am,' Noye replied.

Nettled by Noye's complacency, Charman shot back, 'What you are, Mr Noye, is a man well acquainted with villains, armed robbers and the sort of men who come into large amounts of money, who will come to you to launder their cash. You're trusted to keep your mouth shut, and you share in the profits of crime without having to put yourself up front.'

'I put myself up front the other night, didn't I?' Noye retorted.

'It always goes wrong for these people at one time or another. Why protect them? I suspect that if they were in your position, they wouldn't hesitate to put your name forward. In fact, that's something to bear in mind for the future with this inquiry. A lot of people have been arrested.'

'Then they will have to watch themselves, like Black – won't they?'

Noye then asked if he could see Detective Chief Superintendent Brian Boyce – he had something important to say. Believing he might at last be about to tell them something useful, Boyce agreed to the meeting. When he arrived four hours later with his deputy, DCI John, he was surprised when Noye asked to see him alone. 'If that's what you prefer,' he said. DCI John left the room. Noye told Boyce, 'I want to speak to you off the record. I won't if you write anything down. Have you got a tape recorder going?' Boyce assured the prisoner he had not, and even went so far as to open his briefcase and show Noye his pockets in order to prove this. Noye made some desultory opening remarks. Then, as if gathering himself, he said, 'Can I talk to you?'

Boyce looked at him. 'We are talking. What is it?'

'I've got money,' Noye told him. 'I've done a lot of deals. I'd like to give some money to John Fordham's family.'

Boyce said, 'I understand.'

There was a silence. It seemed to Boyce that Noye was struggling to say what he really wanted to say. Noye tried again. 'If I go to prison for a long time, it's not just my life that gets ruined – it's Brenda and the kids as well.'

Boyce nodded.

'Do you have a family, Mr Boyce?'

'Yes, I do.'

'When do you retire?'

The question surprised Boyce, but he saw no harm in answering it. 'In four years, I will have concluded thirty years' service.'

'You could have a good retirement,' Noye said. 'I could make sure you do.'

A loud alarm bell started ringing in Boyce's head. 'What do you mean?' he demanded.

'I could make sure you have plenty of money after you leave the police. I can put a million quid into any bank account you want in the world. Untraceable. It's yours if you can make sure I don't go to prison.'

Boyce got to his feet, staring at Noye in undisguised contempt. 'You're wasting your time trying to bribe me,' he said. 'The only help I want from you is for you to tell me the whereabouts of the Brink's-Mat bullion.'

Noye shook his head. 'If I told you where that is, I'm a dead man.'

Boyce closed his briefcase, called for the attending officer to unlock the door and strode out.

Noye might be refusing to help the police recover more of the stolen bullion on the grounds that it would get him killed – and attempting to bribe senior police officers into the bargain – but by complete coincidence, on 30 January 1985 – the day after Noye's arrest for the murder of John Fordham – German border police stopped a gold-coloured Mercedes saloon at the Aachen border crossing with Belgium.

At the meeting point between Germany, Belgium and Holland, Aachen is an architecturally rich university town that was once the capital of Charlemagne's European empire. There are plenty of treasures to go and see, and it is a handy base from which to explore the vast and battle-scarred Ardennes forest. But the two occupants of the Mercedes speeding towards the border post on the edge of town that evening had no interest in culture, history, or nature. They were on a mission of a much more prosaic kind.

Business was slack for the German *Bundesgrenzschutz* (BGS) in the cold weeks of the New Year. There was the usual trickle of trucks and vans, but little of the holiday traffic that helped enliven the time during the summer months. Still, here was a nice plump English-plated Mercedes 500 SEL wallowing up to the barrier, like a pig fattened up for the roast. Perhaps it would offer up some diversionary meat for the bored and chilled frontier guards.

One of them, Peter Foerster, walked up to the car as it slid to a halt and glanced inside. The driver was a broadly built, middle-aged man. A woman of similar age sat next to him. Something about the man's appearance sounded a note of alarm in Foerster's mind. Calling over a colleague, he asked the driver to pull into one of the inspection bays. The man said he was en route to Switzerland for a holiday with his wife. His passport identified him as John William Elcombe. It also gave his occupation as 'lorry driver'.

It was this and the crude tattoos on the traveller's forearms and hands that had made the BGS officer decide to take a closer look at him. Berlin or Biarritz, Benin or Bangladesh, amateurishly done tattoos invariably hoist a red flag to law enforcement officers. More often than not, they are the product of chronic boredom. And since when did truck drivers get to drive around in Mercedes 500 SELs? The frontier police had plenty of time on their own hands. Better take a closer look at this beefy *Engländer*. Over in the passenger seat the man's wife was looking a little wide-eyed, a little – how could one put it? – *edgy*. Politely, the guards asked the couple if they would please step out of the vehicle. They wished to search it.

The BGS men did not just search the Mercedes: they more or less took it to pieces. Foerster prised the back seat out of its housing and lifted it clear. There was something – it looked like nothing so much as a pile of house bricks wrapped up in a parcel – hidden in the space beneath. He peeled off the newspaper wrapping. Neat blocks of £50 UK banknotes met his astonished gaze. Brand-new, they were still wrapped in their heat-sealed cellophane Treasury bundles.

Foerster shouted for his colleagues to come and witness the find. As he did so, a second officer raised the storage box lid in the car's boot. The spare wheel, he noticed, was loose. Underneath it was a second currency housing estate, built, like the first, out of mostly brand-new £50 notes, along with some other used sterling banknotes of various denominations. The Germans photographed the banknotes *in situ*, took them out and counted them. The total came to £710,000 – roughly eight times the combined annual income of the men on duty at the crossing post that day. Strongly suspecting they were dealing with the proceeds of a major robbery, the guards noted down the serial numbers on selected sequences of the new £50 banknotes, which formed some 80 per cent of the total. The English couple, meanwhile, were invited to cool their heels in a secure room.

The *Bundesgrenzschutz* sent a telex listing the serial numbers on the banknotes and giving passport details of the detained couple, as well as details of the Mercedes's licence plate, JKJ 353Y, to German Interpol in Wiesbaden, with a request that anything known or suspected about the Elcombes, the car or the money be telexed back to the German authorities at once. Wiesbaden forwarded the information to British Interpol, who in turn sent it on to Scotland Yard. Pretty soon, the answer came back: the Mercedes had passed through the hands of several people in the preceding months, one of whom was a Mr Gordon Parry. The new £50 banknotes had recently been issued by the Bank of England to Barclays Cash Centre, Bristol. The Germans were surprised – and not a little disappointed – to learn that neither the Mercedes nor the money had been reported stolen, and that the Elcombes were not wanted by the British police.

Questioned further, the Elcombes claimed the cash was their life savings, which they were taking to Switzerland for investment, the proceeds of Mr Elcombe's 'antiques business'. Since there was no warrant out on either of the travellers, and no evidence of actual wrongdoing, the border police had no option but to let them go.

The next morning at 0910 a report of the German stop and search operation landed on the desk of a Flying Squad Detective Sergeant. When his superior, DI Brightwell, got back into the office at 1300, the sergeant took it straight in to show him. Brightwell scanned the pages. Slowly, he rose to his feet. All the serial numbers on the new £50 notes logged by the Germans began with the A24 prefix. They were part of the same unique batch detectives had discovered in the possession of Noye, Chappell, Reader and just about everywhere else in the Brink's-Mat laundry chain.

Brightwell picked up the telephone and dialled Roy Ramm at C11. The police knew that the Bank of England had issued every single one of the new A24-prefix £50 notes exclusively to Barclays Cash Centre in Bristol straight from the mint. The Cash Centre had, in turn, forwarded every single one of the new notes directly to its local Bedminster Branch. Barclays Bedminster had issued every single one of the same series to one customer and one customer only: Mr Charles Cooper, real name Garth Chappell, the director of Scadlynn Ltd.

The implications were obvious: the cash found at Aachen was the proceeds of laundered Brink's-Mat gold. The couple driving the Mercedes might be couriers. If so, the money was being ferried into secret Swiss bank accounts by the simple and direct method of driving it there. And last but not least, someone was exporting and managing the cash that had evidently been realized from a large amount of the stolen gold. The Elcombes later successfully defended charges against them on the basis that they had had no knowledge of the true source of the banknotes.

But from now on, any time the police caught anyone in possession of the new A24-series £50 banknotes in any quantity, they were even more sure that the individual concerned had to be a fully paid-up member of the Brink's-Mat conspiracy.

21

Noye's arrest for the murder of DC John Fordham came as an almighty shock to gang leader Michael McAvoy. No less shocking to him was news of the discovery of eleven gold bars in the grounds of Hollywood Cottage. Noye's arrest – and his possession of the bullion – could mean only one thing: someone had taken control of McAvoy's share. Make that *stolen* his share. Someone was trading it without his permission. How could this be? The imprisoned gang leader had made detailed arrangements with his old mate Brian Perry for its safekeeping – what were friends for? The more McAvoy brooded – and for that he had all the time in the world – the angrier he grew. At the same time, he formed a cold resolve: he would find out what was going on. And if somebody out there was messing him about, he might be invited to explain himself.

He asked his partner Kathleen Meacock to find out what she could. She should start with Perry. If anyone would know how the gold had come to be at Hollywood Cottage, it was him. Perry was slippery. His evasiveness, as related by Meacock, confirmed McAvoy's worst fears. Someone was 'at it'. Making free with the leader's golden share. Flouting the unwritten, but to Michael McAvoy, iron, code of *honour among thieves*.

The bad news focused McAvoy's now highly agitated thoughts on the need for renewed negotiations with the police. If his appeal against sentence was to have any hope of succeeding, he needed the deal that he, Brian Robinson and Tony White had been pussyfooting around with for so many months now to get done. Before those clowns on the outside – he spat to think of it – took any further liberties with *his gold*.

A day or two later Detective Superintendent Ramm got another call from Tony White. Ramm was sceptical: he had been through this particular hoop too many times. 'It was,' he says, 'all very frustrating – a complete waste of our valuable time.' And then something happened – something no one at the Yard could have foreseen, and that changed everything. White asked if he could bring someone with him. 'For all we cared,' Ramm remembers, 'he could have brought Santa Claus and all his little helpers, so long as we got the gold back. We agreed to the meet – but only on condition that there would be measurable progress – enough time had been wasted already. As the day of the rendezvous got closer, we even found ourselves looking forward to it: there was always the chance that with this new, if as yet unnamed person in the mix, negotiations might finally come good.'

The meeting took place on 25 March 1986 at the National Theatre on London's South Bank. The slab-sided, ugly concrete temple to Modernism was agreed as safe neutral ground. C11 Commander Brian Worth and Ramm were drinking tea at one of the café tables when White walked in with a second man. The detectives had seen enough photographs and video footage to recognize the new player in the game as Brian Perry. Without being able to stand it up in court, they knew Perry had been behind the attempt to free McAvoy, as well as the 'Oscar will leave him' threat to dissuade crew chief Robin Riseley from giving evidence by separating the guard from his best-loved appendage. White, who looked uncharacteristically nervous said, 'This is Brian Perry.'

The detectives said they knew – they could hardly pretend otherwise. Perry grinned like the Cheshire Cat and took a puff of a fat Havana. His presence did nothing to raise Roy Ramm's hopes of a successful outcome. 'Both these villains knew we were watching them round the clock. They knew that when they got up in the morning somebody would be following them, and they would still be following them when they went to bed for the night. Their expectation was they would not only be followed all day, but that every conversation they had would be recorded. Sometimes they were right and sometimes they were wrong – the problem for them was that they could never be sure when the spyglass was trained on them.

'We sat down at a table, and White said something about the gold being "dealt for". I shot Brian Worth a look. I could see he was as mystified – and frankly as shocked – as I was. I asked White what he meant by that. We had a listening device running right there at the table.'

White: Well as I said, it's been dealt for, you know?

Ramm: Hang on a sec, Tony – what do you mean by that?

Well it's been traded.

You mean you've done a deal for it, in other words?

Eh?

It's all gone? It's been converted into cash?

It's been dealt for. I mean, Mickey thinks he's in control of it, but he ain't.

The two senior detectives sat in silence for a while, struggling to make the necessary mental adjustments. If White was telling the truth, this was serious news. It meant they really had wasted all those weeks of patient negotiations with McAvoy and Robinson; wasted all those trips to Leicester jail; and were most likely wasting their time now.

Perry now took over from White. Where White had been vague and confused, Perry was articulate, focused, and to the point. 'Listen, it's no good being in there and trying to keep everything for yourself, right?' he said. 'Once that cell door's closed, what's he got to trade with?' The police officers stared at him. They doubted McAvoy would take kindly to being duped. Under the circumstances, who would? But as he kept talking, Perry gradually distanced himself from McAvoy and Robinson. Before long, his comments were bordering on the contemptuous: 'Mickey's out of touch, he's not in control. He might think he is, but he's not. They're away.' (He meant McAvoy and Robinson.) 'They're out of the loop.'

Up until this point McAvoy had been convinced – and had convinced the police – that he was still pulling the strings. But as the weeks dragged along and nothing concrete came of the negotiations, the detectives had begun to doubt the extent of his influence. Perry's offhand dismissal of the Brink's-Mat gang leaders confirmed their worst fears.

Disinclined to believe that McAvoy's old friend was now in sole control of some £13 million in stolen gold, Ramm and Worth probed a bit further: Perry might just be jerking their chain, attempting to muddy the investigation. But the minicab driver was unshakeable. 'Mickey's not in control, things have moved on out here, the deal can't be done.' The detectives tried to push him into giving details: was the gold still in its original state? Was it still in the UK? Who had it? Perry was having none of it. He only rose to the bait once, and that was right at the end of the meeting. 'Suppose,' he said, 'it could come back, but it wasn't as it was when it got nicked?'

'What do you mean? Are you talking about cash, or what?'

'Well, just suppose it wasn't in the same form?'

'Providing we can be sure that what we are getting is the proceeds of the Brink's-Mat robbery, then we're relaxed,' Worth told him. 'What we're not about doing is copping twelve or thirteen million pounds from someone that might be the proceeds of a separate crime.'

Worth and Ramm tried to nudge the idea further, but Perry dodged and swerved, refusing to be pinned down when it came to the details of a potential exchange. All he would say was that a deal of the kind the police had been discussing with Robinson and McAvoy might be possible, 'much later'. But it would have to be done with him. He now had control of it. And the gold would be in a different form.

Ramm said, 'If he hasn't got possession, then he [McAvoy] is in trouble.' White grunted, as if McAvoy's interests were the last thing on earth he cared about. 'Well, this is it. Have a nice day.' And with that, he and Perry stood up and walked away.

Yet again, Worth and Ramm were left with nothing to show for the meeting, except the knowledge that the gold was now almost certainly beyond their reach for ever. It was not a good feeling. But there was one glimmer of light: if Perry really was controlling half the gold, then he had to know where it was hidden. Brian Perry now became one of the Yard's top-priority surveillance targets.

When they had time – there was no longer any point in making a special trip – Worth and Ramm paid what was to be their last visit to McAvoy and Robinson in Leicester prison. McAvoy was subdued and wore an angry look – but then that was the way most prisoners looked and behaved most of the time. There was no easy way to go about it, so Ramm came straight to the point. 'About our proposed deal, gentlemen: it looks as if it's off.'

For a moment, McAvoy seemed not to have understood him. 'Off? What do you mean, off?'

'We went to the meeting you set up with Tony White. Tony brought someone along with him – your old friend Brian Perry.'

The look of bewilderment and barely suppressed anger in the gang leader's face intensified. 'Perry? What was Perry doing there with Tony?'

This question, more than anything else McAvoy could have said or done, confirmed to the police that he was being taken for his own fortune. Ramm said, 'Don't ask us, Mickey – these are your people. You tell us what Perry was doing there.'

Exchanging glances with Brian Robinson, McAvoy shook his head. 'I still don't understand. What was Perry doing there? What did he say?'

'White said the gold has been dealt for. He said it has "gone away". Perry said that you two no longer control it. His exact words were, "Mickey's out of touch, he's not in control. He might think he is, but he's not. They're away, they're out of the loop."'

By the time Ramm stopped speaking McAvoy's face was a tight mask of rage. But with a supreme effort of will his tone, when he asked the question, was more or less even. 'Where is the gold? What's Perry done with it?'

The detectives rose and stood back from the table. There was nothing left to say. Worth shrugged his shoulders. 'I wish we knew, Mickey – and not just for your sake. Let us know if you hear anything, won't you?'

Now McAvoy lost it. As they led him away, he shouted, 'Tell Brian Perry to mind his own fucking business and stop having affairs.'

As soon as he was alone in his cell, McAvoy sat down and wrote to his old friend and partner in crime Brian Perry. The letter asked Perry why eleven bars of bullion had been found in Kenneth Noye's possession, why he had been at the meeting with Ramm and Worth, and what he had meant by the remark about the gold being 'dealt for'. Weeks later, when Perry had still not replied, McAvoy took up his pen for the second time.

> Hello mate. Well, you read the last letter, and you know what it is we were told by the police. I don't know what's going on here. I hope for my peace of mind you will tell me. It's our share we're talking about, and with you and fatty out there [he meant Tony White], there should be no one thinking he can hold us up in here. For over a year now I have not settled because of what I am told, and that really is enough with twenty-five years to handle. If I have to have that I will, but what I want is for you to make sure we are not fucked and the game is played.
>
> It seems someone's getting a lot of interest. I won't have anyone else keeping my share for their own needs. He'll be signing his own death warrant if he goes through with it. And if he believes we are away too long to worry about it, well it will be done for me. I have no intention of being fucked for my money here, and still do this sentence. Give my love to your family, mate. Take care.
>
> All the best,
> Mickey.

This letter betrayed some lingering doubt in McAvoy's mind about whether the police had told him the truth about the meeting with White and Perry, or had lied in an effort to sow confusion and dissent in the criminal ranks. But its real purpose was to warn.

'Fucked' is the only word to describe what was now happening to McAvoy. If anything, it was an understatement.

When she went round to see Brian Perry for the second time, Meacock noticed a new addition to Perry's office décor in the form of a specially painted sign. Done in red letters on a white background and encased in a natty golden frame it read:

Remember The Golden Rule –
Whoever has the GOLD makes the RULES.

Perry insisted the sign was just his little joke. But Meacock, who was nobody's fool, understood only too well: the sign was not a joke, it was the literal truth. Perry meant every word of it. He had the whip hand. And there was nothing either she or Michael McAvoy could do about it.

22

Britain has had an official Lottery since 1994 – you pays your money and you takes your chance. But it has had an unofficial lottery for far longer in the form of the criminal justice system. One of the biggest factors in deciding the outcome of a trial – especially a criminal trial – is money. Tony White once complained to his police interviewer, 'I fucking hate lawyers. They're so fucking expensive you've got to go out robbing again to pay for them.' Scrupulous as judges might try to be, few would deny that paying for the best available defence significantly improves the chances of the accused escaping conviction.

Noye's trial for the murder of John Fordham got under way at the Old Bailey in November 1985, almost a year after the detective's death. Until then, Noye had steadfastly refused to answer questions about the murder itself or about the rest of the missing Brink's-Mat gold, repeating only that he would reserve what he had to say for the jury. Now, his moment to speak out had come. Noye did not waste it, and no more did his counsel, John Mathew QC, whose brilliant handling of Tony White's defence had seen his client walk free. On the face of it, this new challenge looked even greater. But Mathew was bullish. It was true that Noye had stabbed John Fordham eleven times, and that Fordham had been a serving police officer. But from the outset, Mathew was confident he would have Noye found 'not guilty' on a plea of legitimate self-defence.

The judge was Mr Justice Caulfield, who presided over the libel suit that the Conservative politician and writer Jeffrey Archer brought against the *Daily Star* newspaper two years later, in 1987. Flatly denying the *Star*'s reports that he had spent a night having 'kinky sex' with prostitute Monica Coughlin in 1986, and had then tried to buy her silence, Archer sued for libel. Summing up in the subsequent case, Caulfield told the jury, 'Remember Mary Archer in the witness box. Your vision of her probably will never disappear. Has she elegance? Has she fragrance? Would she have, without the strain of this trial, radiance? How would she appeal? Has she had a happy married life? Has she been able to enjoy, rather than endure, her husband Jeffrey? Is he in need of cold, unloving, rubber-insulated sex in a seedy hotel round about quarter to one on a Tuesday morning after an evening at the Caprice?'

Quite possibly influenced by this, the jury awarded Archer £500,000 in damages. When it was later alleged that he had asked his secretary at the time to falsify a diary for him, Archer was tried for perjury and sentenced to four years in prison. The *Star* asked for – and got – its money back.

As soon as the jury in Noye's trial for murder had been sworn in, Caulfield told them the police were taking measures to prevent any possibility of conspiracy to pervert the course of justice, or 'jury nobbling'. They would have round-the-clock police protection for the duration of the trial, while all calls to and from their home telephone numbers would be intercepted and monitored.

The trial got going. There was scarcely a reporter in court who did not believe that Noye would be found guilty and sentenced to life imprisonment. Killing police officers tends to produce that result. But they were all wrong. Mathew immediately objected to the prosecution showing jurors daylight photographs of Hollywood Cottage and its grounds. He said that since the killing had taken place at night, daylight shots would give the jury a misleading impression of what had happened under cover of darkness. The shrubbery, which in daylight looked sparse, in reality provided plenty of cover for a nocturnal intruder. Caulfield agreed, and disallowed the daylight shots in evidence. Mathew then asked the judge if he could take jurors to see the scene of the stabbing, in the pitch dark and as it had happened. This, too, got the judicial nod. Hardly able to believe his luck, Mathew at once set up a night-time jury visit to Hollywood Cottage.

Slightly taken aback by this turn of events, prosecuting counsel Nicholas Purnell gave a brief outline of the case against Kenneth

Noye, and the court was adjourned.

That evening, as a rainstorm lashed the Kent countryside, three limousines swept up School Lane, West Kingsdown, and glided to a halt outside the big wrought-iron gates of Hollywood Cottage. Dozens of journalists were waiting. Shielding their faces from the flashbulbs and the driving rain, the jury got out and stood patiently while the Old Bailey clerk reconvened the court in the odd and uncomfortable surroundings. Mr Justice Caulfield, who was wearing a bowler hat, presided. A green prison van flanked by two police cars then pulled up. Handcuffed to a prison officer and escorted by three more, with a back-up guard of no fewer than four policemen, Kenneth Noye was led forward. He was kept well away from the jurors.

Noye, his escort, the judge, the jury, the clerk of the court, a team for the prosecution and one for the defence, and just about anyone else with an excuse for being present, trooped in through the gates and began a tour of the accused man's grounds. They were trailed at a short distance by the press pack, whose police escort had to stop them pushing forward the whole time in an effort to overhear what was being said.

As they drew near the house, everyone looked up to see Brenda Noye and her two young sons framed in a lighted window. It was like a scene from some Victorian melodrama. The boys waved forlornly to their father, and Mrs Noye waved to her husband – or at least what she could see of him, hemmed in as he was by burly law officers. As the procession drew near the house, Brenda Noye handed a pair of Wellington boots and a coat through the front-room window, insisting her husband must have them 'because of the terrible weather'. Following careful examination of these items, Noye was allowed to put them on. This touching interlude concluded, the itinerant court moved on.

What jurors – and the defence – did not know was that Mathew and Milner had already employed a large, physically fit man to dress in a balaclava and camouflage gear of the kind Fordham had been wearing on the night of his death. Illuminated by the light of a powerful torch like the one Noye had been carrying, this man was photographed hiding in the bushes. The jurors reached the belt of scrub where Noye and Fordham had struggled.

When the trial returned to the relative comfort of the Old Bailey, Mathew and Milner produced the staged photographs. Spooky and scary, they had a massive impact on the jury.

It was a brilliant *coup de théâtre*. The question they now had to decide was whether Noye, suddenly confronted in the pitch darkness and in his own garden by a masked figure, had used reasonable force in defending himself. It was not just the number of blows that weighed against Noye – it was their uniform savagery. According to Crown pathologist Dr Rufus Compton, who examined Fordham's body on the morning after the killing, the same single-edged, seven-by-one centimetre blade had inflicted all eleven wounds. Two thrusts had gone deep into the police officer's back.

Why was Noye carrying a knife of that kind in the first place? He told the court he had borrowed the knife from the kitchen earlier that day to 'scrape the battery terminals' of his Ford Granada, which he said were encrusted with chemical residue. His wife had tried to use the car earlier but it had refused to start. On completion of this task, he had accidentally left the knife in the passenger foot well.

When he heard the dogs bark, Noye said he had gone to collect a torch he remembered leaving in the Granada, found the knife lying there, picked it up and carried it with him. This story was crucial in establishing whether or not he had acted in legitimate self-defence. If someone threatened in their home picks up an item in regular use that is lying to hand – a golf club, say – and uses it to resist attack, his or her actions are usually classed as self-defence. If, on the other hand, someone goes deliberately to a kitchen drawer, takes out a knife and uses *that* in self-defence, the law might view this as unjustified assault, on the grounds that it involved a degree of planning or premeditation. So remember, next time you need to stab an intruder in your bedroom, tell the jury the knife was lying ready to hand because you had been using it earlier that day to clean your toenails.

The narrow width of the blade – one centimetre – might have told against Noye's claim that it really had been a kitchen knife. If so, then it must have been a very thin one, of the type used, say, for skinning and filleting fish. It might also very well have been a flick-knife. The police, it was pointed out in court, had found *three* knives in the grounds of Hollywood Cottage: a flick-knife in the driver's door pocket of Noye's Ford Granada, a second in the woods behind the house, and the white-handled kitchen-style knife plunged into the earth near the base of a tree. But forensic tests had been unable to confirm that any of these was the one actually used in the stabbing.

Compton said the first two wounds to be struck had both fatally punctured Fordham's heart, while the first had been enough on its own to render him immobile. Bruising on the flesh suggested all the wounds had been inflicted with tremendous force, so that in each case the knife had been buried up to the hilt.

With so much force and violence evident in the attack, how could any jury find Kenneth Noye 'not guilty' of murder? It seemed an impossible outcome. But gradually, with the deft incisiveness for which he was known, Mathew chipped away at the prosecution's case. He seized on Compton's opinion that the first wound had rendered the victim immobile. Mathew put it to the pathologist, that, if this was true, then John Fordham must have inflicted the bruising and the small cut that Noye had suffered on the night *before he was stabbed*. It seemed to prove that the undercover policeman had struck first, as Noye had consistently claimed – and that he, Noye, had simply been defending himself against unprovoked attack.

In his own evidence, Noye was adamant on this point. He told the court that when he heard the dogs barking, he was concerned in case they were disturbing 'the two old ladies who live next door'. He said he had asked his wife to go and bring the Rottweilers back inside, but she had said, 'I'm not going down there – it's too dark.' While he was putting on his leather jacket in the hallway she said, 'You'll need a torch.'

Noye said he had gone to the Granada, grabbed the torch and spotted the kitchen knife lying beside it in the foot well. 'If Brenda had found it, she would start complaining again about using a kitchen knife on the car,' he told the jury. He had picked it up simply so that he could return it to the kitchen once he had rounded up the dogs. He said he walked down the drive calling to Sam, the elder of the two dogs. As he neared the apple-drying barn, Noye said he saw the two Rottweilers barking at something in the shrubbery. 'I shone my torch around the area to make sure there definitely wasn't anyone around because in the summer I caught some glue-sniffers there.' He then moved into the wooded area by the barn. 'I was looking mainly on the floor. I thought there may be an animal that might be trapped – it's happened before, so I was looking in front of me.' He said he heard a noise to his left and pointed the torch beam in that direction. 'I just froze with horror. All I saw when I flashed my torch on this masked man was just the two eyeholes and the mask. I thought that was my lot. I thought I was going to be a dead man. As far as I was concerned, that was it.'

Noye said the masked figure then hit him in the face with a weapon – although later he could not be certain whether it had been a weapon or a fist. He said he had thought it was a weapon because 'A masked man usually relates with a gun. It [the blow] woke me up. Made me so I could move again. Immediately the blow came across my face I put my hand up. I dropped the torch, obviously, and put my left hand up to his face and grabbed his face or head. I shouted out, "Brenda, help!" and started striking with all my strength, as fast as I could into the masked man. I didn't have to think about using all my might, I thought I was a dead man.

'When he came straight at me I struck into the front of him all of five times. As far as I was concerned, I was fighting for my life. I had struck the man in front, but it didn't seem to have any effect. He was overwhelmingly on top of me. He just looked grotesque, big.

'I am totally amazed at the amount of wounds the man had – I just didn't think it was having any effect. He was just totally overwhelming me ... I suspect in a way I was bringing him towards me because I had hold of him. He looked like a giant. I didn't really relate to the masked man as a human being, I stabbed him in a panic. I don't think I fell under his weight ... It might have been his weight or me losing my foot holding. Over we went. He came down on top of me, I struck him again. This was my only chance to get away because I was having no effect on that person.

'I took it. I got up and started running up the drive, looking over my shoulder to make sure he wasn't coming after me. When I looked, I saw the man [he meant Neil Murphy – by this time Fordham was crawling towards the gate] running towards the front of the wall. My dogs were with him.'

Noye told the court that hearing the commotion and his cry for help, his wife had dashed upstairs, grabbed a shotgun and cartridges and run outside with Reader. (In her initial interviews, Brenda Noye had claimed not to know Reader and denied he had ever been to the house.) Halfway down the drive they had come on Noye, his face covered in blood. Noye shouted, 'There's a masked man down there.' Grabbing the gun from his wife's hands, he ran to the apple barn, picked up the torch and then ran on with this and the shotgun to the front gate, where he could see the figure of a man lying on the ground. Noye said he pointed the shotgun at the man and shouted repeatedly, 'Who are you? Who are you? Take that mask off.' Asked why he wanted to take a shotgun to a man he had stabbed repeatedly, Noye said, 'I didn't want him to get away in case he came back another time, when I wasn't there, to sort Brenda and the children out.'

According to Noye, Fordham then said, 'SAS.' If this was true – and it ran counter to all his training – then it must have been the dying man's desperate attempt to save a catastrophically botched operation from total compromise.

With the man he had stabbed lying at his feet, Noye then turned to his wife and asked her to fetch a camera and flashgun from the house. He wanted a record of the injuries he had sustained as proof that he had been attacked. He also told her to call for an ambulance. He said she went back into the house with Reader.

The trouble with Noye's account was that, except for the stabbing, which he did not deny, he might simply have made it all up. The story about the encrusted battery terminals could have been false. Noye might have inflicted his minor facial injuries on himself when he ran behind the garage. Could he have hidden the gold that was later found in the gutter *and* bashed himself in the face a couple of times? Why else had he dashed from the scene when the police arrived and reappeared a short time later? From the outset, police suspected – but could never hope to prove – that Noye's injuries had been self-inflicted.

For his part, Brian Reader had been charged with murder because of the pathologist's opinion that after the first stab, Fordham had been unable to move. Detectives worked on the assumption that after this initial blow, Reader had held Fordham while Noye stabbed him repeatedly. But there was never any evidence, forensic or otherwise, to prove that Reader had actually been involved.

The main problem for the prosecution was that it had no way of proving whether or not Noye's story was, or was not, a tissue of lies. Only Noye knew what had really taken place that night. Noye was very plausible in court. He came across as charming – a wronged innocent. Mathew told the jury that every statement the police said they had taken from Noye, Reader and Brenda Noye was either fabricated, wrongfully altered, or had simply not, in actual fact, been recorded in the first place. Even Detective Chief Superintendent Brian Boyce, whom Noye had tried to bribe, ended up looking as if it were he, and not the defendant, who was on trial.

And so it was that the whole episode gradually turned into the tale of a terrified man defending his home and family from a gigantic and ferocious masked intruder. You might even have believed that Noye's Rottweilers were gentle, well-behaved dogs, quite incapable of behaving like – well – Rottweilers.

Looking on in Number One Court, Fordham's relatives, friends and colleagues were aghast.

The prosecution did its best to fight back. Purnell put it to Noye that the eleven bars of gold found on his property formed part of the proceeds of the Brink's-Mat robbery: Noye had really been afraid that the masked man in his grounds that night was a rival gangster, who knew about the gold and had come to take it. This was the reason for the savagery of the attack. Noye replied calmly that the gold was smuggled, part of a VAT-avoidance racket, and had nothing to do with the Brink's-Mat heist. He stated that he 'knew nothing about the robbery'. Purnell – who coincidentally would later unsuccessfully defend Jeffrey Archer on a charge of perjury – put it to Noye that this was a lie: Noye knew convicted Brink's-Mat gang member Brian Robinson socially. Noye denied this.

But Purnell thought he had an ace up his sleeve, in the form of a videotape recorded in a South London discothèque. On this tape, Brenda Noye, he alleged, could plainly be seen dancing with Brian Robinson's wife. Mathew knew this evidence might prove disastrous for his client, and asked that the court be cleared while the judge decided whether or not the jury should see it. Once the jury box and the public gallery had been emptied, Mr Justice Caulfield viewed a part of the tape. After a short while he stopped watching, turned to Purnell and said that he could not allow the videotape in evidence: in his opinion, it had no direct relevance to the case in hand.

As a result of this decision, the trial jury never knew about the possible link between Kenneth Noye and at least one member of the Brink's-Mat gang. Nor did Mr Justice Caulfield allow jury members to learn that a Bank of Ireland account in Mrs Noye's maiden name, 'Brenda Tremain', held £1.5 million; or that Noye had opened this account the previous September (1984) at the Bank of Ireland's St Michael's Road, Croydon, branch under the false name 'Sidney Harris'. Noye had made an initial deposit of £200,000 in new £50 notes, following this up with a further four deposits of the same amount, also in new £50s. But none of this evidential trail was allowed in court.

The prosecution's case was falling apart at the seams. As Neil Murphy, John Fordham's partner on that fatal night, put it, 'Our only hope was that a jury would think that eleven stab wounds to John's body were excessive. That was the only real hope we had.'

It was a forlorn hope. After deliberating for twelve and a half hours, the jury found Kenneth Noye and Brian Reader not guilty of murder. In the public gallery, Brenda Noye and Lynn Reader screamed and danced with delight.

Turning to the jury, Noye said, 'Thank you very much. God bless you. Thank you for proving my innocence, for that is what I am, not guilty.' Turning his attention to the Flying Squad officers gathered to hear the verdict at the back of the court, Noye let fly with a few choice epithets. He left court with a grin on his face. His supporters repaired to a local wine bar to celebrate.

But for Kenneth Noye, there were to be no celebrations that night: rearrested immediately, he was remanded in custody to stand trial on the second charge of conspiracy to handle the Brink's-Mat bullion and denied bail. The cell door, once again, slammed shut on him.

Interviewed by Andrew Hogg of the *Sunday Times* two years after the fatal stabbing, Fordham's partner, Neil Murphy, had this to say about events on that night: 'To me it was obvious that we had to move away because [once the dogs started up] somebody was going to come out of the house. We had to get out and try later. I have asked myself a thousand times why John didn't follow. The only thing I can think of is that he had got away with it with dogs before and just stuck it out. He was a very courageous guy. If he had had his way, we would have done the job from a dustbin outside the front door.

'Afterwards, all the problems I had were with what other people were thinking. Family and friends didn't know the full story and thought I had done something wrong, but I always felt I hadn't. There was nothing more I could have done except perhaps at the end, when I saw what was going on near the gate. I could have run across. That's the only thing I reproach myself for, but I didn't want to jeopardize the operation. I thought perhaps he would get a bit of a thumping and then they would kick him out.

'When I did go into the grounds . . . in normal circumstances I would have gone across to help him, but I just couldn't go near him. I felt that I had let him down. But he was too brave for his own good in those circumstances – unnecessarily brave.'

Despite knowing there were three Rottweilers in the house, despite expressing their concern about the dogs, and despite getting specialist advice on how to deal with them, Fordham and Murphy were utterly unprepared when the animals attacked. This is difficult to understand. And given the outcome, terrible.

23

Kenneth Noye had walked on the murder charge, but after five months in prison on remand he now faced trial for handling the stolen bullion, along with a secondary charge of conspiracy to avoid VAT. Chappell, Patch, Reader, the Collector, Adams and Constantino were in court with him at the same time. Between them, the seven defendants had engaged no fewer than fourteen defence lawyers.

The case was heard before Judge Richard Lowry in Number 12 Court of the Old Bailey on 6 May 1986. Lowry told the jury to be 'fair, decisive and courageous' in arriving at its verdicts.

Noye and his six co-defendants were supremely confident that the jury of eight men and four women would find them all not guilty on both counts. They believed the prosecution had no hard evidence proving that the gold they had handled came from the Brink's-Mat raid.

Noye was the key. If prosecuting counsel Michael Corkery QC could convince the jury of his guilt, then he was confident the others would fall over like dominoes. Eleven bars of gold had been found hidden on Noye's property. It was proven that he had bought eleven bars of gold in Jersey, and assumed that this was to provide false documentation in case anyone in the gold chain was caught in possession of stolen bullion. But all signs of the 'gutter' gold's origin had been smelted away. How could anyone say with certainty where it had come from, or if it formed part of the Brink's-Mat heist?

This question was muddied further when two key prosecution witnesses, police forensic expert Trevor Oliver and Johnson Matthey bullion expert John Williams, disagreed about whether or not the bars found at Hollywood Cottage were pure enough to have actually been Brink's-Mat bullion. The disagreement hinged on the tiniest of margins. Oliver stated that the usual margin of error applied in the gold trade was 0.015 per cent, which meant that only bars four, seven, eight, nine and eleven of the 'gutter gold', assayed at between 99.98 and 99.99 per cent pure, could be counted as 'four nines' bullion of the kind that had been stolen.

But to the consternation of the prosecuting team – and the evident delight of the defendants – under cross-examination, Williams told the court that Johnson Matthey's purity measure was more stringent than this: in his view, only bar eight qualified as a 99.99 per cent or 'four nines' bar, while only bar eleven qualified as a 'ten-tola bar' – i.e., a bar that was 99.90 per cent pure. Williams insisted that only these two bars could have come from the robbery – the other nine bars could not.

The prosecution case was not helped, either, by police witnesses showing evident muddle over the precise time at which the instructions for the Alcosa smelter had been found in Noye's apple-drying barn. John Mathew QC, again acting for Noye, was onto these factual discrepancies in a flash, raising doubt about the inherent worth of this evidence.

On top of all this, the prosecution had to contend with the story that Noye and the other defendants now told in an effort to explain both the gold found at Hollywood Cottage and the long inventory of suspicious activities observed and recorded by the police. If they put their hands up to smuggling the gold – and if this was accepted by the court – then they could not be found guilty of handling the Brink's-Mat bullion. And if the police wanted to prosecute them for smuggling, it would mean collecting new evidence, bringing new charges and establishing new guilt. Even if they were all later found guilty of smuggling, the penalties for that were far less severe than they were for handling the proceeds of armed robbery.

When his turn came to take the stand, Noye told the court he had constructed a great global gold-smuggling network, citing all sorts of complicated transactions involving his 'Dutch office' and his 'Florida interests' to lend the account credibility. Chappell and the others sang from the same hymn sheet: they, too, had been part of the smuggling spider's web – but they were not part of any Brink's-Mat laundering conspiracy. Once again in a trial involving Kenneth Noye, things began to look bleak for the prosecution.

But after five weeks of struggling to establish anything like a viable case, the winds of justice suddenly changed. Despite their excellent work in detecting Chappell, Scadlynn and the gold chain, HM Customs had been sidelined once the Metropolitan Police took over the investigation. Now, at the eleventh hour, Customs once again rode to the Flying Squad's rescue.

Although they had seized a vast amount of documentation in the course of the round-up on 'Black Tuesday', the police had made very little progress in analysing and assessing this evidence. Paperwork related to VAT, and VAT-avoidance cases, were hardly the stuff of a Flying Squad officer's dreams. But now, faced with the prospect of defeat, Brink's-Mat detectives invited Customs to take another look at what they had found.

Sifting through the paper trail, Customs officers were able to prove collusion between Chappell and Reader in a conspiracy to avoid VAT on the gold. That might not sound like much, but for the prosecution it was like nailing Al Capone on Inland Revenue offences when charges of organized murder and racketeering had failed to stick. In the eyes of the court, it proved wrongdoing. In the end, for the police, making sure the bad guys end up behind bars matters more than how they get there.

The biggest factor in the trial's 180-degree turnaround was Kenneth Noye's own behaviour. As one observer put it, 'Noye wasn't just confident – he was full of himself.' Even to the untrained ear, Noye's tale of international gold smuggling sounded like something he had concocted from a bad thriller. To explain the huge sums of money discovered in his bank accounts, he told the court that in the single year 1982 the 'Brazilian and Kuwaiti arms of his smuggling empire' had netted his operation some £20 million in profit, of which he had kept £1.3 million. The next year he had made £32 million, of which his share had been £1.6 million. Could he really be blamed for overlooking the odd few hundred thousand quid?

Noye's defence team called in his bank manager, Michael Bryan. Bryan agreed that Noye had told him repeatedly that he held large sums in offshore accounts. But Bryan said he had never actually seen any hard evidence of this. What he *had* seen was the defendant, Kenneth Noye, arriving at his bank in 1984, not very many weeks after the Brink's-Mat robbery, with plastic carrier bags containing cash to the value of some £600,000 in brand-new £50 notes. As the prosecution was happy to point out, it was all very well Noye's *saying* the money had come from pre-1984 foreign-held accounts – but where was the documentary proof these had ever existed?

Worse was to come for Noye. The prosecution was further able to show that in October 1984 he had deposited £150,000 in cash at the Dartford bank, with instructions that it be telegraphically transferred to an account in a Swiss bank held under the name of a Mr I.M. Bottom; the money was to remain in the account until 'Mr Bottom' turned up in person – with British passport number B158417 as proof of ID – to collect it. The court had a bit of a laugh at the expense of the surname, but there was nothing funny about it: the passport had been stolen from an Essex lorry driver of the same name. Bank records proved that Noye, armed with the stolen passport, had turned up in Zurich in person to collect the transferred cash.

Unfazed even by this damning evidence, Noye stuck to his 'big-time gold smuggler' story. The jury, Michael Corkery was pleased to note, showed signs of being less and less impressed by the roguish twinkle in Noye's eye as he related it, and equally unmoved by the 'this-is-all-a-stitch-up' line he fell back on when things went less than well.

In the end, even the redoubtable Mathew seemed to be struggling. Summing up for Noye at the close of his argument for the defence, he said, 'Not paying your taxes and smuggling, in this day and age, you may think possibly unhappily are looked on by many as being in a totally different bracket to the offences of theft and handling stolen property. You may think that most of those people, if not all, who do not declare their profits or all their earning for tax would probably cut their arms off before they would put their hands in the till and *steal* even a 10p piece.'

The syntax may or may not have helped, but by the time Mathew had finished, the jury was stony-faced. For once, Noye's defence had fallen spectacularly flat.

*

Stand by your man: Brenda Noye sits things out in her luxury
Kent mansion
(Rex Features)

McAvoy's mistress Kathleen Meacock stops her £320,000 farmhouse going to the dogs with the help of pedigree Rottweilers Brinks and Mat
(Mirrorpix)

Financial bloodhound Bob McCunn (right)
tracks down the missing millions.
DCS Brian Worth (below left) and DCI Roy
Ramm (below right) tried to do a deal with
the gang leaders for the missing gold.
Unfortunately Brian Perry had already
taken it ...
DS Tony Curtis (bottom right) spent years
on the trail of the villains, seen here
escorting Gordon Parry back from Spain
for trial
(Topfoto)

'Would you mind stepping out of the car, sir?' John Elcombe (above), the man German border police intercepted with £720,000 in the boot of a Mercedes.

Urbane, well-educated and well-nicked ... solicitor Michael Relton (below), whose arrest unlocked the secrets of the laundry business
(Topfoto)

Cold stare – road-rage killer
Kenneth Noye
(Rex Features)

Young and in love
– Danielle
Cable and
Stephen Cameron
shortly before his
murder
(Empics)

The rewards of crime: Noye's blue heaven in Atlanterra, Spain
(*Mirrorpix*)

You can run but you can't hide – the false passport Kenneth Noye alias
Mickey the Builder alias Alan Green used during his time in hiding
(*Empics*)

They get you in the end: Noye arrives at the Old Bailey to stand trial for the murder of Stephen Cameron
(Rex Features)

Staring, not seeing: Brenda Noye leaves court after watching her husband get life imprisonment for murder
(Rex Features)

Chappell was next up in the dock, and fell into the same trap of overconfidence. 'A child,' he announced with breezy pomposity, 'could see that it was smuggled rather than stolen gold.' Sticking to his claim that he had bought the gold legitimately from Matteo Constantino in the face of Constantino's own sworn evidence to the contrary, Chappell insisted, 'Mr Constantino supplied me with £9 million worth of gold. He would carry it to my office, and as far as I was concerned, it was a legitimate transaction. The VAT and Customs and Excise people set up constant observation on me. Do you think that I would be so silly as to deal with stolen gold with those people on my doorstep day and night?' Unfortunately for Chappell, the jury was able to spot the glaring logical flaw in this argument, namely that Chappell had not known the surveillance was in place until *after* Customs had amassed the evidence against him.

Adams elected not to give evidence on his own behalf, but his barrister presented him as an innocent paid courier, employed to carry packages of whose provenance and contents he had absolutely no knowledge. The Collector claimed that the statement in which he had admitted buying the Alcosa smelter for Noye was yet another example of Flying Squad 'verballing'. Patch played the same card as Adams – he was an innocent part-time bookkeeper and courier, who knew nothing of any gold, Brink's-Mat, smuggled or otherwise.

After eleven weeks the jury retired, heads reeling, to consider its verdict. For security reasons jurors were confined to a London hotel costing £80 per head per night – in those days a tidy sum. They started their deliberations on a Thursday. Come Sunday they were still deliberating, but gave notice that they expected to reach agreement by the end of the following day.

It was now that the loss adjusters handling the Brink's-Mat claim for Lloyd's insurance decided to sue each of the seven defendants individually and personally in the civil courts for the full £26 million-plus lost in the robbery – with interest – right down to the value of the leather pouch (£20) that had contained the uncut diamonds. Anthony White, Brian Robinson and Michael McAvoy were also included in the writ.

In a civil lawsuit, the loss adjusters would have to prove the accused had handled the stolen bullion not – as in a criminal trial –

beyond all reasonable doubt but only on the balance of probabilities. At the time, few observers attached much significance to the launch of this civil action. In fact it was a ferocious instrument – and one the insurers would wield until they were satisfied. The stones of a debt mill that would grind almost everyone involved in the robbery into the financial dust had begun to turn.

More than twenty years later, they are still going round.

24

It was Wednesday before the jury, looking haggard after what had evidently been long and hard-fought discussions, returned to court. Speaking in a clear voice, the foreman declared that Kenneth Noye, Garth Chappell and Brian Reader had been found guilty of conspiracy to handle the stolen bullion, as well as to avoid VAT on taxable supplies of gold.

Brenda Noye stood up in the public gallery and yelled out, 'Never has such an injustice been done. There is no fucking justice in this trial.' Not to be outdone, Noye rounded on the jury and shouted, 'I hope you all die of cancer!'

Noye's counsel, John Mathew, was equally furious – at his client, not the verdict. He knew that the outburst would count against Noye when it came to sentencing. Mathew was also taken aback by the man who had just been revealed. This was not the moderate, affable cove he had been defending these past weeks and months. This was a different Noye.

The judge called for order at the top of his voice, but the uproar raged on. Brian Reader shouted, 'You have made one terrible mistake. You have got to live with that for the rest of your lives.' His twenty-year-old son Paul shouted, 'You have been fucking fixed up!' and fought officers who tried to quieten him. Reader junior was arrested, fined £100 for contempt of court and bound over to keep the peace for twelve months. Lynn Reader staggered outside wailing, 'It's not true, it's not true.' She told waiting reporters, 'There has been a terrible injustice.'

The moment he arrived back in his holding cell beneath the courtroom, Customs officers hit Kenneth Noye with a £1 million fine for unpaid VAT. Next in the queue was the Inland Revenue, one of whose officers served him with a second writ for £1 million in unpaid taxes. It was open season on the newly convicted prisoner. As if that wasn't enough to be going on with, news arrived that the loss adjusters had won a High Court injunction freezing all the defendants' assets until further notice. Unable to pay defence fees, Noye was granted legal aid.

Next morning, the convicted men were all back up in court for sentencing. Noye asked for permission to speak. Granted leave to do so, he told Judge Lowry he was sorry for his outburst of the day before, which had been made 'in the heat of the moment'. Lowry listened impassively. When it was his turn, he sentenced Noye to thirteen years in prison plus a £250,000 fine for conspiracy to handle the stolen bullion; one additional consecutive year and a further £250,000 fine for VAT avoidance; and two years to be served concurrently for failing to pay the two fines. This last one was something of a Catch-22 for Noye – with his assets frozen, he could not have paid the fines even had he wanted to. Noye was also ordered to pay £200,000 towards the cost of the trial, estimated at £2 million. In all, he was looking at fourteen years behind bars, fines of £700,000, and massive VAT and tax bills.

Garth Chappell, described by the judge as 'an essential element in turning the gold into cash', was given a total of ten years in prison plus a £200,000 fine and ordered to pay £75,000 towards costs. Reader, described as 'Noye's vigorous right-hand man', was sentenced to nine years. Constantino got one year for VAT fraud, suspended for one year. Thomas Adams, the Collector and Terence Patch were found not guilty.

When Lowry had finished dishing out the punishment, Brenda Noye called out, 'I love you, darling.' Gallantly blowing a kiss, Noye called back, 'I love you, too.' Lynn Reader shouted, 'I will wait for you, Brian.' Outside in the street angry relatives and friends of the imprisoned men scuffled with and swore at the police officers.

One good piece of news for the Noyes came when Michael Corkery told the court that the Crown was dropping the charge of conspiracy to handle stolen bullion in the case of Brenda Noye. But Noye's sister, Hilary Wilder, and her husband Richard were charged with receiving the £50,000 found in their back garden in West Kingsdown. The charge was later dropped, and the money reclaimed by the loss adjusters.

Noye was classed as a Category A prisoner, and sent to Albany maximum-security prison on the Isle of Wight. Deemed likely to attempt escape, Category A prisoners are automatically subjected to strip-search before and after meeting all visitors. They have to be 'in vision' the whole time – i.e., accompanied by a prison officer even when they visit the toilet – and depending on the institution, lights may be kept on in their cells all night, every night. Their cells are regularly 'tumbled' and prisoners may be moved around without notice. Their mail is screened by warders and all telephone calls are taped and monitored. Visitors have to be cleared by police and the Home Office, a process that can, and often does, take weeks. 'Cat A' prisoners are also always the first to be banged up and left to rot in their cells when there are staff shortages. Not a pleasant regime.

The Flying Squad was delighted that 'Cop Killer Kenneth Noye' as one tabloid dubbed him was behind bars – even if it was for less than the full term of a life sentence. They were very much less pleased about the fact that John Palmer, Garth Chappell's former business partner, had so far escaped trial. Nicknamed 'Goldfinger' by the British press, Palmer had never returned from his extended holiday on Tenerife.

But Palmer's golden luck was running out. For years, wanted British criminals had made a beeline for the Spanish *costas* because there was no formal extradition treaty between the two countries. Then, in December 1985 the Spanish interior ministry asked Scotland Yard to draw up a list of Britain's top twenty 'most wanted' fugitives known or suspected to be living in Spain. John Palmer's name figured on it. One month later, in January 1986, Spain introduced a new Aliens Law, which provided that foreign residents only had the right to live in Spain if they held valid passports. The change in the law was aimed squarely at ridding the country of foreign fugitives wanted in their own or other countries. In the case of John Palmer, it did the trick: Palmer's UK passport had expired on 23 December 1985. Acting in close concert with their Spanish counterparts, the UK authorities were not going to renew it any time soon.

Spanish police arrested Palmer at his luxury villa in Tenerife and flew him to Madrid. He was served with a deportation order and told to select a destination country. Hoping to 'do a Ronnie' (Biggs), and live quietly in exile there like the notorious Great Train Robber, Palmer chose Brazil. But well before he set foot on Brazilian soil, Scotland Yard informed the Brazilian authorities that their new would-be immigrant was a wanted man. At Rio de Janeiro airport, Palmer was taken aback to find himself refused entry – on the grounds that his passport had expired. For the second time in two days, he had to choose a destination country. Realizing that there were few countries in the world willing to take a wanted man, and among those none where he actually wanted to live, Palmer gave up and boarded a flight for Britain.

On Wednesday, 2 July 1986, with his former business partner Garth Chappell on trial for handling the Brink's-Mat gold, Palmer arrived back in London. The Flying Squad, in the person of Superintendent Ken John, arrested him at the bottom of the aircraft steps. Taken straight to Kennington police station, Palmer was questioned and charged with 'conspiracy to dishonestly handle stolen bullion'. Claiming repeatedly that he could not remember anything, and careful as always, Palmer said nothing that could be used in evidence against him. Despite offering to post sureties of £1,600,000, he was denied bail and remanded into custody pending trial.

Five months later, on 18 December 1986, Christopher Weyman, the suspected gold courier who had disappeared following Noye's arrest for murder, walked into Cannon Row police station in central London and gave himself up. Weyman was cautioned, charged, and remanded to Wormwood Scrubs prison. The joint trial of both men for handling stolen goods began in March 1987. At the end of the three-and-a-half-week hearing, both Palmer and Weyman were found 'not guilty' on all charges.

25

The major focus of the Brink's-Mat investigation now shifted to Brian Perry, and what had until then been a hunt for the missing gold now became a hunt for the cash and/or property detectives knew had been realized from its fraudulent conversion. Michael McAvoy and Brian Robinson would hardly let any Tom, Dick or Harry control the swag that was costing them the best years of their lives. The fact that Perry *was* in control suggested that he was more than just a trusted friend of the robbers: it suggested that Perry had been on the raid.

The police were convinced that more than four men had taken part in the robbery: but the inevitable confusion – not to say mayhem – of the raid itself, the hooding of the guards, and the fact that the robbers wore masks throughout, meant that no one could be sure of their exact number. The best guess was five men. If Perry had been on the raid, it would explain why some of the gang had entrusted him with their shares of the gold.

Perry duly went under the C11 microscope. But when it came to concealment and evasion, he was a canny and imaginative crook. Like Kenneth Noye, he understood the value of delegation, of allowing others to take the risks while keeping his own hide safe.

But Perry had a weak point: women.

Now that he had sold his partners down the river, any form of contact with them was risky for Perry. The safest thing he could have done was leave his old pals and their dependants to rot. But the consolation he had offered Jacqueline McAvoy when her husband went to prison had by now turned serious. They were in love.

DS Tony Curtis, who had been in on the Brink's-Mat investigation from the very beginning, was at the front of the pack hunting the minicab boss. 'We knew Brian Perry held a lot of money in his hot, sweaty grasp. We didn't just want to recover the cash – we wanted Brian Perry behind bars. We reasoned we might get to him by following back along the cash trail – if we could find a way into it. One thing worked in our favour: like most other people who suddenly get rich, one of the first things robbers tend to do is look after their own. We're talking wives, children, relatives, mistresses and friends, not necessarily in that order. Assuming for investigative purposes that this was happening, we decided, at first in a low-key way, to check up on the wives and girlfriends: find out how they were doing, see whether there were any sudden, unexplained improvements in their personal circumstances. Since he had been the gang's leader, and was therefore most likely to have control of the money, we started with Michael McAvoy's girlfriend, Kathleen Meacock, and his wife, Jacqueline.

'The last known address we had for Meacock was 6 Prioress Street, Lambeth, London SE1. It was a run-down council flat in a grimy, low-rent area just off the Old Kent Road, aka "Robbers' Row". Lo and behold, when we got to this dismal place there was nobody home. According to the neighbours, Meacock had disappeared several months earlier, without leaving a forwarding address. When we went round to see Jacqueline McAvoy, who had lived in a modest flat in Herne Hill, we found the same thing: the bird had flown, leaving no clue to the whereabouts of her new nesting place.

'Concentrating initially on Kent, since for reasons best known to themselves almost all South London criminals make a beeline for that county when they make it into the big time, we set about trying to trace Meacock. A check with the utility companies and the Land Registry turned up a Kathleen Meacock at a place by the name of Turpington Farm, 146 Southborough Lane, Bickley, Kent.

'A couple of us went down to take a discreet shufti at the place. One glance told us we were on the right track: Turpington Farm was a handsome, gabled, six-bedroom, eighteenth-century farmhouse. An estate agent would probably have added that it was "set in large, well-tended and mature grounds at the heart of a lovely village in a coveted corner of the garden of England".

'When we tracked down Jacqueline McAvoy we discovered that she, too, was living in a style to which she had not previously been accustomed. Her new nesting place was 45 Bird-in-Hand Lane, Bickley, Kent: a fine detached property with a nice garden big enough for the little McAvoy children to run about in. Perry later told a jury he had been thinking of moving in there with Jacqueline. But when he got Michael McAvoy's "Tell Brian Perry to mind his own fucking business and stop having affairs" message from the depths of Leicester Prison, his ardour had suddenly cooled. It was a great shame: a bird in the hand is worth two in the bush. By a curious coincidence, Jacqueline McAvoy's splendid new home was just up the road from Turpington Farm. It was like "Happy Families": McAvoy's blonde wife and his brunette mistress were living in the same Kent village, almost within shouting distance of each other. Handy if either woman wanted to borrow a cup of sugar; a shotgun; a wheelbarrow full of cash; or whatever it is you borrow when you are a gangster's moll. The wife's house wasn't quite as big or as comfortable as the mistress's, but then a chap has to get his priorities right.

'It was understandable McAvoy wanted his wife and children looked after – why else had he gone to all that trouble? But Meacock's skyrocket leap from a Lambeth council flat to a $c.$ £300,000 (at 1985 prices) Kent mansion within two years of the robbery's commission was asking for trouble. If all Meacock's relatives had died and left her everything they owned it wouldn't have amounted to two spoons and a penny. On top of that, she had no visible form of income. How, then, could she possibly afford a £300,000 country house?

'They were all spending, that was the thing. Kenneth Noye, for example, not only had two Range Rovers, but when we made entry into the first one we found a pair of sunglasses in the glove box worth £300. Mrs Noye had racks of shoes that had cost her more than £300 a pair.

'A second flip through the Land Registry revealed that Brian Perry, too, had moved up in the world, abandoning his lowly Peckham roots for the leafy suburban charms of Meadowcroft, number 343 Main Road, Biggin Hill. In Kent, naturally.

'We were all so delighted by the improvement in this trio's circumstances we decided to rattle a few cages, beginning with Meacock. On 12 August 1986, Detective Inspector Brightwell and a couple of the boys took a drive out into the Kent countryside. They were suitably impressed by Turpington Farm's air of understated rustic charm. They were much less impressed by the Rottweilers that came rushing at them as they approached the front door. Luckily, these particular dogs were not aggressive, they just jumped about barking and making a show. As Brightwell bent down to pat one of them he noticed a shiny silver nametag gleaming in the black fur at the animal's throat. He turned it to catch the light. The name engraved on the dog tag was "Brinks".' Brightwell stood up to find Kathleen Meacock watching him from the porch. Nodding at the second Rottweiler, he said, 'I suppose the other one's called "Mat", then, is it?'

'Meacock's default setting was "Have no truck with coppers". But the expression on the pretty oval face told Brightwell he was right – naming the dogs "Brinks" and "Mat" was another example of South London gangster humour, on a par with Noye's "Goldfinger" doorbell. Brightwell showed Meacock his warrant card, and with all due reluctance she let him in. He took in the large, gleaming kitchen, into which just about the whole ground floor of the average-sized family home might comfortably fit. "Nice place you have here, Kathleen. You bought it with some of the Brink's-Mat's money, did you?"

'Meacock made no reply. But her silence hardly mattered. She was in big trouble. The Brink's-Mat inquiry was about to get a fresh injection of blood, and they both knew it. There and then, Brightwell arrested Meacock and charged her with "conspiracy to handle stolen goods and handling stolen goods, the proceeds of the Brink's-Mat robbery". On her way to the car, Meacock expressed her gratitude for this interruption to her daily routine in the traditional manner.

'That same day, Jacqueline McAvoy, Brian Perry and a car-dealing associate of Perry's were also arrested. Poring over the back trail, detectives found estate agent's records which showed that the unnamed associate had acted as a front man for Perry in the purchase of Perry's newly acquired Biggin Hill mansion.'

When officers went round to arrest him, Perry's associate seemed to accept their arrival with resigned equanimity. But it immediately became clear that the associate's wife had either not been made aware of her husband's activities, or else had not understood the risk he had been running. When she saw him standing in the middle of the lounge, hands cuffed behind his back and flanked by a couple of burly Flying Squad officers, the reality of what was happening to her comfortable and outwardly respectable existence suddenly hit home. She put her hands over her ears, opened her mouth and started screaming. Nothing anyone could say or do could persuade her to stop. In the end, the attending officers left her standing there, head tilted back and hands pressed flat to her ears, screaming at the living-room ceiling.

Detectives now set out to establish exactly how Turpington Farm had been bought, and by whom. They soon uncovered a devious and deliberately entangled evidential chain, triggered by a telephone call on 13 August 1985 from a London solicitor by the name of Michael Relton. That day, Relton called the solicitors acting for the vendors of Turpington Farm. He had a friend who wanted to buy the house. Would the solicitors act for this friend, too? With no idea of what they were getting mixed up in, they agreed.

Breezing into the solicitors' offices later that same month, Relton's proxy told them that the money for the farm would be coming from an offshore account. He said that for tax purposes he wanted to buy the property using an overseas front company. Could they help him find one? All unsuspecting, the solicitors got in touch with Price Campbell & Co. in the Cayman Islands, who put forward a locally registered company called Sandown. From this moment on, Relton, acting through his proxy, controlled Sandown's shareholdings and directorships and oversaw all of its dealings. Already, the paper chain showed that Relton had paid the fees for Sandown's acquisition from a US dollar account held in his own name. In a letter dated 24 May that was intercepted by the prison authorities and passed on to the police, Meacock told Michael McAvoy she had viewed Turpington Farm and wanted to buy it.

On 16 December 1985 Relton's proxy paid the vendor's solicitors £25,000 by banker's draft as a 10 per cent deposit on Turpington Farm. Detectives discovered that Relton had collected the money that same day from a branch of the Midland Bank at 41 Horseferry Road, London SW1. The money had been drawn on the 'Lynn Relton Client

Account (2)'. Lynn Relton, it immediately transpired, was Michael Relton's wife. When police checked the details of *her* account, they discovered that £35,000 had been transferred into it on 26 November from something called 'The Burton Account'. This account was held by a Mr Gordon Parry at the Hong Kong and Shanghai Bank in Zurich, Switzerland.

Detectives did not know who Gordon Parry was, and neither did they know very much about the solicitor Michael Relton. The Flying Squad now had a very strong urge to find out as much as it could about both men. Offshore bank accounts channelling money through proxies into a property deal on behalf of jailed gang leader Michael McAvoy's girlfriend – that was a solid lead. Watching him, detectives saw that Relton had an office in Verney Road, just the other side of the Old Kent Road from the flat occupied by Kathleen Meacock before she had joined the 'Homes and Gardens' set.

Well-educated, charming and plausible, Relton was the director of a company called Selective Estates, which developed properties mainly in London and Spain. The Spanish connection was interesting – if it did not end up in South-East London or Kent, a lot of the capital's hot money washed up on one or other of the *costas*. To find out exactly what Relton was up to in Spain, Scotland Yard applied to the Spanish authorities for a *commission rogatoire*, the international legal protocol whereby one national police force can ask another to investigate a suspect or suspects on its behalf, including details of their bank accounts and financial dealings. The Spanish authorities agreed to help.

'The Flying Squad had only had eyeballs on Relton for a couple of weeks,' recalls Curtis, 'when he suddenly disappeared. Just went, like that – dropped right out of sight overnight. It might have been that he got wind of our interest in him, or spotted a watcher. At any rate, he made a run for it with his wife to Spain. Then, on 15 October, we got word from the Ports people that Relton was in a car on his way back to England.

'The Spanish police had served the *commission rogatoire* on Relton, and were preparing a report for the Yard. But they had not arrested or charged him. Perhaps Relton thought we had lost interest in him and it was safe to return. If so, he could hardly have been more mistaken.

The second his daintily shod Jermyn Street feet touched UK soil we put him back under surveillance.

'He drove to London. We tailed him. He was drifting around, seeing old friends, doing nothing special. To nudge things along we decided to get proactive on Relton. We lifted him that night, cautioned him, put him in a cell, and let him cook for a few hours. When we thought he was nicely done, we hauled him out and started asking him a few searching questions, such as: How did he know Kathleen Meacock? Did he know Michael McAvoy? If so, how? Why had the money for Sandown come from his personal account? Why had he felt it necessary to acquire an offshore vehicle for the purchase of Turpington Farm? and so on. Although he did his best to stall and block, Relton was like a rabbit in the headlights. And he looked as guilty as hell.

'While he was being grilled, we searched his car. In the boot we found dozens of documents. Stashed in large brown manila envelopes, they were all neatly sorted according to their type and labelled with the Spanish address where Relton had been lying low.

'It only took a glance to see that we had hit the jackpot. The documents detailed a series of bank accounts – including the "Burton Account" – held by Gordon Parry, Michael Relton and other named individuals in the UK, Switzerland, Liechtenstein, Spain, the Cayman Islands and the US. They itemized cash transfers between these accounts and banks in Britain and abroad, and gave chapter and verse on any number of property deals that had been executed worldwide since the beginning of 1984. The sums detailed on the pages made your eyes water. What really got everyone going was the fact that the names of Jacqueline McAvoy, Kathleen Meacock and Brian Perry cropped up at regular intervals in the paperwork.

'A lot of police work is hard slog; you can go for a long time on a case without getting anywhere. But sometimes you get a slice of luck. This was more than just a slice, it was pretty near the whole cake – and it was about to get even better. We had not just come by a lucky find that revealed how Kathleen Meacock had managed to go up in the world: we had a detailed inventory of where at least some of the laundered Brink's-Mat millions had gone and were going.

'Relton cut a sorry figure after his long slow broil in the cell. Before falling in among thieves, Relton had been a reasonably successful and perfectly respectable criminal lawyer who had defended many serving police officers. He had also acted for Gordon Parry on legitimate property deals. Relton's clients might risk spending time in prison, he did not. He had never been locked up before, and the experience hit him like an express train. You have to try one of the filing-cabinet dungeons we had put him in to know how unpleasant they are. Anthony Black had not taken well to cell-block living; Relton liked it even less.

'We asked our lawyer friend to tell us about Gordon Parry. Relton explained that Parry's son and Brian Perry's daughter were what he called "an item". In the natural course of things the fathers had met and become acquainted. (It was a little confusing on the surname side of things, but then you can't have everything.) When they met in the last week of 1983, Gordon Parry had been doing business in London's ancient docks, or "Docklands" as they were then being rebranded. When we say "business", Parry was employing a team of people to go around buying up the rent books of the area's mainly aged residents. When it came to buying the new flats and houses that were going to be built, special discounts were available to residents. Parry could buy at a discount and sell at the full price – simple.'

In the mid-1980s, the whole Docklands area was a kind of property Wild West, perfect for the cowboy speculators then roaming loose. Ill-suited to the demands of modern containerized shipping, London's once mighty docks had gradually fallen into disuse. They were bankrupt and falling derelict. This is what the London Docklands Development Corporation (LDDC) had to say about the eight-and-a-half-square-mile site:

In 1981 the Royal Docks . . . were areas of economic and social deprivation, characterised by inadequate and poor social and community facilities. The area was physically isolated with few and poor public transport links, whether to elsewhere in Newham or to the City and West End. Some industry continued after the closure, but much of it was there for reasons such as low rents in poor quality property. There were, of course, notable exceptions such as sugar refiners . . . But for the rest, it is hard to convey the

sheer desolation of the area in the period after the closure of the
Royal Docks: so close to the City and West End, yet so remote.
Most Londoners remained ignorant of this huge and blighted area
of their city.

They did indeed. But some of those realized that the old docks
were not all that far from the centre of London, or that they actually
adjoined the City, its financial heart. Hordes of well-heeled upwardly
mobile professionals commuted into the Square Mile every day, often
from inconveniently far-flung suburbs. Here, then, were several
square miles of prime real estate with enormous potential ready for
the taking. You could throw up apartments and offices, shove in a
few roads and some basic infrastructure, and before you could say
'EastEnders' a property phoenix would rise from the Docklands ashes
and shift the whole axis of London.

Over a few meetings and many drinks, Parry regaled Perry with his
own version of the Docklands Dream, impressing on him how much
money someone with the necessary capital stood to make, and how
much like falling off a log it would be to make it. Like many
criminals, Perry was a clever man with one significant area of
blindness. This did not lie in the part of his brain that controlled his
business acumen – he knew a good deal when he saw it.

Parry and Relton suggested Perry take a little walk with them
down Docklands way, to view the crusty bones of the past and peer
into the glittering future. Standing on the empty quay of Odessa
Wharf, letting his imagination freewheel while Parry conjured offices
and apartment blocks, conference centres and marinas from the cold
London clay beneath their feet, Perry felt an old familiar stirring deep
in his soul. It was greed. Why not buy into the Docklands Dream,
then going dirt-cheap at £35 a square foot? Why not make a huge
profit; accumulate shedloads of cash; double or even quadruple the
money he was meant to be holding in trust for his friends in jail?
Then, when they finally came out – if they came out – he could
always give Mick and Brian back their money. He might even throw
in a little interest, and hope Mick would forgive him for bedding
Jackie and making off with the gold. At any rate, investing – and at
the same time concealing – some of the Brink's-Mat millions in the

new Docklands development would keep the rozzers guessing.

One day, 'Docklands' might have its own airport; a dedicated monorail linking it to central London; an Underground spur; and hip designer cafés where young, good-looking junk bond traders could exchange lightly steamed glances with perfectly stilettoed secretaries. It might have towering skyscrapers bristling with knowledge workers and classy restaurants and loft apartments and all manner of other wonderful things. Manhattan-on-Thames – why not?

Parry broke in on Perry's daydreaming, but only to give it the lifeblood of hard fact. He suggested they buy up half-a-dozen wharves, hire a firm of architects, and pay them to draw up plans for mixed housing and office space. When they had outline planning permission, they could sell on the sites at a big profit. Naturally, they would set up a few offshore companies to disguise these transactions, and make sure that they themselves stayed out of sight.

It sounded good to Perry. Sprinkle a few dozen bars of Brink's-Mat gold over this dismal wasteland, and they would multiply. Everybody would be rich and happy. What could go wrong?

In fact the idea was not at all bad: Parry was an excellent businessman. If Relton had been a bit more careful about how he acquired Turpington Farm, and not left a paper trail that had led detectives directly to Michael McAvoy, they might just have got away with it. As it was, the dodgy solicitor *had* been tracked down, and here he was spilling the old *haricots verts* all over the police station linoleum.

Aware that the slightly built, foxy-faced man in front of him was frightened half to death, DI Brightwell started the interview with what he thought might be a relatively easy question. Tapping the stacks of files laid out in front of him, he said, 'Why did you send all this material to Spain?' No one, least of all Brightwell, expected an immediate confession. But the effect on Relton was extraordinary. Raising his eyes from the documents where they had been fixed, he said, 'I'll tell you everything.'

Curtis was there when Relton started to talk. 'We started getting ready to take his statement, but Relton held up his hand. "The financial dealings," he told us, "are so complex I'd never be able to explain them. Wouldn't it be better if I wrote out the statements myself?" Not half: a handwritten confession from one of the chief handlers? From our point of view, this was the dream ticket.

'Supplied with copious quantities of pen and paper, Relton duly set to work writing his statement out longhand. And what a tale he had to tell. Although we had the documents to back up what he said, in terms of its sheer size and complexity the web of transactions, accounts and investments the solicitor now laid out for us was hard to credit.

'Relton was the linchpin of a huge and far-reaching financial empire built on laundered Brink's-Mat cash. Gordon Parry was chief business adviser. And – the topping on the cake – Relton named Brian Perry as the person in overall charge.'

The flow charts and diagrams used to track the network of illegal accounts, payments, deals and acquisitions gradually expanded to cover the walls of the Brink's-Mat inquiry offices. As the days went by and the solicitor turned launderer kept on writing, detectives were able to see how much gold had been converted into cash; who had handled it; where it was banked; who controlled it; where it had been invested; how it had been spent and by whom. The financial accounts of the Byzantine Empire could hardly have been more complex.

26

It rapidly became clear to Scotland Yard that some ways of laundering the proceeds of a successful raid had been thought out well in advance. Just before the robbery, on 23 November 1983, three men had arranged a £100,000 loan from the Bank of Ireland (BoI) to buy a nightclub called 'Reflections' at 8 Bridge Road, Stratford, London E15. They were a man named Patrick Clark, John 'Little Legs' Lloyd and an associate. The loan was secured by the personal guarantees of Lloyd, Patrick Clark and his wife; term assurance on the lives of the two men (the benefit of which was assigned to the Bank of Ireland in the event of their deaths); and on Patrick and Mrs Clark's home at 3 The Greenwalk, Chingford, Essex – as well as on the premises of 'Reflections'.

At the same time, two companies, Centavale Ltd and Cotgrave Ltd, were incorporated, with Patrick Clark named as a director of both. Lloyd's common-law wife, Jean Savage, was made a director of both companies on 30 December that year. Another new company, Barbe Ltd, controlled by and for the benefit of Patrick Clark, John 'Little Legs' Lloyd and two other conspirators, was incorporated in Jersey on 5 June 1984. On 29 June, in a further attempt to muddy the waters, a husband-and-wife team replaced Clark and Savage as directors of Centavale and Cotgrave. Lloyd and Savage lived in Noye's old West Kingsdown home.

'Reflections' nightclub, a string of other front companies, and the individuals controlling them were the first attempt to launder and conceal the cash river that, for the next six years, would stream from the stolen gold.

The network quickly prospered. Between December 1983 and 3 March 1986 Patrick Clark and others received from Noye, Lloyd and a host of willing go-betweens sums totalling £4,461,029. These were deposited into and subsequently withdrawn from various bank accounts.

Kenneth Noye ferried large cash sums in person. Only eleven days after the robbery – and less than a week after Johnson Matthey bought the first batch of resmelted gold from Scadlynn – he paid £15,000 in new £50s into his current account at Barclays Bank, Dartford. The next day, a courier deposited £30,000 in cash into a BoI, Isle of Man (IoM) account held jointly with a second man. On 14 January 1984, Noye paid a further £95,000 into his Dartford account. Three days later, Clark popped up again, hitting his Ilford account with a round £100,000. On 7 February 1984, an unidentified person paid £304,000 cash into a new account at the Mercantile Overseas Bank Ltd, Isle of Man. On 15 February, Clark deposited another £50,000, and on the 20th he purchased a banker's draft made out to John Lloyd in the sum of £300,000, paid from 'Sundries Suspense', another account held at Ilford.

Relton explained how he, too, had been in on the laundering act from the start, opening the Lynn Relton Client Account, Bank of Ireland, Balham, on 29 February 1984 with £122,500 in cash. The money was used to buy Hever Cottage, Kent, in the name of a third and ostensibly unconnected person. On 2 March 1984, Patrick Clark collected the £300,000 'John Lloyd draft' he had arranged at the Bank of Ireland, Ilford, and transferred it by proxy to the Mercantile Overseas Bank on the Isle of Man. Kenneth Noye ultimately controlled this account jointly with other named individuals.

Gordon Parry entered the picture on 7 March 1984, when he paid £260,000 cash into a new account opened in his own name at the Bank of Ireland, Isle of Man, and promptly awarded himself an American Express Gold Card. Parry deposited a further £120,000 in cash into yet another account in a Dublin bank. In order to explain the source of his wealth, Parry later told bank officials that his father ran a string of South London betting shops, and that he himself owned a nightclub in the same area. On 23 March, £30,000 cash was used to open the 'Jean Savage' account at the Bank of Ireland's Croydon, South London, branch – near where she lived.

On 30 April Noye put a further £300,000 into his Dartford account. Five months after the robbery he had close on £1 million in that one bank account.

And so it went on, as a network of couriers and proxies channelled various tributaries of the cash river flowing out of Bedminster. On 22 May 1984 Noye bought his eleven bars of gold from Charterhouse Japhet in Jersey, creating what the gang hoped would be a blind for possession of the stolen bullion. After that, the carousel ran faster: £137,848 to the Coleman Street branch a few days later; £87,400 by telegraphic transfer to Waterson Todman, NatWest Bank, 31 The Promenade, Cheltenham; and £150,000 cash into a named Balham account.

Noye paid £200,000 into the Royal Bank of Canada, Lothbury, in the City of London on 21 July 1984 and the same again into the Lothbury account on the 23rd for onward transfer to the Mercantile (IoM) account. Always in cash, almost all of the money was paid across in new, A24-prefix, consecutively numbered £50 notes issued exclusively by the Treasury to Barclays Operations Centre in Bristol, supplied extensively to Barclays Bedminster branch and paid exclusively by that bank into the Scadlynn account.

The crooks were still looking for any and every way to launder the cash, not least by acquiring – and then either occupying or selling – property. Relton told police he had attended a meeting on 31 July in Jersey at a company called Centre Services to discuss buying premises that had until recently been occupied by Cheltenham Ladies' College. The idea – subsequently implemented – was to convert the former school buildings into luxury flats. If you were trying to hide your ill-gotten gains in an outwardly respectable place, it did not get much better than that.

Clutching one of the heavy-duty plastic carrier bags she routinely used to ferry Brink's-Mat cash, on 2 August Jean Savage – one of the gang's busiest couriers – paid £200,000 in A24-prefix £50s into her Croydon account, followed by £269,950 eleven days later and £75,000 after that.

As the year wore on the tempo upped again. So far, all of the illegal bank accounts had been opened in the UK or the Republic of Ireland. This changed on 3 August 1984, when Gordon Parry arrived at the plush Zurich offices of the Hong Kong and Shanghai Banking Corporation (HSBC) armed with a letter of introduction from Lynn Relton. A third man introduced Parry and told the bank what an upstanding citizen he was. To look at rather like Mr Cheeryble, the fictional character in Charles Dickens's *Nicholas Nickleby*, the third man was hired precisely for his ability to put a good-looking front on a shady bit of business.

Parry got the new Swiss account off to an auspicious start by stacking £850,435 in brand-new banknotes on the delighted manager's desk and inviting him to count them. The £50 tower blocks did nothing to stop business reaching a swift and successful conclusion. Brian Perry and his new recruits now had their first secret, numbered Swiss bank account. Its coded access word was 'Burton', and from then on it was known as the 'Burton' account. Bank records show that Michael Weber Relton had power of attorney over the account from its inception.

On 15 August 1984 an anonymous bagman arrived at the front desk of the Hong Kong and Shanghai Bank, Bishopsgate, London, dumped £500,000 in cash on the counter, and told the bemused clerk that the money, 'Once you've counted it, should be sent to the Burton account, HSBC, Zurich'. Before anyone could ask him questions like where the money had come from or what his name was, the stranger turned on his heel and walked out again. Bank officials transferred the money. The Burton account was now in the black to the tune of £1,350,435. Hotel and restaurant records show that Relton, Parry and two others were in Zurich on 29 and 30 August, and bank records show that an unnamed person deposited a further £490,000 in cash in the Burton account during that same two-day period.

Nine months after the Brink's-Mat robbery, everyone associated with it was swimming in money – except for the leaders of the gang that had stolen it in the first place.

27

Switzerland is a nice place to be if you have a truckload of money. These guys had several, and they made sure they enjoyed it, staying in Zurich's best hotels, travelling first class and eating at the kind of restaurant that has among the highest 'millionaire per table' counts in the entire world. They tended to pay their substantial bills in new £50 banknotes.

Perry was careful to cover his tracks. On 29 August 1984 he shared room 24 of Zurich's Hotel Dolder Grand with Gordon Parry. They hardly needed to economize – but then, the Dolder Grand, a five-star hotel complete with indoor and outdoor swimming pools, a superb restaurant and views of both the city and the nearby mountains, was so spacious and comfortable that the two men probably did not feel the squeeze. They shared because Perry, wily as ever, wanted to keep his name out of the hotel's records. When they checked out, Parry paid the bill with his new American Express 'gold' card.

Parry and Perry drove across the border into Liechtenstein in the same well-rummaged Mercedes that had been used to transport much of the laundered cash. The gang opened two new accounts in a bank in the country's capital city, Vaduz, paying £45,000 in cash into each account. The first was codenamed 'Como' – not after the Italian lake, but in a sardonic reference to the popular 1950s crooner, whose songs and singing style Perry intensely disliked. The second was named the 'Glad' account after Gordon Perry's mother. On 31 August, Parry paid just under a million pounds into the Burton account, while Jean Savage kept things ticking over on the home front by depositing £130,000 back in Croydon.

Opening the new accounts, Parry wrote 'layabout' in the box marked 'employment'. Self-confessed idler though he might be, on 4

September 1984 he found sufficient energy to whack a further £490,000 crisp ones into the Burton account.

While his friends were doing their bit on the Continent, in the first week of September Noye paid a total of £1,000,000 into his swelling Croydon nest-egg. Savage, meanwhile, had a couple of days off – a welcome break, no doubt, given how busy she had been hauling massive bags of banknotes around for the past many weeks. While she rested, John Elcombe, who later said he thought all the banknotes were simply 'black tax money', stood in for the 'Bag Lady', as some detectives would later call her, banking £500,000 at Balham while another proxy paid £286,000 into his Finchley account.

Gordon Parry and John Elcombe were back at the Bank of Liechtenstein in Vaduz on 20 September. When detectives asked him who Elcombe was and how he was connected with Perry and Parry, Relton pointed out that Parry's common-law wife was Elcombe's first cousin. While they were in Vaduz, Parry paid £500,000 cash into the Glad account, numbered 052-608-8, while Elcombe opened the Elcombe (Liechtenstein) account with a cash deposit of £1,697,946.

Just in case anyone in this headlong gangster scramble should prove to be dishonest, Parry made sure that he was joint signatory to the Elcombe account. Even so, the arrangement meant that Elcombe would no longer need to trouble Gordon Parry with the huge bundles of cash he was ferrying from the UK: he could take them straight to one of the banks in Switzerland or Liechtenstein and pay them in under his own name.

Relton told detectives that Elcombe's January 1985 detention – and the discovery of £710,000 in cash in the back of the Mercedes – had both alarmed and angered Brian Perry. The stop and search had been routine, but there was no way Perry could be sure the German police had not been working for – or might at the very least have been alerted by – Scotland Yard. Terrified that the Swiss accounts were about to be discovered, Perry decided to move all of the money to Liechtenstein. In the process, he made one small slip for detective kind: the car hired to transport Parry, Relton and Perry from the Dolder Grand Hotel to Zurich airport on 24 September for the flight to Vaduz was charged to Perry's personal debit card.

Perry named the new Liechtenstein umbrella account the 'Moyet Foundation' after his favourite champagne, Moët, whose name he was unable either to spell or pronounce correctly. Immediately, Gordon Parry transferred £3,167,407 to the Moyet Foundation from the three existing Swiss bank accounts. He also paid in cash to the tune of £1,150,010.60. He then transferred £152,126 into the UK bank account of Selective Estates Ltd. This was to pay for a new property – Gowles Farm Barn, St Mary Platt, Kent. Like the rest of the properties the trio would now go on to acquire, Gowles Farm Barn was intended as a quick-turnaround investment that when sold at a profit would increase the take from the Brink's-Mat job and help muddy the back-trail.

The Moyet Foundation's Articles of Association provided that Perry should become its sole beneficiary in the event of Gordon Parry's death. The agreement further provided that 'Perry and Relton were empowered, in addition to Parry and both during his life and after his death, to impart instructions to the Moyet Foundation and/or its delegates'. Parry, Relton and Perry all signed the Moyet Agreement in their own handwriting. Behind the scenes, it was Perry who worked the levers, but if anything went wrong, Parry and Relton were likely to take the fall.

Moving all this money around had become a full-time occupation for the conspirators, but as Relton pointed out, it wasn't all hard graft: they were having the time of their lives, drinking vast quantities of the finest champagne and living off the fat of the land. Life was a big bowl of cherries. The only slight crack being the basilisk gaze of Scotland Yard, which Perry knew only too well would always be fixed on him. Detectives now had documentary evidence that he controlled the money. He was now – officially – the key to breaking the case.

At the same time as they were busy banking it Perry, Parry and Relton got busy spending the cash by means of still more front companies. These included Selective Estates; Platform 22; Feberion (Panama) Ltd; and Melchester Ltd – all of them officially controlled by Parry alone or by Parry and Relton. Between 6 August 1984 and 4 September 1986, these companies were used to acquire New

Caledonia Wharf, Odessa Street, London SE1; Globe Wharf; Upper Globe Wharf; Lower King and Queen Wharf, and Cyclops Wharf, 170–174 West Ferry Road, E14. A phoenix London Docklands was rising, and a fat chunk of it was stretching skyward on the proceeds of the stolen Brink's-Mat gold. In Margaret Thatcher's 'There is no such thing as society' Britain, this was and remains beyond irony.

The list of properties Parry, Relton and Perry now acquired is too long to detail in full, but along with Gowles Farm Barn and the Docklands wharves it included: The Courtyard, Montpelier Street, Cheltenham; 2/10 High Street, Cheltenham; Credon House, Verney Road, London SE1 (where Relton had his offices); nos. 2, 3, 4 & 5 London Road, London SE1; Flat 7, 57/59 Lisson Street, London NW1; the Auclaye Brickworks, Horsham Road, Capel, Surrey; and Crockham House in Westerham, Kent. Following expensive and extensive renovations, Gordon Parry, his common-law wife Irene and their two children moved into the £400,000 Crockham House.

Striking out on the foreign front in 1984, Relton bought two plots of prime building land at Torremar, Spain, for £135,000. On 18 December he transferred US$3,000,000 from the Burton account to a joint account held in his own name and that of a US proxy at the South East Bank, Sarasota, Florida, for the purchase of a giant condominium.

For his part, Perry bought plot 105, Marbessa, for £27,000 in cash and spent £48,000 building a new villa on it.

Despite trying as hard as they could to spend big bundles of it, the tidal waves of cash from the sale of the stolen gold kept pouring out of the Scadlynn account: more than half a million pounds in the second week of November 1984 alone. On 5 December 1984 – the day after McAvoy and Robinson were sentenced to twenty-five years apiece for armed robbery – Garth Chappell withdrew £384,000 in cash and moved it down the line to Perry and chums. The next day, Chappell – posing as 'Mr Cooper' – took £270,000 more from the money machine his newly imprisoned colleagues had so successfully created.

And so it went on – and on. By the New Year of 1985, it was raining money on everyone involved in the cash chain. Efforts to dispose of and disguise the deluge became ever more brazen, careless or desperate – and frequently all three at the same time.

Following down the trail of payments made from the Moyet (Liechtenstein) account, detectives saw that on 13 June 1985, £113,000 had been transferred from that account via Credit Suisse, Zurich, by means of draft no. 3037864 to the same intermediary who records showed had visited Turpington Farm on 27 July on behalf of Kathleen Meacock.

That same day, £160,000 was transferred to the Lynn Relton Client Account from the Moyet Foundation, and a further £450,000 remitted from the Moyet Foundation to something called the 'Medayil' account. The Medayil account – another financial hidey-hole – was used to buy 45 Bird-in-Hand Lane for Jacqueline McAvoy. Like Kathleen Meacock, Jacqueline McAvoy did her best to conceal the fact that the money for her new home derived ultimately from the Brink's-Mat heist. Like Meacock, she needed a little help from her friends to spin a false accounting trail.

This started in May 1985 when a male go-between approached an employee of Lockwood's estate agents to see if they had a local property for sale at about £150,000. Lockwood's gave him details of a property at 45 Bird-in-Hand Lane, Bickley, that might suit. Brian Perry took Jacqueline McAvoy to view it in person. The house was very nice indeed. Thrilled, McAvoy asked her go-between to proceed. The deal went ahead.

Medayil Ltd arranged a £50,000 mortgage from the Bradford and Bingley Building Society for Jacqueline McAvoy, who called herself 'Jacqueline Sheffield' for the purposes of the transaction. Falsely declaring an income of £18,000 a year as a fashion model, McAvoy stated that Gordon Parry – who gave her a glowing reference – was her current landlord.

A proxy paid the vendor's solicitors £8,000 in cash on 31 July 1985 – a sum Relton had withdrawn that very morning from his wife Lynn's account. This was in rude good health, detectives were able to see, because Relton had transferred £170,000 into it from the Moyet account on 19 July. On 9 August, Brian Perry arrived at the solicitors in person with £70,000 in cash and a banker's draft for £20,000 to complete the sale. His fingerprints were literally all over the deal.

Turning to McAvoy's mistress, detectives saw that once Meacock had made her one visit to Turpington Farm on 24 May 1985, she deliberately dropped out of sight. Using Sandown, the Cayman Islands front company bought to disguise Perry's and Meacock's invol-vement, the proxy now stepped in and took her place as the buyer.

Meacock moved in with Brinks and Mat, her pedigree Rottweilers, and for a while everything in the garden was lovely. Roses bloomed, the birds sang, and friends came to wonder at the manifold delights of her new home. Then, one cold dark morning in February 1986, Turpington Farm's vendor, who still lived in the area, came round to see if there was any post for her. Instead of being greeted by the man to whom she had sold the house, the vendor was surprised to be met by Kathleen Meacock. The vendor remembered showing Meacock round the house and how much the Londoner had liked it. But surely – surely she had sold her farm to a man? Why was Meacock living in the house? What was going on here?

Meacock told her bemused visitor that she was simply renting the property, and got rid of her as quickly as possible. As soon as the woman had disappeared, Meacock sat down and wrote another letter to Michael McAvoy, telling him about her unwelcome visitor and her own explanation for being resident at the farm. This letter, too, was intercepted by the prison authorities and a copy of it passed to Scotland Yard.

Spooked by the visit and terrified her occupation might come to the attention of someone in authority, Meacock asked her solicitors to take out an advertisement in the property section of the London *Evening Standard*. This purported to offer a two-year lease on Turpington Farm with immediate effect. Writing from her old address at 6 Prioress Walk, Lambeth, under her maiden name of O'Connell, Meacock herself then applied for – and duly obtained – the lease. Oddly, she never paid Sandown Ltd – the nominal landlord – a penny in rent. Relton showed the police how he had transferred £233,000 from the Burton account to the solicitors as a final payment for Turpington Farm.

Matching Relton's evidence with the information they had already collected, detectives could now see the shape of the whole conspiracy. It fitted together as neatly as a jigsaw – albeit the complicated kind. From now on, no matter how hard their quarry might twist and turn, it was only a matter of time before they ran Brian Perry and the rest of the pack to earth.

28

There was now almost a surplus of information available for the purposes of a laundering prosecution, but in the huge and fiendishly complex job of recovering the illegally held cash and property and getting the conspirators behind bars, the police had a secret weapon: Bob McCunn. In return for access to the Relton papers, McCunn's separate and exhaustive investigations helped detectives compile what they hoped would be a series of watertight cases in respect of Perry and the rest.

McCunn had already applied for – and been granted – Mareva injunctions. Described by a Lord Chief Justice as 'the nearest thing the law has to a nuclear weapon', the Mareva injunction is a legal instrument specifically designed to stop suspiciously acquired funds from being spent before due investigation. It freezes the target's financial assets. Bank and building society accounts stop working; debit and credit cards revert to worthless plastic; even piggy banks fall into the legal net. Any property – including a home or for that matter a television set – is also seized.

Granted by Mr Justice Roach on 9 December 1986, Mareva injunctions were applied to the assets of Gordon Parry, Michael Relton, John Elcombe and Brian Perry, to include all of their individual and collective bank accounts and all of the properties they had bought either in their own names or under the numerous company flags of convenience. If a property had been sold on, it was still subject to the blanket financial stop order until its fate could be decided in court. This must have come as a nasty surprise to any new – and entirely innocent – owner.

A financial steamroller was rumbling that threatened to crush the conspirators. Increasingly confident of success, on 11 December 1986 the Crown Prosecution Service authorized Brian Perry's arrest on a charge of dishonestly handling the Brink's-Mat gold. He was remanded in custody.

A warrant was also issued for the arrest of Gordon Parry; but Parry, who could hardly have failed to see which way the wind was blowing, had already fled to Spain.

On 18 June 1987, Brian Perry, Kathleen Meacock and Michael Relton were committed for trial at Lambeth Magistrates Court. In a letter to Michael McAvoy written nine days before her arrest, Meacock wrote:

> I really do think I've got no way out, darling, from what I've heard. But really, darling, I want you to be as strong as me when it comes to it. It really won't bother me about going away. We will both get through this, won't we, sweetheart? We are both strong people and we have one another.

A few weeks later, shortly before her case came to court, Meacock and McAvoy were married in Leicester jail. Videotaped for posterity by doting prison officers, the civil ceremony was brief, sparsely attended – and lent a certain poignancy by the newlyweds' knowledge that McAvoy still had another twenty years or so left behind bars. Love is a wildflower – it blooms in the most unlikely places.

Even as the committal proceedings got under way, two previously hidden accounts held in the names of two other launderers were credited with just another £500,000 in cash. The police and McCunn were sticking a spoke in its wheels, but the money-go-round was still turning. In 1987 one of these new accounts took receipt of £440,000 – as much as had been deposited into it in the three preceding years. These accounts, too, were now frozen.

On 16 December 1987, Brian Perry closed the Como account and authorized the transfer of the remaining £60,401 to a named proxy account held at Barclays Bank, Sidcup.

In the run-up to his trial in the summer of 1988, Relton was set on pleading 'guilty' in the hope of receiving a reduced sentence. But as the fateful day approached his counsel advised him against this, pointing out that the police had offered him no assurances or deals in return for his cooperation. Persuaded by this logic, Relton changed his plea to one of 'not guilty'. With no other defence to fall back on, he told the court his statements had all either been manufactured by the police or obtained under duress. Relton seemed to have forgotten that the statements had all been written out longhand *in his own handwriting* and in the presence of his own solicitor – who had not only approved the handwritten statements, but countersigned them on behalf of his client as a true record, voluntarily obtained. As the prosecution was happy to point out, in these circumstances there could be no question of duress, 'verballing', or any other such invented nonsense. The jury agreed, and found Relton guilty as charged. Possibly reflecting official annoyance at Relton's last-minute change of plea and the extra cost and effort this had entailed, the judge sentenced him to twelve years. He described the shocked and distraught Relton as 'a rich parasite'.

Tried a few weeks later, Kathleen Meacock was luckier. Sticking to a 'not guilty' plea throughout, she got eighteen months suspended for handling the stolen gold. She would not, despite her own worst premonitions, be spending any time in HMP Holloway.

Brian Perry's ploy of hiding behind Parry and Relton paid off: his trial ended in a hung jury. But the circumstantial evidence against him was so strong that the court remanded him in custody pending a retrial.

29

Even with McCunn's help, it took the police and the CPS three years to unravel Perry's elaborate illegal financial web and construct prosecutions they believed would stand up to the rigours of a new Old Bailey trial. The Yard learned the hard way that Brink's-Mat defendants always hired the best lawyers in the land.

On 7 April 1989 Spanish police arrested Gordon Parry on the Costa del Sol. Extradition proceedings started at once. Alarmed by what was happening to so many members of the gang, on 15 May Jean Savage arrived with a male companion for a meeting at the Bank of Ireland in Dublin. She closed her own account and transferred the £4,110,026.62 balance into a new account opened there and then by her friend. The next day, this man transferred £1,060,026.62 into an account opened by a third new conspirator at the Abu Dhabi Commercial Bank. This new handler swore a deposition in front of a notary public that the money was not the proceeds of the Brink's-Mat robbery. This was a lie.

If the idea was to get a million or so safely out of reach of the UK authorities and keep it as a back-stop in case all the rest of the cash was seized, it was doomed to failure: on 12 October 1989 Flying Squad officers arrested Jean Savage, Patrick Clark and an unnamed third person. All three were charged with handling stolen goods – and the two new-established accounts instantly frozen.

Brian Perry's retrial started at the Central Criminal Court on 1 June 1992. As before, Perry tried to shift the blame for the creation and management of the Brink's-Mat money-laundering empire onto Relton and Parry, insisting that he had been nothing more than a kind of bemused bystander. The following statement, taken from the trial transcript, is typical: 'Parry told me he went there [to Switzerland] to open up the [Moyet] Foundation, which I didn't fully understand. He asked me to be a signatory on it just in the event of anything happening to him – it would all come into my possession.'

The prosecution counsel retorted: 'I suggest that is a total lie. Do you understand what I am suggesting?'

'I do understand what you are suggesting,' Perry countered, 'but you are wrong.'

The trial dragged on into the New Year of 1993. Perry began to complain of feeling unwell – the pressure of lying his head off day by day was proving a strain. He felt even worse when the prosecution landed a right hook by exposing his cold-hearted and faithless betrayal of Michael McAvoy. In a scathing attack on Perry's duplicitous behaviour, prosecuting counsel said, 'The reality, unknown to poor old McAvoy on the inside, is that the gold had been traded – had it not?'

Perry looked grim. 'No, it hadn't.'

'That's why McAvoy got so cross with you, and said there was "some low life", as he described it, on the outside. That was referring to you, was it not?'

Perry shook his head. 'No, it wasn't.'

Everyone in court could see different. Everyone could see that, despite Michael McAvoy's honourable silence when it came to Perry's role in the robbery, for Brian Perry there was no such thing as honour among thieves.

The outlook grew bleaker for Perry when John Elcombe (who had earlier been acquitted with his wife on the grounds of not knowing the money's source) confessed to having ferried large sums of money from the UK to Switzerland and Liechtenstein and delivering them to Parry and Relton. Not enough, of itself, to convict Perry of handling. But the prosecution revealed that Gordon Parry had once bought the Mercedes stopped by German border police and found to contain £710,000 in A24-prefix £50 notes, the proven proceeds of the Brink's-Mat robbery. Elcombe also admitted paying more than £1,000,000 into the Moyet Foundation, one of whose co-signatories was Brian Perry.

Try as he might to squeeze through it, the door of Perry's prison cell remained firmly locked.

Bank records proved that £175,000 of the £275,000 paid for Perry's Biggin Hill home had come from a £1,000,000 banker's draft Parry had personally instructed to be paid from the Moyet Foundation. The remaining £100,000 had been transferred out of the Lynn Relton Client Account (2), and paid to the solicitors conveyancing the sale.

Other little details counted against Perry, like the fact that he had viewed 45 Bird-in-Hand Lane with Jacqueline McAvoy, wife of the convicted Brink's-Mat gang leader – and a woman he admitted in open court to bedding. The final straw came when Jean Savage, confronted by the massive weight of evidence against her, admitted that between 27 March and 8 November 1984 she had made cash payments totalling £2,541,720 into the various accounts she controlled. She also admitted transferring £4,110,026 to her unnamed male companion at the Bank of Ireland in Dublin on 15 May and closing her account.

Savage could hardly deny having acted as a courier for the Brink's-Mat gang. Making one of her routine cash runs to the bank one day, the Bag Lady decided to make a detour via her daughter's home in Chislehurst, Kent. Strolling down the High Street after the visit, Savage, carrying £300,000 in a plastic shopping bag, managed to drop £12,500 on the pavement. As always, it was in brand-new, A24-series £50 notes. When she got to Croydon, Savage watched in increasing alarm and confusion as the bank clerk counted out £287,500 instead of the expected £300,000. Terrified the gang might think she had pocketed the missing cash and that reprisals might follow, Savage hurried back to Chislehurst.

If you have dropped a lot of money in the street, the first place to look for it is the local police station. Even today, there are still plenty of honest souls who will hand in any money they might find. Savage was certainly in luck: one upright citizen had done his duty, and the Chislehurst police had the missing £12,500 safely in store.

Savage asked if she might please have the cash back, as it was hers and she had lost it, whereupon an officer appeared at her elbow and clutched it in a steely grasp, while a second snapped handcuffs round her wrists. By this time, the police knew that *all* mint A24-series £50 banknotes had to be and were proceeds of the Brink's-Mat robbery. Anyone caught in possession of large quantities of these notes was by definition a Brink's-Mat laundry worker. Which was how Jean Savage ended up in the Gothic corridors of the Old Bailey. The mistake cost more than Savage dear: in an out-of-court settlement, her common-law husband, John 'Little Legs' Lloyd, later agreed to pay the loss adjusters a whopping £4.2 million.

The press had a field day with Savage during her trial. Nicknamed 'Lady Goldfinger' and 'Grandmother Savage', she was lampooned for her expensive designer clothing, waterfalls of gold jewellery and gold-painted finger- and toenails. A fighter, she remained defiant to the last.

Prosecution lawyers established that Brian Perry was a long-standing friend of Jean Savage's. (On the death of Perry's mother-in-law in October 1985, Savage had sent him a sympathy card.) They also showed that Perry had known Michael and Jacqueline McAvoy since the early 1970s, that Perry had had a sexual relationship with Jacqueline McAvoy following her husband's imprisonment, and that Savage, Lloyd, Robinson, Black, Kenneth and Mrs Noye were all close acquaintances or friends, as was shown not least by the fact that Lloyd and Savage lived in Noye's former home.

At the back of all the prosecutions was the rock-solid evidence of the A24-prefix £50 banknotes. There was also the fact that none of the defendants, with the possible exception of Gordon Parry, could account honestly for the huge sums of money they had had under their control, nor for the spectacular spending sprees they had indulged in during the months and years following the robbery. Worn down by the weight of evidence against him, Brian Perry finally admitted that he had personally paid £45,000 worth of new £50s into the Como account. He also owned up to authorizing the transfer of £60,407.16 from the Como account to a firm of London solicitors.

It was enough. At the conclusion of the trial, Brian Perry, Gordon Parry, Jean Savage and Patrick Clark were all convicted of conspiracy to handle stolen goods. Perry, who had already served the best part of two years in prison on remand, was sentenced to nine years in a Category A prison. Gordon Parry stood impassively as the judge gave him eleven years in the same accommodation for ten counts of the same crime.

Jean Savage got five years for handling stolen goods – but given that she would serve the bulk of her sentence in HMP Holloway, in terms of the hardship involved it was probably worth more.

30

The police were unimpressed by the fact that, despite his admission that he had used the smelter in his back garden to process bullion, John Palmer had been found 'not guilty' of handling the stolen gold. They had neither forgiven nor forgotten Palmer's failure to return from Tenerife for questioning; his unsuccessful attempt to flee to Brazil; and, despite the fact they did not of themselves prove he was guilty of handling the gold, the two warm bars of the yellow stuff found snuggling under his sofa cushions.

By now promoted Commander, Roy Ramm picked up Palmer's trail again in the summer of 1994.

'After Perry was sent away I got promoted, went to the West End division and dropped out of the [Brink's-Mat] chase for a while. I came back on it a year or so later as a member of SO1, the Serious and Organized Crimes Branch. [All of the Met's branch designations had by now been changed from 'C' to 'SO'.] That summer, *The Cook Report* [a popular investigative TV programme presented by Australian journalist Roger Cook] ran an exposé of a massive timeshare fraud run by John Palmer and his underlings on Tenerife. By chance, I knew Clive Entwistle, the producer. Clive told me they thought they could turn Palmer over live on national TV – both for the timeshare scam and for offering to launder money for a "drugs baron".'

The Cook Report had employed a man with the inventive code name 'Smith' – he was a former member of the US Drugs Enforcement Agency (DEA) – to investigate Palmer. One of the least noticeable and most unassuming characters you could ever expect to meet, 'Smith' looked quite unlike a law enforcement officer of any kind. But as a crook he was very convincing, spinning John Palmer a long yarn about a fictitious Burmese drugs baron named 'Kun-Sah'. According to Smith, Kun-Sah had made millions of dollars trafficking heroin in the Golden Triangle. Now he needed someone who could help him launder it. Naturally, the successful intermediary would be very well rewarded. Was Palmer interested? Palmer agreed to a meeting at the Ritz Hotel.

'Entwistle and his team set up concealed cameras. These recorded Palmer boasting to Kun-Sah – played by a professional actor – that he could "launder any amount you want – between $3m and $4m [£2.1–£2.8 million] straight away. And I can clean up $50m [£35 million] twice a year, provided you give me six weeks' notice."

'Palmer said he owned plenty of legitimate companies that could be used to mix the illegal money with clean cash. The fact that the dollars derived from the trade in heroin made no difference to him: he was happy to take in any amount of dirty washing as long as he got his cut. At the end of the programme, Roger Cook walked into the hotel room, introduced himself, and there was Palmer, caught bang to rights.

'After this programme we started to focus hard on Palmer for money laundering. But any evidence of his involvement in that was buried under the avalanche of information that suggested he was committing a huge timeshare fraud in the Canary Islands. Investigating further, we found that Palmer was employing more than 200 agents to prowl the streets of Tenerife and other resorts. They called it "working the deck". Young, attractive and extremely plausible individuals trained in high-pressure sales techniques, they accosted unsuspecting holidaymakers and set out to win their confidence through tactics like offering them a "free" scratchcard with a "guaranteed win"; free alcoholic drinks; and ladles of flattery. Once the victims – usually older, white middle-class couples – were hooked, they were asked: "Would you like to buy a timeshare?"'

As the industry was well established on Tenerife before Palmer got his hooks into it, most people replied, 'No thanks, I already own one.' It was exactly the reply Palmer's agents were hoping for. Glib, slick, and with the goad of a fat commission ensuring they never gave up, they sprang the fraud known in the confidence game as the 'buy/sell'.

'This went along the lines of, "OK, fine – if you've already bought one, what we'd really like to do is take your old timeshare off your hands. We'll buy it from you, sell it at a profit and allow you to use that money as a deposit on this brand-new, bigger and much better property we have here." Over a round or two of drinks, touts showed their victims lovely glossy pictures of a new complex on the island called "Island Village" – impressing on them how much grander and better value it was than their existing timeshare. Many were taken there on tours.

'Holidaymakers are by definition in a relaxed and happy mood: they tend to be much less cautious than they would be at home, and much more receptive to the kind of expert and extremely persistent sales pitch to which they were subjected by Palmer's goons. This could last several hours – in some cases it went on all day. Bewildered and worn down by the relentless patter, the more vulnerable and often elderly victims who gave in were escorted to the nearest bank machine to withdraw the "registration fee" or "deposit" they were told had to be paid before the deal could go forward. This was usually in the region of £100.

'Some people wanted to make sure this seemingly wonderful and foolproof offer was for real. No problem – they could visit the new complex in person: look around the apartments, admire the lovely swimming pool, the excellent on-site facilities and so on. Palmer had a couple of attractive timeshares ready for inspection. To clinch the deal, victims were given a "no-lose guarantee" in writing. The idea was, "trade up, enjoy your much better timeshare property and live happily ever after". What could possibly go wrong?

'Lured into what looked like the perfectly respectable offices of a legitimate business, potential victims with the strength of mind to hold out against the fraudsters thus far were subjected to further persuasion, often by older agents posing as "senior managers". A staged sale with selected touts posing as holidaymakers would be in full swing, and while the next batch of financial lambs awaited slaughter the fictitious "sale" reached a successful conclusion. Cue the popping of champagne corks, bell ringing and a "spur-of-the-moment" party everyone was encouraged to join.

'Few people made it past this stage without signing. Out would come the legal forms: "Sign here for the sale of your current timeshare, Property A, and sign here for the purchase of your new one, Property B."

'Of course, Palmer's companies – and they were numerous – made no attempt to honour the deal they had just pretended to strike. They never sold Property A on behalf of the benighted victim. They held on to it, so that they could sell it all over again as a timeshare to some other unsuspecting innocent. As for Property B, it did not exist.

'Between 1989 and 1997, more than 16,000 people fell for the "buy/sell" con. But, honest as they were, systematically confused as they were, most felt obliged to keep to their part of the bargain. They had signed contracts – and Palmer's minions were not slow to threaten legal action if victims tried to get out of what was in fact an entirely illegal agreement.

'Some holidaymakers – incredibly – were ensnared for a second time. Convinced by the hustlers that the first entrapment had all been a terrible mistake, for which the company in question was heartily sorry and now wished to make amends, they were persuaded to part with yet more money for a *third* fictional timeshare.

'A less common, but no less successful fraud employed by Palmer and his agents was the "rental trick". Holidaymakers new to the timeshare market were persuaded to buy a timeshare apartment, which one or other of Palmer's companies promised it would help them rent out. Sales agents assured buyers they could be certain of getting as much as £900 per week in rent, fifty-two weeks a year. With this supposedly steady and guaranteed income they would quickly recover the purchase price of the apartment and be into clean profit for life. There was only one snag: once they had bought the property, the company that had sold it to them made no effort whatsoever to help the owners find tenants.

'Customers who tried to complain or take legal action were confronted with a baffling web of front companies that passed their complaints around between one another and ran the holidaymakers' time, effort and money into the sand. Eventually, unable to derive any rental income, indebted, sick to the back teeth and thoroughly disheartened, many sold their properties back to the timeshare companies they had bought them from in the first place at a massive loss. The swindle cost the average victim several thousand pounds, with some unlucky enough to lose more than £15,000.

'The frauds brought violence, intimidation and an ugly, Wild West atmosphere to what had previously been a peaceful and idyllic chain of holiday islands. In battles to control the lucrative trade, rival gangs shot, beat and even blinded one another, trashed offices and set fire to cars. In one incident, a timeshare company manager who had already been injured in one of these attacks was assaulted for a second time in the clinic where he had been taken for treatment. One of the "security guards" employed to protect the deck agents from irate holidaymakers – and from their rivals – died in dubious circumstances on the end of a rope in a Tenerife jail cell.

'Infuriated by the steadily worsening violence, as well as by the negative effect on Tenerife's reputation, in 2000 Spanish authorities asked Judge Baltasar Garzon to investigate the alleged collusion between the fraudsters and unscrupulous elements of the island's police force, put a stop to the violence, and arrest, imprison and deport timeshare touts as necessary. Garzon had a ferocious reputation in Madrid, where he had done much to stamp out organized crime. Slowly, he started to clean things up.'

Launching 'Operation Beryk', Scotland Yard now began to investigate Palmer's business affairs in detail. Originally seconded to the case in April 1994, Detective Constable Gordon Walker and Detective Constable Herbie Fryer of the Met's Serious and Organized Crime Group would spend the next seven years amassing evidence of timeshare fraud against Palmer and his associates. Their inquiry, which spanned four continents and led them to a host of different countries, eventually turned out to be one of the biggest fraud investigations ever undertaken in the UK. Walker and Fryer discovered that Palmer controlled his timeshare empire through a complex web of companies registered in Madeira and the Isle of Man. They also identified a company called Island Financial Services Ltd, based in Brentwood, Essex, the timeshare fraud's main financial hub.

The case against Palmer and five senior executives of his timeshare companies came to trial at the Old Bailey in 1999. After a hearing lasting eight months – and at huge public expense – managers

Malcolm Wallace, Simon Stephens, Michael Harbison, Martin Addington Smith and Alexander Thompson were convicted of conspiracy to defraud and jailed for terms of between fourteen and eighteen months apiece. But Palmer's counsel argued successfully that the adverse publicity linking his client to a separate and coincidental murder trial had prejudiced his chances of a fair hearing. The judge agreed and ordered a retrial. As he left the courtroom, a delighted John Palmer blew the newly redundant jury an extravagant kiss.

DCs Walker and Fryer, who had spent years working on the case, were, to use the vernacular, gutted. 'We were due to begin the closing speeches of an eight-month trial,' Fryer said. 'It was soul-destroying – I had spent *four weeks* giving evidence.'

Yet again, one of the big fish had slipped free. But the show wasn't over till the timeshare victim sang: Walker and Fryer went back to their task, compiling still more evidence against Palmer. By the time they had finished work, it filled five cells and three detention rooms at a London police station.

Palmer was brought back to the Old Bailey for retrial in October 2000. With what was described by press observers at the time as 'overweening confidence', Palmer decided to defend himself. Quite why, when he could afford the best defence lawyers in the world – and when one of them had recently got him off the hook on a technicality – was something only he could explain.

Whatever his reasoning, it was a mistake. Palmer began his defence reasonably well by telling the court, 'I have been portrayed as a gangster. I am not a gangster nor ever have been a gangster.' But he then tried to convince jurors that he was the subject of a long-running vendetta on the part of the Metropolitan Police. The Met, he claimed, was determined to 'get' him after he had been cleared of handling the Brink's-Mat gold. 'They have done anything to try and get me, and have spent millions and millions of pounds – public money – to get me. I am not guilty, nor is Miss Ketley [his associate and co-accused] and nor is [his nephew] Andrew Palmer.' He went on, 'I created the largest timeshare company in Europe – and, I think, the best. I am proud of what I achieved. I have enough money and do not need to make more defrauding people.'

David Farrer QC, for the prosecution, countered that Palmer was the architect and boss of a huge timeshare fraud even then being perpetrated by his agents in no fewer than thirteen Canary Islands resorts. He said the buy/sell con was the main plank of this fraud, characterizing it as 'a slick, well-orchestrated and thoroughly dishonest sales operation'. Farrer also described the rental trick. 'It involved high pressure, glib, untruthful salesmen who had been trained to latch on to the unwary – or even the wary. Customers were faced with a confusing network of companies which purported to be independent of one another but which were in fact all under the one umbrella. In return for their cash, customers were given deliberately over-complicated and misleading documentation.'

Farrer now called witnesses. 'Victims,' he said in a telling address, 'who were of quite ordinary means . . . Some were pensioners who like that sort of climate for their health. This was not an exotic fraud of finance houses or banks, but of people like any sitting in this court. It could be you, or the person sitting next to you.'

Pensioner Constance Bartram told the jury how she had been cheated out of £17,000. When she went to the timeshare company offices to try and get her money back she had been variously ignored, patronized, bullied and belittled. When she burst into tears, the timeshare touts had ordered security guards to remove her from the premises.

The next witnesses were the Mumbys, a married couple from Pudsey, West Yorkshire. Bernard Mumby told the jury he and his wife had been holidaying in Tenerife in 1993. One of Palmer's touts came up and handed them a scratchcard, which he said had just won them a big prize. The 'big prize' turned out to be a tour of a timeshare complex called Club La Paz. The tout insisted the Mumbys go and see it, ignoring their repeated protestations that they already owned a timeshare apartment in the north of the island. At the end of a long, hard and very tiring day, the salesman convinced the Mumbys that one of the 'resales experts' who worked with him could sell their existing timeshare on for £5,000 – realizing a £1,500 profit on the £3,500 they had originally paid for it. The whole deal, he assured them, was 'guaranteed failsafe' and their rights were legally protected. If by some amazing chance their first timeshare did not sell, then the agreed sum of £5,000 would be returned to them immediately and without question.

Needless to say, the touts banked the £5,000 for the second timeshare, grabbed the Mumbys' original apartment and sold it on. Agents ignored the couple's increasingly desperate pleas for information, and increasingly insistent demands for their money back. They were left paying for two timeshares – neither of which they now owned or could visit – for the same two weeks in August. Frustrated, angry and worried to death, they returned to Tenerife in September 1995, where they found the same rogue timeshare company still operating out of the same office with many of the same staff – including the salesman who had fleeced them in the first place. An argument ensued, at the end of which Mr Mumby shouted, 'Everything you told us was lies.' Shrugging his shoulders, the tout replied, 'Well, that is just good salesmanship.'

To pay for the second timeshare the Mumbys had taken out a £5,000 bank loan and spent five lean years trying to repay it. DC Fryer drove home the heartless nature of the crime. 'All the victims were induced to buy on the spot in Tenerife. Their vulnerability was exploited by misleading sales talk, alcohol and other tricks.'

Ruffled by the visible effect all this was having on the jury, Palmer tried another tack. He claimed his business had grown so large it had simply run away from him. How could he possibly be expected to know about or be blamed for anything bad done in his name when the business had grown so unwieldy? When this line of argument looked as if it, too, might fail, Palmer tried to incriminate his business partners, especially Brendan Hannon. Palmer said he had poached Hannon from a rival company and made him group sales director. According to Palmer, Hannon had brought his own 'dream team' with him when he jumped ship: these 'rogue' sales reps had committed all this fraud behind his, Palmer's, back and without his knowledge.

Hannon had fled Tenerife in 1996, following a disagreement with other members of the organization. It was an everyday sort of affair: a flurry of death threats, followed by the firebombing of Hannon's luxury villa. Arrested in Morocco two years later, Hannon was extradited to the UK, where he pleaded guilty to fraud and got four years in jail.

In a short, sharp reply, Farrer dismissed Palmer's attempts to shift the blame: 'He [Palmer] was at the pinnacle of the organization and knew perfectly well what was going on.'

Palmer's next line of defence was to say that he had been too busy learning to fly his personal Learjet and his helicopters to notice what was happening. The millionaire lifestyle was no idle boast: in the 2001 *Sunday Times* rich list he figured in 105th place, with an estimated fortune of £300 million – next to Queen Elizabeth II. Along with the Learjet and helicopters, he owned several large houses in various countries; a £6 million seagoing yacht, *Brave Goose of Essex*; a collection of classic cars and several expensive modern sports cars. Not bad for a dyslexic boy from the back streets of Solihull who had left school at fifteen to sell paraffin door-to-door. One of seven children, Palmer had gone on to deal in scrap metal, second-hand cars, jewellery and finally gold. Here he was in court at the age of fifty-one, a multi-millionaire once again fighting to stay out of jail.

It was beginning to look as if it might be third time unlucky for Palmer. His old adversary, Roy Ramm, now took the stand. Ramm told the jury how Palmer had been videotaped in the Ritz Hotel, London, offering to launder drugs money on behalf of a man he had apparently accepted was a drugs baron. Ramm said, 'Our view is that you were a serious organized criminal trapped by his own words into admitting laundering money.'

Palmer retorted that Scotland Yard and *The Cook Report* had concocted a huge conspiracy whose sole purpose had been falsely to incriminate him, and that Ramm's main concern in driving the investigation had been 'lining his own pockets'.

At seven and a half months, it was one of the longest fraud trials in British legal history. It was also – at a cost of more than £10 million – one of the most expensive. It took the jury twenty-one days to find John Palmer guilty.

In his plea for mitigation on 23 May 2001, Palmer told Judge Gerald Gordon, 'I acknowledge I have a strong, dominant personality, probably from my background. I have always relied on my wits for the benefit of those nearest and dearest to me.' Sentencing him to eight years in jail, Gordon commented, 'This was clearly a fraud on a substantial scale.' Gordon ordered Palmer to pay £266,000 towards the costs of the trial – less than 3 per cent of the total.

The Crown immediately announced its intention to seize John Palmer's disposable assets. In April 2002, the High Court in London duly imposed a £33,243,812 confiscation order on Palmer. To the estimated 17,000 people who had been defrauded by him, this came as very welcome news, especially as some £2 million was earmarked to compensate timeshare victims. But their pleasure was to be short-lived. In one of those strange twists the legal system sometimes delivers, in 2003 the Court of Appeal overturned the confiscation order. There had, the judges asserted, been 'crucial procedural flaws' in the case.

A further Appeal Court judgement delivered by the Lord Chief Justice, Lord Woolf, ruled that the judgement overturning the compensation order had itself been wrong in law. Woolf said, 'The court considers the law was misunderstood and misapplied in Palmer.'

Despite desperate legal arguments put forward by the Crown, the upshot in simple terms was that, despite having been found guilty of conspiracy to defraud 17,000 people of an estimated £30 million, John Palmer was allowed to keep the £33 million he had originally been ordered to pay to the Treasury.

Listening to all this, serving police officer and director of the Victims of Crime Trust Norman Brennan struggled to believe the evidence of his own ears. 'A lot of vulnerable people who worked hard all their lives lost their life savings,' he said. 'At the end of the day his sentence, eight years, was not that long anyway. Now Palmer is sticking two fingers up to all of us and the courts are allowing him to do it.' There was a public and press outcry. Finally, the Home Office announced that 'attempts would be made to reclaim the money by invoking new laws recently passed by Home Secretary David Blunkett'. Whether anything comes of this official bravado remains to be seen.

More than 200 victims of the timeshare fraud have since banded together and are suing John Palmer in the civil courts for compensation. Speaking to the BBC in 2003, one solicitor said, 'Perhaps perversely, the court ruling improves the chances of claimants getting compensation from the civil courts – because there are now more of Palmer's assets available.' Dismissing John Palmer's appeal against sentence in November 2002, Judge Finlay Baker told him, 'Those who enter into complex international conspiracies should not expect sympathy when the process of being called to account turns out to be burdensome.'

31

While all this was going on, Anthony White, the man who had been found 'not guilty' of involvement in the Brink's–Mat raid, was doing nicely for himself. At the time of the robbery he and his wife Margaret were renting a council house at 45 Redlaw Way, Rotherhithe, London SE16. White was unemployed and had been on social security benefit for more than six months. His wife had also been out of work. Despite their apparent poverty, in January 1985 the couple paid £33,000 cash for 192 Brockley Road, London SE4, converted it into flats and sold it on three months later at a handsome profit. In May that same year Anthony White bought 'Monalee', a house in Beckenham Palace Road, Beckenham, Kent, for £146,000, paying £134,000 in cash and raising a short-term mortgage on the rest. He repaid the mortgage with a quick-turnaround resale, moving onwards and upwards into the burgeoning mid-1980s property market by acquiring 195 Sandhurst Road, London SE6. He paid £134,000 of the asking price with an Allied Irish Investment Bank draft and the balance in cash.

Between 1984 and 1986 large sums of money began to appear in accounts held both singly and jointly in the names of Anthony and Margaret White at Allied Irish Investment Bank (AIIB) branches in Lewisham, South London, and Dublin, Ireland. These grew until they amounted to more than £1,000,000. In November 1986 that year the couple moved to Spain, where they bought Urbanización Marberia, 14 Plot C, Lower Semat.

Living in Spain did not stop White's speculations on the home front: he bought 394 Baring Road, Lee, SE12 for £87,000, and another property at 200 Jamaica Road, Rotherhithe, London SE16, for an undisclosed sum. In March 1989 he bought 2 Sambrook Mews,

Inchmery Road, Catford, SE6, for £129,000. Transferring this property into his wife's name, he and his family moved into it. The Whites acquired 'Mixtures', a shoe shop at 7 Catford Bridge Road, SE6, again for an undisclosed sum. They took out a £25,000 lease on a wine bar at Rushey Green, Catford, which they renovated at a cost of £100,000 and renamed the Blancos Tapas Bar. Arrested in Spain on 19 October 1989 for currency violations, White was found in possession of jewellery to a value of £108,000 as well as £100,000 in cash. Spanish police impounded the lot, 'pending claims to ownership'.

What White did not know – but was about to find out – was that McCunn and the legal team at the insurance loss adjusters were now hot on his trail. The 1994 joint civil action on behalf of 'Brinks', as the Brink's-Mat company had renamed itself, demanded 'Delivery up of such of the gold, or proceeds of sale thereof or property purchased with such proceeds as they [the defendants] have received and/or dealt with together with any profit they have made by the use of the same . . .'

As we've already seen, each of the named individuals became liable for the full £27 million, plus legal and other costs, plus interest.

The list included Anthony Michael White and Margaret Sheila White.

When it came to the balance of probability, McCunn and his team pointed out that the Whites could only have obtained the huge sums of money they had demonstrably handled and used to buy property by illegal means. Arrested after six months on the dole, White had spent the year December 1983 to December 1984 on remand in prison, where he could hardly have earned the small fortune he had since been splashing out on property.

Other tiny details tended to catch the defendants out – in White's case, the fact that in the course of his tape-recorded 1986 South Bank meeting with DCI Ramm and Commander Worth – and in the company of Brian Perry – he had admitted some knowledge of the stolen gold.

McCunn won the civil action on behalf of Brinks Ltd, which meant that almost everyone named in the writ had to pay up. With a £27 million financial sword of Damocles hanging over their heads, many of the defendants wisely opted for an out-of-court settlement. Kenneth and Brenda Noye agreed to repay £3 million. In return, they were allowed to sell Hollywood Cottage for £1 million – making a profit of some £500,000 in the process – and buy a new £300,000 house in Sevenoaks close to the town's police station. This arrangement was not quite as indulgent as it sounds: like many of the Brink's-Mat gang, Noye was a good businessman who had made a lot of money legitimately in the years before the robbery.

Faced with the prospect of having all their worldly goods seized, and hoping it would help them hang on to the odd million or so, Chappell and Patch declared themselves bankrupt. Their hopes of financial escape were dashed when the loss adjusters simply used the courts to pursue the trustees in bankruptcy for the money. In a last-ditch effort to hang on to what they had, one or two other people on the list, like Anthony White, did go to law. White lost his case. High Court judge Mr Justice Rimmer ordered him to pay the loss adjusters £2,188,600. Margaret White had to repay £1,084,344. White, who also incurred massive legal costs, blamed Noye for this expensive reverse, convinced that Noye had been far too willing to agree a deal, and in the process set what was for the Whites a very inconvenient legal precedent.

When it came to the companies and corporations named in the civil action, the most spectacular example was Barclays Bank. The loss adjusters sued Barclays for '£14,234,893.91, alternatively £10,315,500, alternatively damages and/or equitable compensation, further or alternatively a declaration that Barclays is bound to restore the said sum to the account in the name of Scadlynn at the Bedminster Branch . . .'

The loss adjusters' lawyers contended that Barclays Bank had failed in its duty to question the activities of Scadlynn and its officers, especially the behaviour of Garth Chappell, aka 'Charles Cooper', as huge sums of money poured into – and out of – the Scadlynn account.

A series of internal Barclays Bank memos showed that while managers had raised the odd eyebrow at the gigantic cash sums the Bedminster branch had paid out, they had taken no effective action. A letter dated 9 July 1984 stated:

We have seen evidence that Mr Cooper's bookkeeper has been less than honest . . . following which we have spoken to Mr Cooper [i.e. Garth Chappell] about the whole matter. If we are to believe him he is making very substantial profits at this time from the company [Scadlynn] and indeed has diverted funds to purchase properties valued at £152,000. Our immediate thought is that there is a tax problem and we are by no means convinced that Mr Cooper is being entirely frank with the Authorities.

A second diary note on 6 July 1984 included the statement:

I have discussed the whole situation with Mr Drewett [then Barclays, Bedminster, branch manager] and Mr Macdonald and Mr Drewett have ruled that in future all cheques drawn by Mr Cooper on behalf of Scadlynn Limited requiring encashment will require Mr Cooper's presence at our counter.

The proposed requirement was never enforced. The sports bags, bin liners and boxes kept coming across the counter, and bank staff kept right on filling them.

The civil writ went on: 'Brinks will contend . . . that by no later than 9th July 1984 Barclays had grounds to suspect, and in fact did suspect, that Scadlynn was owned or controlled by dishonest people and/or was being used as a vehicle for dishonest and unlawful activities.'

It did not help Barclays' case that yet another internal memo dated Christmas Eve 1984 revealed that the police had just paid a visit to the Bedminster branch: '. . . police officers from the Fraud Squad visited Mr Drewett on 21st December 1984, saying that they were investigating Scadlynn's activities and that they believed that Cooper was an alias of Chappell.'

Did Barclays Bank settle with the loss adjusters? No one will say. But if it did, then the sum paid by way of settlement must have been pretty big.

32

Right about now the prison service was releasing Kenneth Noye. He had served only eight years of his fourteen-year sentence for handling the gold. 'Rave culture' had come into fashion during his time away, fuelled by the drug known as 'ecstasy', or 'e'.

Before going to prison, Noye had steered clear of the drugs trade. But as his release date drew near and his status changed from Category A to low-risk, he was transferred from Swaleside jail in Kent to Latchmere House, a resettlement centre in Surrey. Nothing puts years on a man faster than prison time, and although he was still in prime physical shape because of the gruelling, self-imposed fitness regime he followed daily, Noye's hair was turning grey and some of the brilliance had begun to fade from the piercing blue eyes.

Granted day release in 1994 in order to help him in the process of social rehabilitation, Noye began working for a skip-hire firm based in Dartford, Kent. The company was run by one of Noye's friends. The idea was to help him find a job, get back on his feet and go straight. Giving every appearance of playing ball, Noye left promptly for work every day in a borrowed BMW. There is some doubt as to whether he was actually helping the owner hire out skips.

Noye returned to family life in Sevenoaks. He did not, however, find a steady nine-to-five job and settle down. In 1996, several men were convicted of conspiracy to steal £800 million from high-street cash machines using counterfeit bank debit cards. Strongly suspected of involvement in the conspiracy, Noye escaped arrest and possible imprisonment because of insufficient evidence. But detectives believed that an elaborate, expensive and time-consuming attempt to make money had come unstuck for him. Frustrating, annoying, and unlikely to improve his mood – but no excuse for what happened next.

33

At around 1.15 p.m. on Sunday, 19 May 1996, Kenneth Noye was driving down a slip road onto the very same A20/M25 Swanley interchange south of London where C11 had lost track of the Collector, his Rolls-Royce and the Alcosa gold smelter back in the winter of 1983. As he took the slip road, Noye decided he had been cut up by a nineteen-year-old blonde driving a red Bedford Rascal van. Her name was Danielle Cable. Sitting next to Cable in the passenger seat was her fiancé, Stephen Cameron, a 21-year-old electrician.

Noye overtook the van at high speed and cut in front of it, forcing Cable to brake sharply. Cameron may – or may not – have made a hand gesture signifying his annoyance at the other driver's behaviour. By now, both vehicles were approaching the traffic lights at the bottom of the slip road. These turned red, forcing both Cable in the Rascal van and Noye in the Land-Rover Discovery to stop. Noye leapt out of the vehicle. Cameron also got out. The slip road was busy, with a steady stream of Sunday afternoon traffic passing the terrifying scene that now took place.

According to Cable, Noye strode straight up to Cameron and punched him hard in the eye. Cameron staggered back, at the same time kicking out with his feet to defend himself. There was a short scuffle, in which it looked as if Cameron, who was tall and strongly built, might be gaining the upper hand. Cable said Noye then turned and ran back to the Discovery, reached down into the driver's door pocket and pulled something out of it. He ran back up to Cameron and lunged at him twice. Cameron half turned under the force of the blows. Cable could only watch as the fight now came to a terrible end. 'I saw Steve clutching his chest. He said, "He stabbed me Dan, take his number plate." I saw blood on his chest. It was dreadful. I was screaming and crying for someone to help me. Then Stephen collapsed on the floor.'

Stabbed through the liver and heart, Stephen Cameron died in his fiancée's arms – right there by the roadside. His opponent downed, Noye hopped back in his car and drove away at high speed.

Dozens of people had seen snatches of the killing as they drove past the scene. Many dialled 999 – including a lorry driver who had been behind both vehicles when the fight started. He watched as the two men struggled, sounding his air horn in an effort to shock them out of it. When that failed, he overtook the Land-Rover and stopped again. Watching in his rear-view mirror, the truck driver saw the older man's arm move twice like a piston, and the younger man slump down in front of the red van. He had seen much of what happened. But in common with everyone except Danielle Cable, he had not witnessed the whole vicious scene from start to finish.

Many witnesses gave more or less accurate descriptions of the man who had been driving the Land-Rover. Several gave versions of its licence plate. Not one person got the combination of numbers and letters exactly right, but witnesses did agree that the vehicle was 'L' registration and had been dark in colour, and almost all agreed it was black.

News of Britain's first 'road rage' murder hit the airwaves.

Fleeing the scene at top speed, Noye was in a panic. He called his wife Brenda, his sons, and his old friend John Palmer. From the sharp tone of the caller's voice, Palmer knew something was very wrong. 'What is it?' he asked. 'Are you in trouble?'

'Nah,' said Noye. 'Nothing serious.'

'What?'

'I need to lie low for a while. You know.'

Palmer did not need it spelled out – Noye needed to skip the country there and then. Palmer gave him swift instructions, including the telephone number of the aviation company that garaged and serviced his personal helicopters. Noye shoved a few clothes and a pile of cash into a suitcase, donned a flat cap as a form of rudimentary disguise, bid a hasty goodbye to Brenda Noye and drove straight to Palmer's mansion near Bath.

The next day, Palmer flew Noye by helicopter to a golf course he owned near Caen, Normandy. The two men caught the evening train to Paris. The day after that, Palmer's Learjet took them to Le Bourget airport, on to Madrid, and from there to Tenerife in the Canary Islands. Noye spent a day or two lying low at one of Palmer's villas outside Lanzarote – there was no shortage of empty timeshares to choose from – and then started running again.

And well he might. Back in the UK, a massive police manhunt was on for the owner of the black Land-Rover Discovery driven by Stephen Cameron's killer. Detectives investigating the incident at once began a painstaking trawl through the details of no fewer than 17,000 privately owned vehicles of the type. It took weeks before they found one registered in the name of a man named 'Anthony Francis', but when they did, they had a real stroke of luck. DI Brightwell, the detective who had launched the Brink's-Mat investigation all those years ago, happened to be looking at the list of names. He recognized the name Anthony Francis – it was a favourite alias of Kenneth James Noye.

The full focus of the murder investigation now switched to Noye. Led by Detective Superintendent Nick Biddiss, Kent police discovered that on the day after Stephen Cameron's murder, a convoy of vehicles had been seen going into the skip-hire firm for which Noye had ostensibly worked on day release from prison. A witness said she had seen a black 'L'-reg Land-Rover Discovery identical to the one owned by Noye in the middle of the convoy. She stood and watched as the yard gates closed on the procession, then heard the sound of heavy machinery starting up in the yard. If true, it was a damning account – but was it?

There was more evidence to back it up: that same day a man using the alias John Grittens had turned up at a car showroom in Finchley, North London. 'Mr Grittens' took £12,000 in cash from a plastic carrier bag and used it to buy a black 'L'-reg Discovery identical to the one Noye had been driving at the time of the killing. He then drove this vehicle to Noye's home and left it outside his front door.

Mobile phone records showed that Noye had been near the Swanley roundabout in the immediate aftermath of the killing.

Kent police now knew that their prime suspect was Noye. But the last thing Superintendent Biddiss wanted was for Noye to find out they were on to him. It would just make him harder to catch. Biddiss told his team to keep a tight lid on everything they knew. He might as well have saved his breath: almost immediately, someone in the know sold the information that Noye was wanted for the murder of Stephen Cameron to a tabloid newspaper. Although it was obvious that doing so would jeopardize the chances of catching him, the newspaper went ahead and named Noye.

The hue and cry now began in earnest. With Interpol, Kent Constabulary, Scotland Yard and the British press corps all hot on his tail, Noye's immediate priority was to keep moving. He spent the last two weeks of May and most of June staying in the Turkish enclave of Northern Cyprus. He may have spent some of his time there at the Jasmine Court Hotel, the sometime base of another fugitive from British justice, Asil Nadir. (A Cypriot-born businessman, Nadir is still wanted by the Metropolitan Police. Head of Polly Peck, a fruit-to-electronics conglomerate with 24,000 shareholders that collapsed in dubious financial circumstances in 1990, Nadir absconded to Northern Cyprus before his scheduled Old Bailey trial on charges of theft and fraud. Police believe he is still hiding out somewhere in the island's Turkish sector.)

Noye quit Cyprus just as the British authorities were about to contact their Turkish counterparts with a view to having him arrested and extradited. Kent police now lost track of him – but speculation raged unabated in the British press. One tabloid claimed that he had skipped to Brazil following plastic surgery; another had him running a timeshare fraud in Northern Cyprus; while in a third leap of the imagination, Noye was busy masterminding a drug-smuggling ring in Russia. This last guess, it turned out, was nearest the truth. Detectives discovered that Noye had travelled to Tangier and Jamaica on a false passport and tried – unsuccessfully – to set up drug deals in both places. He had then flown to Aruba in the Dutch Antilles, where he was suspected of opening bank accounts in a false name.

In Aruba, the trail went cold. And despite the 'Public Enemy Number One' label now attached to Noye, it stayed cold. A dedicated unit of the Kent police, with help from civilian specialists and members of other police forces, kept on his trail, as did an equally dedicated section of the British press, but at the end of 1996 he had quite simply vanished. Throughout 1997 and for the first six months of 1998, no one could find any trace of 'Britain's most wanted'. It looked as if he had found himself a permanent place in which to lie low. The question for Biddiss was 'where?' It was hardly worthwhile looking for him on the Costa del Sol. Far too many 'faces' on the crime coast would recognize Noye and be ready – perhaps even willing – to give him up to the police. There were also too many sharp-eyed, tabloid-reading British holidaymakers in the area, armed with mobile telephones for his safety.

While they kept up the hunt for Noye abroad, Biddiss and his team were obliged to check a string of reported sightings in the UK: now for the wedding of a friend's daughter, now for the funeral of an old mate. Looking back wryly on this period, Biddiss remarked, 'We actually went to more weddings and funerals than Hugh Grant – and that's with all the repeats as well.' But despite extending the search to no fewer than ten countries, no one could find hide nor hair of the wanted man.

34

The western side of the peninsula that forms Spain's southernmost tip could hardly be more different from the brash, bacon-sandwich Costa del Sol that lies to the east. As yet largely unspoilt and sparsely populated, the Costa de la Luz, stretching from Gibraltar up to Cadiz, has a contained and secret beauty all its own. Perhaps the strong and persistent Atlantic wind keeps them at bay, but few outsiders discover its spectacular coastline. The windsurfers, whipping their brightly coloured craft across the bays, keep the secret to themselves.

After renting a succession of secluded properties in this area, Noye found what he was looking for: an unobtrusive two-storey villa set on a promontory 2 kilometres south of Zahara de los Atunes, a remote coastal village some 50 km south of Cadiz. The spectacular cliff-top view the property enjoyed included the adjoining section of coastal road, which dwindled to a dead end some little way beyond the house. Isolated, rugged, and unequivocally Spanish, it was the kind of backwater where the average British policeman would stand out like the proverbial sore thumb. Nelson had known these seas; Noye was hoping everyone would suffer from a bad case of the blind eye.

Not far from the small, friendly seaside town of Barbate, with its smattering of family-run bars and restaurants, the house overlooked the tiny beachside hamlet of Atlanterra. The villa came with a swimming pool, a taciturn handyman-gardener who lived just across the road – and good stout shutters and doors. It was also handy for Morocco and points south in case Noye ever needed to make another run for it.

The villa had been owned by a wealthy German businessman, Hans Bartom, who had bought it as a refuge from the Hamburg rat-race. But after a couple of years in the sun, Bartom decided he preferred the bracing, bustling streets of his home town to the leisurely, picturesque surrounds of the cliff-top at Atlanterra. He would sell the place and take his Mercedes convertible back where it came from. As luck would have it, at the very moment he was looking to move, a jaunty, square-set Britisher calling himself Michael Mayne, or alternatively Mickey the Builder, turned up ready and eager to buy.

'Mickey' explained that he was looking to take it easy, having made a bit of a killing in the British property market. Would Hans accept an offer of 50 million pesetas for the villa? In cash, of course, and as between friends? Hans was willing. Noye paid the £200,000 in used £20 notes and promptly moved in.

After a cautious start, Mickey the Builder was soon in thick with a select handful of the expats who lived in the local area, and had discovered El Campero, an excellent fish restaurant in Barbate that rapidly became a favourite port of call. He did not have to suffer the indignity of eating there alone: after a few weeks, Mina Altiabato, his dark, attractive – we must not call her sultry – mistress came to join him. A Spanish citizen of Franco-Lebanese or possibly Brazilian extraction – the details are slippery – it was rumoured that Altiabato had a flat in Madrid provided by her wealthy British benefactor. The couple liked to dine out in the evening on El Campero's cosy terrace, romantically cocooned amidst its covering of trailing vines.

By day, the new arrival favoured Las Dunas, a thatched, open-air beach bar a short walk down the cliff from his Atlanterra home. The days went by, the living was lush, and a man could watch the windsurfers tack and skim from the safety and comfort of a long, cold Estrella beer. What clouds might trouble such a peaceful existence?

An entire weather front. Some people said it stemmed from Brenda Noye, who had decided to visit her husband and been followed to his lair by the Kent police. Others told how a British holidaymaker had recognized Noye from a newspaper photograph and contacted the authorities. Then again, local expatriate tongues had certainly been wagging: the juiciest rumour of all had it that this 'Mickey the Builder' might not be all he was cracked up to be. He might – and wouldn't that spice up the dull round of expat days – be a *wanted criminal* in hiding.

The most likely explanation is that Noye was betrayed by a criminal informant. According to this version of events, the grass told

Kent police he knew a Kent-based criminal associate of Noye's who was in regular telephone contact with the fugitive. Ever since his disappearance, the police had been bugging anyone and everyone associated with Noye in an effort to pick up his trail – without the faintest whisper of success. But this new informant seemed serious, not least in demanding a £100,000 reward for revealing the name of Noye's supposed contact.

If that is what actually happened – and Biddiss, who wants to write a book on the hunt for Noye, will not say – then police took the new information very seriously. We don't know if they actually paid out the £100,000 reward, but reportedly with the help of GCHQ, the huge British government listening station just outside Cheltenham, they set about monitoring the mobile and home telephone calls of Noye's associate. Four weeks later – and just as they were about to give up the costly job of round-the-clock eavesdropping – Noye identified himself by name in a call placed to the target number. Canny as ever, he was using a pay-as-you-go mobile, which at the time made it impossible to pin down his location – even by country.

But the police now had a second stroke of luck: Noye asked his contact to send some documents he needed to a post box in Zahara de los Atunes. The worldwide hunt for Noye had suddenly narrowed down to a tiny corner of south-west Spain – in the process turning from dull grey to white hot. In July 1998, Biddiss took the biggest gamble of his professional career. Without informing the Spanish authorities that they were in the country – and without any back-up in case of trouble – he sent two trusted detectives down to see if they could locate and identify Noye. Sworn to absolute secrecy, the officers were not even allowed to tell immediate family members where they were going.

Biddiss had good reason for taking such a monumental chance. Where Noye was concerned, someone always took the press shilling. The fewer people who knew where he might be hiding, the better. And there was always the possibility it would turn out to be another false lead.

Throughout his detectives' venture to southern Spain, Biddiss was on tenterhooks. His real fear was for his officers' safety if Noye spotted them. No one could forget what the fugitive had done to John Fordham.

In the event, Biddiss need not have lost so much sleep. Three days later, one of his detectives called him on his home number. 'We've just seen him, guv. It's him.'

There was no mistake: they had found Noye. For Biddiss, it was the Eureka moment. He was on the phone in a flash: with Noye's identification confirmed, he could now go to the Spanish authorities and ask for an arrest warrant. The Spanish immediately agreed to issue a warrant – on condition that their own men took part in the arrest.

British and Spanish police now mounted a massive covert surveillance operation. At the same time, they began to formulate a series of arrest plans, or 'actions on'. The obvious and urgent priority was to watch Noye round-the-clock and make absolutely sure he did not go to ground again. In the meantime, Kent police asked Danielle Cable – still the most important eyewitness to the murder – if she would be prepared to make a positive, first-hand identification of the man she had watched kill her fiancé. Only if she did this officially, and to the satisfaction of the Spanish courts, would the British authorities be able to extradite Noye.

Cable had seen at first hand what Noye could do. Already, it was rumoured, there was a £300,000 contract on her head. Some rumours put the reward for her murder as high as £1 million. There was every chance that the bounty on her life would remain in force, perhaps indefinitely. But Cable refused to be intimidated. To the delight and relief of the police, and despite the enormous personal risk, she agreed to make the trip.

The moment she agreed to try and identify Noye, Cable's life changed for all time. Giving her no more than a few minutes to pack her belongings, armed police drove her to a safe house. From this moment on, Cable would have to live out her days in the bleak and soulless desert of the witness protection programme. She would never go home again.

Over the next few days and weeks, Cable changed her identity, her appearance, her habits, the way she dressed, her hobbies, her reading matter, and just about everything else. Allowed very little contact with her immediate family, and none with her former friends, even her authorized telephone calls were kept to the barest minimum. Her letters were screened and took a week to reach her. Danielle Cable was under no illusions. Given who Noye was and what he had done, she would always have to live with a corner of fear.

In total secrecy, a small party of police officers escorted Cable – told at the start that she was headed for northern England – to south-west Spain. For a few days, the party kept a low profile, acclimatizing, eating in secluded restaurants, waiting for the moment when the surveillance team tracked Noye to a location where the identification could take place as safely as possible. This was a tall order: detectives had to get Cable close enough to Noye to give her the best possible chance of recognizing him, but not so close as to put her at risk. This – roughly speaking – is what happened next.

On the evening of Thursday, 27 August 1998, two Kent detectives and a Spanish colleague watching Noye's villa saw him leave the house and get into his car. They followed his Belgian-plated blue Shogun along the coast road, out through Barbate and on to the apartment Mina Altiabato rented on the beachfront in the village of Los Canos de Meca. Noye's mistress, who had obviously been waiting for him, emerged as he pulled up. She was dolled up ready for an evening out. The police followed the couple out through the pinewoods bordering the coast. They were heading towards Cadiz. It was plain they were going out for dinner. The only question now was, where?

The answer was not long in coming. At 2300, Noye pulled up and parked outside El Forno, a well-known restaurant in the nearby town of La Muela. Noye ordered a bottle of rioja. He looked happy and relaxed. He also looked hungry. There was every reason to believe he would stay in the restaurant for at least the next hour. Immersed in conversation with his companion, he did not look like a man who was suspecting trouble. Cable was with her escort in one of the nearby unmarked police vehicles. It was now or never.

Flanked by detectives, Cable got out of the unmarked car. Dredging up her courage, she propelled herself towards the restaurant. Blonde, attractive and slender, Cable had a tendency to turn heads. For this reason she was escorted in through El Forno's back door. One of her armed bodyguards scouted ahead to see if Noye was still in place – and still focused on Mina Altiabato. He was.

It was the moment of truth. If Cable failed to identify Noye now, then the whole operation would have been so much wasted time and money. Cable was in a back room. She leaned slightly, looked through an aperture in the dividing wall and scanned the faces of the crowd in the main eating area. Cable went dead still. She recognized a man at one of the tables. Deep in conversation with a woman she did not know, it was the man she had last seen assaulting her fiancé. She stepped back out of sight and turned to the detective beside her. 'That's him,' she said, almost inaudibly, 'that's the man I saw kill Stephen.' At once, detectives escorted her back outside and whisked her away to safety.

The Kent detectives were jubilant. The arrest plan in place was finalized for execution at the next best available opportunity. It came the following night, on Friday, 28 August when Noye and his mistress repeated virtually the same pattern as the evening before.

This time, they headed for his favourite place, El Campero in Barbate. A waiter showed Noye and Altiabato to a table at the side of the restaurant's small terrace. After more than two years on the run, Noye may not have felt he was wholly safe, but his guard had certainly dropped, if only by a fraction: even in the short time they had been watching him, detectives had seen Noye visit El Campero twice before. He had settled into a predictable routine.

A cut-off group – a large force of armed British and Spanish plain-clothes police officers – now deployed around the restaurant's perimeter to prevent any possibility of escape. At the same time, the snatch squad tasked with Noye's actual arrest put their game plan into action. Half a dozen officers in this core group were already making merry at one of El Campero's large tables. Others now drifted in to join them, some clutching half-empty bottles of beer. Casually dressed, and, it seemed, already well lubricated with alcohol, the burly Englishmen's conversation made it clear to anyone who might be listening that they'd played a rugby match against a local Spanish team that same afternoon. Post-match, they were cementing Anglo-Spanish friendship over a few jars of sangria and an extremely large platter of paella. The tourist season was at its peak and El Campero was full. Waiters bustled past, trays piled high with food, there was a smell of fine cooking in the air and glasses chinked a counterpoint to the steady conversational buzz. As time went by the rugby players grew increasingly boisterous. Eventually, their spirits soared so high they fell to singing.

To the varied annoyance and amusement of the other customers, the British and Spanish rugby players now launched into a rousing chorus of Prodigy's 'Firestarter'. Still chatting happily with Altiabato, Noye ignored them. Raising his hand, the operational commander made as if to adjust his shirt collar. In fact, he thumbed the 'transmit' key of the concealed radio he was wearing twice. A vigilant observer might have noticed members of the 'rugby team' check for a split-second, as if they had just received a message.

The singing began to tail off. The rugby players rose to their feet. They no longer looked like harmless drunks. They looked like men with a cause. With the slickness won by long and hard rehearsal, they padded up to Noye's table. Taken by surprise, he glanced up. The rugby players had vanished. In their place was a solid wall of armed police. As the fear flooded into Noye's face, they pounced.

One officer grabbed Noye in a headlock. The momentum knocked him clean out of his chair. Both men fell to the floor with an almighty crash. Shocked by what was happening, the other diners fell silent. Altiabato sat back and put her hand to her mouth. As Noye struggled to get free, letting rip with a string of four-letter words, Miguel Fernandez, an eighteen-stone Spanish Special Branch officer, sat down squarely on his back. Two of the British detectives caught an arm each, yanked Noye's wrists up behind his back and snapped on handcuffs. Coolly, as if she formed no part of the chaos that had now overtaken the El Campero, Mina Altiabato stood up and walked off into the night. Detectives let her go – she was not wanted. But for Kenneth James Noye, the fun was over. The Kent police had pulled off a remarkable coup. They had him. And this time they were not going to let him get away.

Searched at the local police station, Noye was found to be carrying more than £6,000 in cash and a passport in the name of Alan Edward Green. To rule out any chance of escape, detectives decided to move him 50 kilometres north to Cadiz that same night and incarcerate him in the notorious El Puerto de Santa Maria maximum-security prison.

The British authorities now moved as fast as they could to secure Noye's extradition. Preliminary extradition hearings took place in the Spanish high court in Madrid on 16 November. The presiding judge was Baltasar Garzon – the same man who had led the clean-up of the Canary Islands.

Bullish as ever, Noye insisted he would 'fight tooth and nail' any attempt to remove him from Spain. He was as good as his word. At the full hearing in the *Audiencia Nacional* high court on 1 February 1999, his solicitor, Henry Milner, informed the court that Noye's arrest was illegal, and that Scotland Yard had no evidence linking Noye to the murder of Stephen Cameron. He further claimed that his client would not get a fair trial in the UK, having already been tried and found guilty by the British media. Seated right at the front of the public gallery, and separated from her lover only by the bulletproof glass screens that encased him, Mina Altiabato nodded enthusiastic agreement.

One thing was true: since his arrest, the British press had been ripping Noye to shreds. The court adjourned while the judges considered their verdict in camera. Noye went back to his cell. One month later, Garzon announced the court's decision: Noye's appeal against extradition was refused.

It was one thing winning the verdict – it was another getting Noye back to the UK. Kent police were so worried that someone might try to free him on the journey that they asked for – and got – the unprecedented use of a BAE 146 aircraft from the Queen's Flight. As if it really were carrying royalty, the plane was routed down the special ultra-VIP 'blue corridor'. Among other things, this meant that no other aircraft was allowed to come within 200 miles of it. To keep things extra tight the plane landed at RAF Manston, in Kent, where it was met by an armed police convoy. Kenneth Noye, one of the most wanted criminals in British history, was getting the royal treatment.

On 21 May 1999, Noye appeared before Dartford Magistrates Court for committal. Bearing in mind his reputation, extensive criminal contacts and massive financial resources, a squad of heavily armed police surrounded the court building while the evidence was heard. Dartford magistrates took little time in arriving at the same conclusion as their Spanish counterparts: there was a clear case to be answered. Two weeks later, Noye was remanded to HMP Belmarsh. In July he was committed for trial at the Old Bailey.

Now anxious to distance himself from 'Britain's Most Notorious Criminal', Noye's old friend Palmer gave a newspaper interview in which he said, 'Kenneth bloody Noye! A drink or two at a boxing match. I've met him once or twice. I never knew him. I don't want to know him.'

35

Noye's trial for the murder of Stephen Cameron began on 29 March 2000, in the Old Bailey's Number Two court, adjoining Court One where he had been cleared fifteen years previously of murdering Detective Constable John Fordham.

Opening the case for the prosecution, Julian Bevan QC told the court that Cameron 'was unarmed at the time he was stabbed, indeed he was empty-handed. The driver of that other vehicle was this defendant Kenneth Noye, as he now admits.'

Bevan made clear how brutal, violent and cold-blooded the murder had been. 'Stephen Cameron's decision to get out of that red van and deal with this potentially ugly situation cost him his life. He broke away from Mr Cameron. He went towards his Discovery . . . and it appears he acquired a knife. He returned to face Stephen with the knife in his hand ready for use with the blade out. Stephen Cameron remained unarmed, indeed empty-handed. He [Noye] lunged at [Cameron] and stabbed him twice in the chest.'

The first stab wound penetrated to a depth of 16cm, fatally puncturing Cameron's heart. 'The direction of the wound was upwards, backwards and inwards. The second wound went to a depth of 18cm and penetrated his liver. According to one of the pathologists, [Cameron] was rotating away from the knife when he was stabbed. Danielle Cable was hysterical.'

Heavily protected by armed police firearms specialists, Cable, now aged twenty-one, told the court in a low, hesitant voice how she had been driving her red Bedford Rascal van on the slip road of the M20/M25 interchange near Swanley, Kent, when the driver of a black Land-Rover Discovery she had just overtaken accelerated and cut in front of her at high speed. As the traffic lights at the junction ahead of them turned red he braked sharply, forcing her to brake hard in turn. Her fiancé, Stephen Cameron, had shaken his head in disapproval at the other man's reckless and aggressive driving. Noticing this – and apparently infuriated by it – the motorist jumped out of his car and strode towards them. Alarmed and wishing to protect her, Cable told how Cameron got out of the van.

Cable said the stranger had come straight up and, without uttering so much as a single word, 'punched Stephen hard in the eye. Stephen stumbled and staggered back. The other man fumbled in his jacket pockets and went towards the Land-Rover. By this time I had got out of the van. I pleaded with Stephen to get back in but he told me to stand back. I was going towards Steve. As I approached, the other man was standing looking at me. He had a blank expression on his face. I saw something in the man's hand which I believed was a knife, so I ran round the other cars [passing by on the slip road] screaming and shouting "Can you help us?" I saw the blade. It was about four inches long. Stephen tried to kick the knife from the man's hand.'

By now the court was rapt – appalled at how easily the mask of civilization could slip, and a silly little incident spiral from a standing start to murder in the space of a few seconds. After stabbing Cameron, Cable said, the other driver walked calmly back to his vehicle, climbed into it and drove off at high speed.

There was a long silence after Cable had finished speaking. Telling as it had been, honest as she appeared to most of the listening court, Cable's evidence on its own might have been enough to convict Noye. But Bevan, who had studied Noye's earlier trials, knew how plausible, persuasive and charming this particular defendant could be. He called a second eyewitness, a man named Alan Decabral. This was something of a risky decision. From his vantage point immediately behind the two cars, Decabral had witnessed the entire incident. But the forty-year old father of three's arrival in court caused a sensation. For a start there was his appearance: overweight, with unkempt, shoulder-length hair and a straggly white beard, he wore a lurid red-and-black striped sweater that made him look like a cross between a superannuated Hell's Angel and a giant bumblebee. The Hell's Angel element wasn't imaginary – in his younger days, Decabral had been a fully initiated gang member.

The new witness described himself as an antiques dealer. But this was no ordinary Sunday motorist. Shortly before his appearance in court a police raid on his home had brought to light a hidden cache of fifty-six firearms – enough to start a small war. The arsenal included late model automatic pistols, assault rifles and machine guns. Detectives also found £160,000 in cash and 36g of cocaine. Like most of the Brink's-Mat story, this was wilder than just about anything even the most imaginative Hollywood scriptwriter might have dreamed up. Decabral was arrested and charged with possession of firearms and a Class A narcotic. When he agreed to give evidence against Kenneth Noye, detectives dropped all charges, put the firearms beyond use – and returned them to Decabral along with the cash. They kept the coke.

Police suspected that Decabral was an underworld 'fixer', or armourer, selling or renting out firearms to violent criminals by the job. They also knew – because HM Customs and Excise had recently told them – that he was involved in a large-scale smuggling racket importing bootleg alcohol and tobacco from the Continent. Decabral certainly acted the part of the big-time crook. Arriving at court in a Rolls-Royce, he also owned a Jaguar, and had paid cash for the £250,000 home he had recently moved to in the small village of Pluckley, Kent – a location so picturesque it had starred in the TV serial based on H.E. Bates's book *The Darling Buds of May*.

So much for the credibility of the new witness. But Bevan must have known what he was doing: under questioning the big man was impressive and unshakeable. Describing what he had seen in graphic and chilling detail, he told the court. 'I saw a bright flash and I realized it was a knife because I could see the sun glinting off the blade. I saw the knife go into his chest. I saw the blood. I'll never forget his face.' He said Noye closed the knife and walked past him. 'As he walked past my car he nodded to me as if to say: "That sorted him out, you've got yours mate," that sort of thing.'

Decabral said he had called 999 and reported the stabbing, then tried to follow Noye's Discovery in his Rolls-Royce, but lost him because Noye had been driving so fast. In the middle of his testimony Decabral's mobile telephone started ringing. A ripple of laughter, quickly smothered, ran through the court. It was the only moment of levity in a relentlessly grim trial.

Before the trial, someone had dropped three bullets through Decabral's letterbox. 'Gangsters', he told the court, had told him to 'shut up or we will shut you up'. The police had offered him protection, but despite living in constant fear of assassination he had refused this. He said the strain on him imposed by the intimidation was so great he had been forced to close the vintage motorbike shop he owned in Acton, West London, and move to Pluckley so that he could lie low. He also said his marriage had broken down. His final comment was, 'I always look over my shoulder when I go into Sainsbury's.'

Bevan had a couple of other aces up his sleeve. Phone records proved that in the immediate aftermath of the stabbing, Noye made repeated calls to two men – from one of whom Noye had bought the Discovery in 1995, registering it under the alias 'Anthony Francis' at an address in Brigden Road in Bexley. In reality, this property belonged to the second person Noye had called. Said Bevan, 'As Mr Cameron's life slipped away, Mr Noye was busy on his mobile phone, probably believing that someone had taken down the registration number of his car. He took the necessary steps to stop anyone telling the police the true identity of the driver.'

Noye's mobile phone records further showed that at 2242 that same day he had called a private aviation company owned by 'a friend'. Bevan recounted how Noye had stuffed a briefcase with cash, jumped into one of his other cars and dashed across country to meet the 'friend' who lived near Bath. (At this point, for legal reasons, Bevan was unable to name John Palmer.) The next day, the friend had flown Noye by private helicopter to a golf course in France and then on to Madrid in his private jet. 'What he did following this [stabbing] clearly tells its own story,' Bevan said.

None of this either looked or sounded good for Noye, and there was more to come. Bevan next called a car valet named Carl Simcox to the witness box. Simcox told the court that in the course of cleaning a Land-Rover Discovery and a Mercedes brought in for cleaning by Noye, he had found a flick-knife with a black handle in the Discovery and a second flick-knife with a brown handle in the Mercedes. But Noye had a first-class defence team, and he could afford it: declared bankrupt following his imprisonment for handling the Brink's-Mat gold, he had been awarded legal aid to the tune of £250,000.

Noye's counsel, Stephen Batten QC, wasted no time in proposing that it was Cameron who had started the fight, and subjected his client Kenneth Noye to an unprovoked assault. Grilling Danielle Cable, Batten succeeded in getting her to admit that Noye had 'not looked angry' when he had been walking towards Cameron. Batten tried to suggest that out of loyalty to her dead fiancé, Cable had given an incomplete and one-sided version of events. 'Is it the fact that you told the police, and indeed told us, far less than you really saw because you found it, perhaps totally naturally, difficult to admit that any of this was Stephen's fault?'

Cable stuck to her guns: 'No, I don't believe it was his fault at all.'

Batten then asked, 'Is it not the case that your fiancé had something of a temper?' Cable then replied that she had never seen Cameron in a bad temper. Batten, who had done his research, pounced. Had Cable somehow forgotten Cameron losing his temper at their engagement party? Hadn't Cameron, in fact, fallen into a vicious argument with his next-door neighbour, urinated on that neighbour's fence, hammered his fist on the neighbour's door, and to cap it all, fought with the man? Cable was forced to admit she did remember these events taking place. Driving home his advantage, Batten urged, 'Would you say that Stephen was a young man who thought he could take care of himself without too much difficulty?' Given what the court had just heard, Cable could hardly deny it.

'Yes, I suppose he thought he could take care of himself.'

Batten then called Noye to the stand. Dressed in a light-blue shirt, blue trousers and a grey cardigan, Noye's clothes had been carefully chosen to lend him a friendly, nice-guy-next-door kind of look. Would a man in a baggy Marks & Spencer's cardigan come at you with a four-inch knife? With the eyes of every single person in the packed courtroom fixed intently on him, Noye started to speak. In a pleasant, conversational tone he said he had been driving home that Sunday lunchtime to have a drink with friends at a pub in Chislehurst, Kent. He remembered passing a red Bedford Rascal van, but claimed he did not recall 'cutting it up' as the prosecution alleged.

He said he thought he had recognized the driver as a woman he had recently met in a nightclub.

When he pulled up at the traffic lights, Noye said the driver had flashed the van's lights at him, as if she was annoyed by his driving. He got out to say hello, but as he drew near the van he realized he had made a mistake: he did not, in fact, know the woman behind the wheel. He agreed it was the woman pointed out to him in court, Danielle Cable.

Noye said Cable's passenger, Stephen Cameron, had stepped out of the van and started walking towards him. Noye told the court, 'I said, "Sorry mate, I thought you were someone else." He just stared. I said, "Sorry," and he said, "You will be, you c-u-n-t, I will kill you." As he came at me I see his face, and I knew I was in trouble. I have done nothing. Nothing. I have not antagonized or done anything.'

Noye said Cameron had lashed out at him, kicking and punching him back into the line of the oncoming traffic so that he feared for his life. He claimed a 'full-frontal' blow had knocked him to his knees, leaving him clinging to the bumper of the Discovery. 'I tried to get away, but he come up behind me and done me in the back.' Afraid, he said, that Cameron might kill him, Noye said he had reached in his pockets for the four-inch (10-cm) lock knife he carried. 'He was facing me. I said, "Don't come near me, you nutcase." I was holding it outstretched. He stood there for a second or two. His girlfriend got out of the van and said, "Don't go near him." That just fired him up. He came straight at me. The fight started again. He has punched me and given a few kicks and then I said, "Hold up, hold up!" He's telling me he's going to kill me. He was in a completely wild rage. He grabbed me and started smashing me in the face. I was trying to get back, to get away from him . . .

'I was worn out. I didn't have nothing left. I thought, I cannot take much more and no one has tried to stop the fight. I thought if he catches me again, then I'm out. He will take the knife and definitely use it on me. So I struck out with the knife. I can't remember exactly how I done it, but I accept it was twice.' Asked if he was by nature violent, Noye said, 'I've never hurt anyone. I've never hurt an animal.'

There was total silence in the court.

Noye said he had got back into the Discovery and driven away wondering, '"Why would a person fight like that?" I was shaking. I had a bloody face, I was just devastated.'

When he arrived home, his wife, Brenda, had seen the state he was in, the blood all over his face and clothes. 'She has seen my face. I said, "I have been in a fight." She was not too happy. She said, "I've heard, it was on the news. The chap's dead."'

Noye said he had called a friend for advice later on that evening, but refused to name the contact for fear of incriminating him. They agreed he should flee the country, on the grounds that he would not receive a fair trial. 'If I go down the police station I knew myself what would happen,' Noye said. 'I would never be believed. I would never get a fair trial. All those witness statements would, without a shadow of a doubt, have been tainted against me.' He said the friend had taken charge of the Discovery and the knife when they met, telling him, 'Leave them with me.' Neither the car nor the murder weapon had been seen since.

In an effort to get around the problem of his client's well-known criminal record and notorious reputation, Batten asked Noye if he felt the media coverage of the Fordham case had been fair and reasonable. Noye replied, 'It was absolutely scandalous, there's no other word for it.' He said he had been taken to court, 'like a monkey in a box'. Once there, warders had told him that the jurors, who had been ordered by the judge not to fraternize with their protection officers, had been seen 'laughing and joking with them during trips to Marks & Spencer'. Noye said the kind of coverage he had recently been getting in the British press meant he could never hope for a fair trial. By now, he was the Great British Bogeyman, Public Enemy Number One, up there with Crippen and Jack the Ripper in the public mind.

He said that ever since his release from jail in 1994 he had been afraid that the police, still angered by the Fordham killing, would try to 'fit him up'. He lived in fear of kidnap and torture at the hands of criminals who believed he might know where the missing ton of Brink's-Mat's gold was hidden. A good friend of his, Nicky Whiting, had been abducted and stabbed to death by a person or persons unknown, perhaps in the mistaken belief that Noye had told him where the gold was hidden. 'I was in fear of my life from two sources,' he said. 'The police definitely detested me and I had it in mind that they would pull in a villain who had done something really serious and would get them to do something to me.' It was fear of all these possible enemies that made him carry a knife. 'I would have preferred a stun gun or CS canister but they are illegal. A stun gun would have been much better, really.'

He complained that the police were continually on his tail, hounding and attempting to entrap him. He gave the example of a US citizen serving time with him in prison, who had asked if Noye would swap the missing gold for a large amount of cocaine. 'I found out later,' Noye alleged, 'that he was working for the FBI.'

Asked again about the fight, Noye said, 'I didn't want to fight. I can't fight. I was forced into something I did not want to do. I said to my sons from the time they were little, "If you ever get into a fight, just walk away. You are not being a coward; you never know what will happen."' Invited to explain why he had registered the Discovery in a false name at a false address, Noye fell back on his story that he felt threatened both by the police and by possible gold hunters. 'I didn't want anyone to know where I lived. I didn't want anyone to know what cars I drove.'

Cross-examining the defendant for the prosecution, Bevan immediately set about itemizing Noye's incriminating behaviour after the stabbing, beginning with the fact that Noye had made a run for it. 'How did you come to have a false passport under the name of a Mr Green?' Noye had a ready answer: 'I bought it off a mate of mine. When he came to Spain he brought it with him.' Bevan wanted to know how Noye had managed to support himself while he was on the run. 'I had money in Spain,' Noye replied. 'As much as I wanted. I'd been doing deals previously.' Bevan reminded the jury that during his extradition hearing, Noye had told Spanish magistrates he had not been at the scene of the stabbing.

Bevan: 'That was a total lie on your part?'

Noye: 'Yes.'

'Which you told to help your cause at the time?'

'Yes.'

'Since then you have completely changed tack and put forward a defence of self-defence?'

'Well, that is true.'

'You thought nothing of telling the Spanish court a complete lie to help your position?'

'Yes.'

'So if you hadn't been found by the police in Spain you were never going to come back?'

'Yes.'

'And face some responsibility as you had? Leaving the parents of this boy totally ignorant?'

'Yes, they would have been.'

'Mr Noye, the truth is that so far as this incident is concerned you became angry with that young man and deliberately stabbed him, didn't you?'

'No, I am quite a placid man. I did not do that. It is not true.'

'And you ran away in fear, not fear of not having a fair trial, you ran away in fear of the truth emerging from all the people at that junction.'

'Well,' said Noye, 'the truth has emerged.'

The jurors certainly thought so. On 14 April, after a trial lasting two weeks, the jury of eight men and four women found Kenneth James Noye guilty of Stephen Cameron's murder by a majority of 11 to 1. The judge, Lord Justice Latham, wasted few words in sentencing Noye. 'The jury have found you guilty of murder. There is only one sentence I can impose and that is life. I don't propose to say anything further at this stage.' He did not need to. To the satisfaction of the police and the British press, Noye was sentenced to life in a maximum-security prison.

As the prison officers led Noye down to the cells, Stephen Cameron's parents turned and hugged each other. Speaking at a news conference later, Mrs Cameron said, 'This is not a joyous occasion. Our lovely son Stephen is dead and our lives will never be the same again. We will never feel the happiness that we once had. We are still experiencing overwhelming grief, as any parents who have lost a child will understand. For our beloved Stephen to lose his life – a life with so much future – and in such a wicked, senseless way, is very difficult to bear.' Cameron's father, Ken, said, 'Our family has undergone torment in the four years since the killing. The uncertainty of not knowing whether we would get justice for our son tore us apart.'

Cable, who was not in court when the verdict was announced, told the *Daily Express*: 'When the police officer phoned me from the court to tell me about the guilty verdict I was overjoyed. I could not believe it at first. But it will never bring back my Steve. I just hope he's looking down from heaven today and smiling. This is for him.'

Speaking on behalf of Kent police, Detective Superintendent Dennis McGookin also expressed satisfaction at the outcome of the trial. 'Noye thought he was above the law and would never be brought to court. This shows you can run from justice but you cannot hide.' Praising Cable's courage, he went on: 'she watched her fiancé get stabbed to death when she was only seventeen. Her courage in sticking by the investigation and coming to court and giving evidence against a man like Kenneth Noye is somewhat outstanding, and is a great tribute to that young lady.'

Given the ordeal she had been through – and the prospect of a lifetime in the witness protection programme – 'somewhat outstanding' was something of an understatement. As Cable told the *Daily Mail*, 'I have lost twice – Stephen and my old life.'

36

Murder runs through the Brink's-Mat story like a sclerotic vein. Next to that of John Fordham, the killing that best sums up the general viciousness is Brian Perry's. Early on the morning of 16 November 2001, Perry pulled up outside his minicab office at Credon House, Verney Road, Peckham. It was his habit to arrive early for work, at pretty much the same time every day. The predictable routine would now cost him his life.

Since his release from prison a few months earlier, Perry had gone full circle. Back in his old Peckham stamping ground, back running his rotten old minicab business from his decrepit office in Queen's Road, it was almost as if the Brink's-Mat robbery had never happened. As if he had never been in control of a £13 million fortune; never been a criminal mastermind; never snapped his fingers in the faces of Michael McAvoy and Brian Robinson in Leicester prison or Roy Ramm and Brian Worth outside the National Theatre; never helped kick-start the great Docklands renaissance; never whooped it up in Switzerland with Relton and Parry; never had the girls and the booze and the Bentley Turbo and the fancy home in Biggin Hill. Never had the gang leader's money and the gang leader's wife.

Here he was now, on a cold winter's morning almost exactly seventeen years to the day since the robbery, making his way to work as if the heist had never happened and nothing had ever changed. But everything had changed. In Anthony White's memorable phrase, the gold had been 'dealt for'. With an army of willing helpers Perry had turned it into cash, into property and back into yet more cash.

Perry had done it all – and in so doing, he had crossed the invisible line.

Perry locked the Mercedes and began walking towards his office.

As he drew near the door, two masked men strode up to him. At least one raised an automatic pistol and fired – three bullets slammed into his head and chest. They left him lying face-down in the gutter in a pool of his own blood.

Brian Perry was sixty-three years old.

Detectives questioned the major Brink's-Mat players at length, but could prove no link between any one of them and the assassination. Mired in the usual silence, the murder investigation went on hold.

There were other killings, some more directly related to the Brink's-Mat robbery than others. Two days after Noye skipped the country, on 20 May 1996, the body of a man named John Marshall was found under some bales of straw in the back of his Range Rover. A 34-year-old suspected drug dealer, Marshall, who also dealt in used cars and scrap metal, described himself as a 'salvage operator'. In what had all the hallmarks of a professional killing, Marshall had been shot through the head and then casually concealed. The Range Rover was found parked in a sidestreet not far from his office. Detectives found £5,000 in cash on the vehicle's dashboard, left there, as the *Sunday Times* put it, 'almost as a mark of contempt'.

Police believe that Marshall's killing was the work of a professional. No one has ever been arrested in connection with it.

In December 1998, Hatton Garden jeweller Solly Nahome was found shot dead outside his London home. A friend of Tommy Adams, Nahome was suspected of money laundering, fencing and fraud. Some detectives who worked on the case believe that Nahome played some kind of role in the Brink's-Mat robbery, possibly helping to store and/or smelt the other half of the gold. A professional killer fired four bullets into him before escaping on a motorcycle.

No one has been arrested in connection with the murder.

Then there is Alan Decabral. For the several months since he had given the evidence that had helped convict Kenneth Noye, Decabral, on his own account, had lived in daily fear of violent reprisal. His terror was well grounded: on Thursday, 5 October 2000, Decabral left his handsome new Pluckley home to go shopping at the Warren Retail Park in Ashford, Kent. He parked his black Peugeot 206 between two other vehicles outside a branch of Halfords. As he sat in the car, someone stepped up to the driver's window, held a gun to his head and blew his brains out. Witnesses said they saw a man in his early twenties wearing a light-green jacket running from the scene. Police believe the murder to be the work of a professional. No one has been arrested in connection with it.

At 0500 on the morning of 14 May 2003 a man named George Francis arrived back at his home in Lynton Road, Bermondsey, following an all-night drinking session with friends. Francis was a major London face, the nearest thing the UK had to a criminal 'godfather' of the kind often caricatured in film and television. Flying Squad detectives strongly suspected that he had been part of the gold-laundering syndicate: very possibly, a key player in helping to launder the other half of the stolen gold. As Francis opened the door to step out of his green Rover 75 saloon, someone put four bullets through his head. Fired at point-blank range, the 9mm slugs left Francis's blood and brains all over the interior of the brand-new car. Four men in a dark saloon were seen speeding away from the scene.

Some Scotland Yard detectives believe that Francis, convicted in 1990 for his role in a large-scale cocaine-smuggling operation, was killed because, like Perry, he had helped himself to a golden share. There had been at least one attempt on his life back in 1985, when he was shot at a pub he owned in Hever Castle, Kent. On that occasion he was lucky – the bullet just lodged in his shoulder without doing serious harm.

Three weeks before his death, Francis told a detective: 'I expect to die with my boots on. My old man was a villain and I hope my kids will grow up to be villains. I have lived by violence, been close to violence all my life and in the end I will die by it. I would rather die quickly by the bullet than slowly in some old people's home that stinks of cabbage water.'

He got his wish.

Police believe that his murder was the work of professionals. No one has been arrested in connection with it.

Futile as they are, there may yet be more killings. For so many people involved in the robbery, it was a death warrant.

*

In the autumn of 1998 Thomas Adams, acquitted in 1986 of handling the gold, was sentenced to seven and a half years in prison for drugs smuggling.

For everyone involved in it, the Brink's-Mat heist was like some giant lucky dip seeded with gold bars. The robbers and their associates all dived in and grabbed what they could. Out they all came again covered in blood and sawdust. Few have grown old basking in the golden afterglow of the robbery. One, or maybe two, gang members may have escaped the law. If so, then they are presumably trying to while away the lingering days in some exotic foreign hidey-hole.

All of the immediate or suspected gang members and most of the wider circle of conspirators either made swingeing payments in out-of-court settlements or face a lifetime of pursuit by the financial Rottweilers unleashed by the loss adjusters. Anthony Black remains in hiding. Noye is still in prison. On 17 August 2005 John Palmer was released on parole from Highdown jail in Surrey. Described as 'a model prisoner', he had served roughly half of his eight-year sentence. He went home to the vast country pile near Brentwood in Essex that he shares with his partner.

In 2004, the High Court found against Palmer in a civil suit brought by a group of 350 timeshare victims and ordered him to repay £3.25 million, plus costs. Subsequently declaring him bankrupt, the court seized and sold one of his timeshare resorts for £3.4 million. Other actions are in the pipeline. There are still timeshare touts out there working the decks. Michael McAvoy and Kathleen Meacock are still married and were last heard of living in Surrey. Brian Robinson is thought to be living on a Greek island. Gordon Parry got to stay in Crockham House. At least seven people directly connected or associated with the robbery have been shot dead.

Brian Perry was the last person to be convicted in a criminal case linked to the Brink's-Mat robbery. The epic nine-year struggle between the police and the conspirators had ended in something of a score draw. If you counted Anthony Black, then three – and with the imprisonment of Brian Perry possibly four – of the original gang had been put behind bars, along with many of the handlers. Police suspect at least one more is still on the run.

The Brink's-Mat gang showed great daring, flashes of brilliance and examples of extreme stupidity. The detectives who spent so many years hunting them showed great daring, flashes of brilliance and made some terrible decisions.

37

Like a virus that goes on mutating, Brink's-Mat is one of those stories that won't go away, but that keeps coming back in some new and unexpected form. On 8 February 2001, a police team led by Scotland Yard's Superintendent John Shatford arrived at R. Winchester & Co., a timber yard in Graystone Lane, off Old London Road, Ore. Ore is a pleasant village near Hastings on the south coast of England. Acting on a tip-off, the police brought along a mechanical digger, ground-penetrating radar, shovels, pickaxes, spades – and a lot of optimism. They started digging in a corner of the yard, and spent the next several weeks excavating. They did not find a single ounce of the 1,000-odd kilos of gold that are still presumed missing. The joke, all the time, was probably on Scotland Yard: *'l'or'* is French for gold.

If it has not already been turned into cash, where is the rest of the missing bullion hidden? In one of those big walk-in safes in the vaults of a dodgy jeweller in Hatton Garden? Buried somewhere in the Kent countryside close to Kenneth Noye's old West Kingsdown home? In a rented flat somewhere in or near London? (Somewhere back in the mists of time, a news story claimed that some of the heist was hidden in a first-floor flat on the Finchley Road. The story goes that an ex-member of a failing rock band – and at the time one of Britain's poorest men – lived on the ground floor beneath the glittering hoard. When the police arrived to search the first-floor flat, our man was mightily surprised to learn that he might have been eking out his penury a few feet away from an almighty fortune.)

Is it really stashed somewhere amusing like Ore – somewhere with a name that is easy to remember, and that brings a secret little smile to the lips of the person, or persons, who are in on the joke? On the principle of 'never keep all your eggs in one basket', the missing hoard, if it exists, is almost certainly not hidden in a single location.

Perhaps it lies in one great golden pile, guarded by a dragon named 'Brinks'. Or a Rottweiler named 'Mat'. Will it ever be recovered and laundered like the rest of the heist? Gold is much harder to shift these days. You can't just smelt it down, bung it into the Assay Office and wait for the cheques to arrive – the police would be feeling your collar before you knew it. In the Age of Terrorism, 'doing the laundry' is a lot harder: all those tiresome questions about your identity. Where exactly did you come by that van load of gold you are looking to convert into spending money? Better leave the bullion lying where it is until everyone has forgotten about it. It might take twenty years, or thirty, or even fifty, but one day, some lucky relative or friend might just go out with a spade and a map and start digging; or come by the key to one of the rented flats or vaults where what's left of the heist has been sitting, year after year, biding its time. If the heirs to the hoard are really lucky, the rest of the Brink's-Mat bullion might even still be there. It will be worth having: gold has increased in value by 11 per cent in the past year alone. If they are really smart, they will be able to launder it. But the chances of any of that happening have to be worse than even.

Like some gaunt warning to criminal kind, Whitemoor maximum-security prison rears its ugly mass from the middle of a barren, windswept Cambridgeshire moor. At the heart of the prison lies a big red-brick block known as the Special Secure Unit. A prison within a prison, its walls breathe that sickly-stale, trapped-animal smell peculiar to human beings kept in long-term close confinement. One of the bleakest, most hostile places on the face of the earth, the constant rattle of the prison's keys, the endless crashing of its steel doors, and the occasional desperate howls of its inmates are the stuff of a bad horror movie.

One of no more than a dozen lifers locked up in the SSU, during the four years he spent at Whitemoor Noye was allowed minimal contact with his fellow inmates or with anyone else. Even the warders were changed on a random basis to prevent him from corrupting anyone. Entirely self-contained, SSUs have their own mini-library, recreational facilities and catering arrangements. Noye couldn't have any of the social, work or educational opportunities enjoyed by inmates of the wider prison.

Noye's High Court appeal against sentence – on the grounds that Alan Decabral's testimony about the road-rage murder was tainted because of Decabral's criminal record – failed in October 2001. After the ruling, Stephen Cameron's father Kenneth said of Noye: 'I hope he spends the rest of his life in jail. I hope he comes out in a wooden box.' He may just get his wish. Faced with the prospect of a further twenty-odd years in the SSU, Noye complained about the harsh conditions of his imprisonment, seeking judicial review to challenge them under the terms of the European Human Rights Act, 1998. This appeal, too, has failed.

Is this the end of the story? Not quite. In the first week of February 2005, a Whitemoor warder carrying out a routine 'tumble' of Noye's cell discovered a mobile phone hidden in a packet of Weetabix. It meant that Britain's most notorious prisoner had almost certainly turned one of the people who had contact with him. Since the search procedures for all visitors at maximum-security facilities are extremely stringent, it is very unlikely that a visitor could have smuggled in a mobile. It is far more likely that someone who worked inside the prison had been trying to help Noye escape.

How had Noye meant to do it? Would a team of heavily armed men clustered on the back of a hurtling JCB have smashed through the prison's outer wall, flattened the SSU's towering chain-link perimeter and threatened or shot their way up to his cell? Would a second squad of armed men in a helicopter have given top cover, and then plucked Noye out of the stinking mire and away to freedom? Or had the plan been less fanciful than that, more subtle? The hurried call on the smuggled mobile; the bent insider slipping into his cell with the keys and a warder's uniform, a pistol to make sure on the way out? What had Noye been planning?

No one but the man himself can say.

Whatever had been in the works, the upshot was immediate: Noye was moved that same day – out of the Whitemoor frying pan and into the fire of a second, almost identical, Special Secure Unit. Just like the first, it lies at the cold concrete heart of a maximum-security prison: Full Sutton, on the rolling upland moors a few miles from the city of York. Furious at the foiling of his escape plans, outraged at the sudden move that would take him even further from his relatives and friends, Noye languishes in his cell, smacking the punch-bag and lifting the weights . . . waiting for the day when he can step outside a free man, set his face to the keening wind and catch up on unfinished business.

Word is, you can make yourself a cool £5 million if you help Kenneth Noye bust out of jail. Hardly surprising that someone at Whitemoor might have been ready to help.

One more ripple on the golden pond, and then we are done. Without even knowing it, many of us are part of the Brink's-Mat heist. Anyone who bought gold jewellery in the UK after November 1983 stands every chance of wearing – or should that be handling – stolen goods.

Index